'An honest and incredibly rela
journey during his first year o

C000115194

'Absolutely brilliant. A hilarious and accurate insight to
the ups and downs of first-time fatherhood'
(not so) Secret Dads Business

'A funny and heart-warming daddy diary. A great gift
for any expectant father'
Ellie, Editor My Baba

'Calling all parents – this is a must read'
MANtenatal

'A no-holds-barred memoir that gives true insight into
what parenting can be like'
Reedsy Discovery

'An outrageously cute read … captures the emotions and
the roller coaster ride of a newbie father perfectly'
Mary Anthony, Au Rendezvous Podcast

'A witty and honest look at the ups and downs of
fatherhood'
Working Dads

*Be prepared to stifle giggles in your pillow and to be touched by thoughtful insights on parenting from the underrepresented point-of-view of a first-time dad.*

Laura Miller. The Library Laura Podcast

*'Simply delicious, an easy read for all parents'*

Babyhour Podcast

# DEAR ARLO

Adventures in Dadding

# TOM KREFFER

Charlie Cat Books
Kemp House, 160 City Road
London, EC1V 2NX

CCB

First published in Great Britain in 2021 by Charlie Cat Books

Cover Design and layout by MiblArt.
Illustrations and cover artwork by Chandana Wanasekara.
A CIP catalogue record for this book is available from the British
Library.

ISBN 978-1-8382225-6-7

For Arlo

*My son – my teacher – my small-sized buddy*

# Also by Tom Kreffer

*Adventures in Dadding*

DEAR DORY: JOURNAL OF A SOON-TO-BE FIRST-TIME DAD

TODDLER INC. *(coming 2022)*

# Table of Contents

# Before we get started ...

It's worth pointing out a few things that this book is not, in the hope of reducing the number of complaints from parents telling me that I don't know what I'm doing.

Because I don't know what I'm doing.

I haven't written this as a guidebook on how to look after a baby. And I certainly don't believe that every decision I made as a father during the first year was the right one.

If my first book, *Dear Dory*, was an insight into the experiences of a first-time father bumbling his way *towards* parenthood, then *Dear Arlo* is an insight into that same father bumbling *through* his first year of parenthood – 70 per cent of which he spent winging it with his partner.

When your midwife hands you your newborn baby, she's also handing you an invisible contract that you mentally sign when you hold your child for the first time. It's a contract that says you agree to be responsible for that child's safety, to love them, to care for them, to share with them everything that you know, so that they can forge their way in the world without repeating your mistakes. But not once anywhere on that contract does it say you have to be perfect, or that you can't make errors – a good job, otherwise I'd have multiple lawsuits on my hands.

Life is spectacularly precious, and I can think of no higher honour than being a dad.

Enjoy!

PS: if you thought the profanity was too much in *Dear Dory*, it's probably worth regifting this copy of *Dear Arlo* immediately, because I use a lot of profanity in this book too. Like, a fucking lot. Fucking tons, in fact. What? You try and refrain from dropping a few F-bombs when you've had as much sleep as I've had this year.

# November

## Happy Birthday
### Tuesday, 19 November 2019

**0 days old**

Stillness.

Peace.

Calm.

Love.

There exists no human experience that will elevate you higher than the first time you hold your newborn baby in your arms. I am certain of this. Hopefully, you will experience it for yourself one day.

A few minutes ago, at 4.26 p.m., you were born. I'm sitting, holding you in my arms.

Time has reached a standstill.

You are the CPR machine that I never knew I needed.

You're awake, staring into my eyes, alert for someone who's minutes old. Your gaze is filled with endless curiosity.

Mine is filled with wonderment.

I could spend the rest of my life trying to etch this experience into words, but a lifetime's commitment to such a task could only ever result in failure. What I will say is that at this exact moment my life is in a state of impenetrable tranquillity.

It's difficult to see it, but you have an almost transparent, cloudy film over your left eye. I'm not sure what it is: possible remnants of your former lodgings perhaps.

Your arrival in our lives has been dramatic. It's why Mummy is lying on a bed nearby while doctors repair the incision that was made below her tummy to retrieve you, by way of an emergency C-section. Don't worry about Mummy, though, her durability makes diamonds seem like the biscuit base of a cheesecake.

Until 4.26 p.m., we called you Dory – your pre-birth name. Now we know you're a boy, we've named you Arlo, and you are the most beautiful baby boy – a biological marvel. People say parents are biased about how cute their babies are. I agree they are, but that doesn't mean that some parents don't make beautiful babies, and you are one of them, Arlo.

The midwife, who also happens to be a friend of ours, Rebecca, says you look like your mother, but I can't recognise either of us in you yet. In my defence, you are only a few minutes old, my eyes are misty and my emotional state is packing enough energy to fuel eight return trips to the moon.

I stand up so that I can lay you on Mummy's chest. As I do, I catch an unwanted glimpse behind the curtain (called a 'sterile drape') that was erected over Mummy ahead of the surgery. The curtain had a dual purpose: it helped keep the operating environment (Mummy's tummy) sterile, and it prevented the soon-to-be parents from seeing the doctor slice Mummy open – you risk seeing more than you need or want to if you stand up, which of course is what I've just done.

The surgery team are progressing through their repairs, but they still have a long way to go. In my peripheral vision I can see silver instruments flashing under high-intensity LED light bulbs, quick-moving hands wrapped in blue surgical gloves, and blood. A lot of blood.

I avert my gaze before the image can solidify, and I focus my attention instead on my family.

My amazing family.

And to think we were told that the chances of making a baby naturally were slim to none.

More time passes. Nothing can penetrate this bubble. But then ...

'Would Daddy like to get Arlo changed?' says someone in the room.

*What?*

Panic.

Anxiety.

Fear.

Imagine you're Sleeping Beauty. You've woken up and experienced love at first sight – you can't describe the sensation, but you feel like you're connecting with the world on a spiritual level. And then someone severs that connection by swinging a spiked mace right up into your nether regions.

We don't jump right into this parenthood gig ... do we? Isn't there some sort of transition phase for new parents?

Before I can begin listing reasons why this is a terrible idea, someone lifts you away from Mummy and gently lays you down in a cot, which is then wheeled over to me while someone else hands me your nappy-changing bag.

I now have a baby and baby clothes. I have everything I need apart from confidence and experience.

My hands are shaking. I try and hide it. It's not that I don't want to do this – on the contrary, nothing would give me more pleasure than being the first one to dress you. It's an honour, and there exists only one opportunity to dress your first child for the first time, but I've hardly slept in three days, I've watched Mummy go ten rounds in the ring with life, I've just held you myself for the first time and I'm an emotional wreck. I'm surprised that I'm being allowed to operate a few-minutes-old baby, given my serious lack of qualifications and current mental state.

But everyone in the room is smiling at me – encouraging me. I can't comprehend if they're all sadists or if they're unable to appreciate what's going on inside my head.

*Surely they know what I'm feeling. They see this every day.*

Am I a terrible person for wishing a patient in another room to go into cardiac arrest so that the population of spectators is thinned out a bit? *Probably.*

I guess this is it, then.

Fatherhood begins today.

Right now.

There's no transition period, no trial run, no supervised training, no e-learning module you can consult, and no simulation that you can fuck up as many times as you need to until you get it right. This is now my life. I'm a dad, and your upkeep is my responsibility. Besides, how the fuck can I bow out of something like this when I've just watched Mummy go through what she's gone through over the last hour, three days, nine months?

So I mentally sign the employment contract that's hanging in front of me, and then I mentally travel to the offices of Dadding Inc. I meet a friendly smiling receptionist, Julie, who confirms I've been successfully registered on to the system, and that I'm now an official employee of Dadding Inc. She tells me not to be nervous, wishes me luck, and then she hands me my work-pass badge. I swipe it through the scanner. It beeps and the turnstile clicks into place, telling me that access to my new office has been granted.

I pass through and officially commence my dadding job, the one I'll have for the rest of my life, and one that begins immediately as I exit the world of the metaphorical and return to the land of the literal.

*One baby, one nappy-changing bag. I can do this.*

Here we go.

I put your outfit ready to one side. Then I extract from the bag a clean nappy that's marginally bigger than my passport.

'Remember, the animal goes on his bottom,' Mummy slurs. Despite being out of her head on enough drugs to secure world peace for twenty minutes, she is still in my corner, cheering me on, waving an imaginary sign that reads: 'You can do it!'

I flounder my way through the entire process of putting your nappy on but I somehow complete that part of the task. Next, I slide your Babygro underneath you. I'm OK-ish threading your legs through, but not your arms. They terrify me. Actually, threading any infant's arm through the sleeve of a Babygro terrifies me ... let alone a newborn baby ... *my* newborn baby. Why aren't gilets mandatory attire for infants?

A few minutes later, you're dressed, which means I've completed my first task as a daddy.

One down, ten trillion to go.

Soon after, you and Mummy are relocated from theatre to recovery ward, where you both settle in before receiving a speedy breastfeeding tutorial.

Unsurprisingly, you guys nail it.

I use this as an excuse to take my leave and visit the bathroom, even though I don't need to. I walk in, lock the door and burst into tears. I can't remember uncontrollably sobbing like this since I was a child.

After I'm done having my moment, I return to my family. Now that you're dressed and fed, I can relax for a second and maybe see about returning to that cloud in the sky.

And return I do. It feels like only minutes have passed but in reality it's a lot longer. One of the midwives approaches and says, 'Hi. Just to let you know, it's almost 10 p.m., which is when visiting hours end.'

'I have to go home?'

'I'm sorry, but yes.'

Now that you're here, following a successful delivery, NHS regulations stipulate that partners can only be at the mum's bedside between the hours of 10 a.m. and 10 p.m.

This doesn't sit right with me, Arlo. Mummy can't move, and you're a newborn baby. I want to stay and look after my family, I want to cuddle my son and I want to remind Mummy how amazing she's been through all of this.

I do not want to leave.

I've heard staff complain many times about how busy the wards are and how they don't have enough midwives to look after all the mummies and their babies. It would make sense, to me at least, to allow partners to stay so they can help with the care.

But my view is irrelevant, and I have to go.

And so, with great reluctance, I say goodbye to you and Mummy for the night.

Fortunately, I'm leaving you in the care of yet another extraordinary midwife. She will watch over my family tonight: she will look after you, and she will look after Mummy.

Sleep well, my boy.

You're gonna need it.

## My First Day At Work
Wednesday, 20 November 2019

I day old

I set two alarms for this morning, but I must have turned them both off in my sleep. Your Granny

Smurf – my mummy, who's temporarily living with us – wakes me at 8.40 a.m. with a coffee.

After a few seconds, it dawns on me that I've become the thing I've spent over two years dreaming about, the thing that doctors told me wouldn't happen, the thing that I've wanted more than anything else in my history of wanting stuff.

I am a daddy. I am your daddy. *I have a son.*

What a feeling.

I drink my coffee and snap to it. There's work to be done.

Mummy has sent me a summary of the first night. Apparently, you have excellent jaw functionality – a little too excellent. Mummy's food factories already have several mechanical fault issues, which translates to 'they fucking hurt'. She requires nipple shields.

Fast-forward thirty minutes, and I find myself in the vastness of an unknown wilderness – without a map. I'm sitting on the shop floor of Boots with a staff member, a young girl: my guide, I suppose, though she's never been to this particular wilderness either. Together we're trying to wrap our heads around the various nipple-shield products that are available. Neither of us has the foggiest about them so I hedge my bets, buy two different versions of everything, and then make my way to the hospital. Worst-case scenario, I can suction the spares to the fridge and hang a couple of cute baby photos from them.

I tiptoe into the ward to find you and Mummy having a cuddle. Mummy has a smile on her face that, until 4.26 p.m. yesterday, I'd never seen her wear before. I savour the sight before making an entry.

'Fancy a cuddle?' she says.

Do I ever.

I lift you up and into my arms, and once again, I find myself transported to a place of deep serenity.

I could do this forever.

I debrief Mummy on my mission to acquire nipple shields without taking my eyes off you.

Soon after, a member of staff arrives to tell us that Arlo's grandmothers are here to see him, but staff have refused them entry because it's not visiting hours – something I know they're aware of because I told them myself. I head out to meet your Granny Smurf and Mummy's mummy, Granny Feeder.

'I thought a box of chocolates would work,' says Granny Feeder, living up to her nickname.

'Ten points for effort,' I say. 'But you need to come back at four.'

I'm back in the ward with Mummy, and it's time for me to change my first dirty nappy. The contents resemble that of thick black tar. Don't worry, this is normal and expected. Your first poo is a meconium one, made up of fluid and cells that you ingested while in the womb. It's one of the most freakish sights I've ever encountered, which is not an insubstantial claim given that I've just witnessed childbirth.

*Yay.*

A natural I am not. My movements are clunky and uncoordinated, and I have little confidence. You're crying as well, which does not help matters. The pitch is like a thousand tiny pins rapidly and repeatedly stabbing at my eardrums like the needle on a sewing machine.

Mummy fails to conjure up even a particle of patience watching me fumble through a task that she could perform in mere nanoseconds, thanks to ten years of experience working in childcare. In her defence, she remains beyond exhausted from labour, and hearing your baby cry in distress is not a pleasant feeling.

'Do you want some help?' Mummy says.

'No, stay where you are. I need to learn how to do this.'

I'm ignored. Mummy hobbles over and prepares to take the reins. But as she does, she accidentally knocks the cannula embedded in the back of her hand on to the side of your cot. And now her hand is bleeding. Several droplets of blood land on you, making the entire scene look like some sort of voodoo ceremony. Mummy starts crying, which allows me to keep hold of the reins until I've changed your nappy, for which I score a D-minus at best.

'Did you bring the right-sized vests with you?' Mummy says.

*Shit! No, I didn't.* 'Yeah … about the vests … you know, I was really hoping you'd bring that up. I sort of forgot them.'

'Sort of forgot them?'

'I did that funny thing where I meant to pack them to bring them with me but then I didn't. Because I forgot.'

'But the ones we've got here are too big.'

Damn it, Daddy will need to be better organised.

After things calm down, Mummy and I have a cuddle and we agree to take it an hour at a time. Once we're all at home, and Mummy recovers from her surgery, we'll have both space and time to adjust to being a family. Until then, we'll have to stumble forward.

We spend the afternoon watching you sleep. The cot is made of transparent plastic, so we can see you at all times. I'm transfixed by the rise and fall of your chest. It's hypnotic. As are the subtle movements in your face, creasing ever so slightly at intervals. Your nascent feet, legs, hands and body. Everything about you is brand new. And your tiny newborn fingers: they grip my index finger, telling me that you need me – as a guide to take you through the early years of your life. I will be that for you. *And more.* Your new life is a blank slate, an empty canvas, a chance to grow into something awe-inspiring and to achieve something astonishing. Everything is a possibility to you. Who will you become, what will you accomplish? None of us knows the answers yet, but the journey we will all take together in discovering them will be an incredible adventure.

At 4 p.m. the grannies return, accompanied by Grandad Tools (Mummy's daddy) and your Auntie Lisa (Mummy's sister).

The introduction is extraordinary. Not for the first time in the last twenty-four hours, I watch another person – in this case four people – fall instantly in love with you.

Soon after, I change your nappy for the second time today, and you urinate all over me. I'm neither surprised nor bothered, which is a good job, as I presume this will be happening often.

It's evening, and you're asleep. Today has zipped by quicker than a rabbit fleeing from a hungry fox. It won't be long before I have to leave you again.

But not yet.

There is just enough time for Mummy and me to enjoy date night.

In the past, our dates have consisted of trips to the cinema and meals out.

But we're not doing anything like that.

Tonight's romantic activity sees us undergo a fun little exercise called colostrum harvesting. Colostrum is the first milk that a mummy produces after giving birth. It is full of nutrients and contains a high white blood cell count, equipping a baby's immune system with enough heavy artillery to ward off any early nasties.

The harvesting process is simple: Mummy applies pressure to certain regions of her food factories, teasing out prized colostrum, while I arm myself with a sterilised syringe and linger nearby, ready to capture every precious drop.

Despite the simple mission brief, this is a delicate affair. Remember, Mummy underwent major surgery a little over twenty-four hours ago. In addition, you have done a number on poor Mummy's milking parlours. I think the breastfeeding specialist referred to you as having 'an aggressive suck'.

Nevertheless, Mummy begins to extract the first drop. She winces in pain, but I can't see any colostrum.

'There. Quickly, this really hurts,' Mummy says

'Where ... oh, I see it! Come here, you little fuck.'

'Catch it.'

'Stop talking then, dickhead!'

The droplet, in a desperate attempt to evade capture, constantly alters its speed, but it's no match for my determination and skill set as I successfully suction the first drop in the syringe.

'Why are you pulling that face?' Mummy says, trying not to laugh.

'I think it's because shut up and stop questioning my methods, woman. Now, how about you get back to squeezing those tits? This syringe ain't gonna fill itself.'

After a successful date night (we harvested 3 ml), I change your nappy for the third time today. I'm already getting better. I'm more relaxed. I even manage to avoid you pissing on me.

It's now 10 p.m. and it's time for me to leave. My first day of being a daddy is over. Only the rest of my life to go. To an outsider, it probably doesn't amount to an event deserving global media coverage, or even a cursory one-liner mention in the back of the local paper, but to me, it's a day that I will never forget. My first day of dadding.

## A Curveball Of Boob-Shaped Proportions
Thursday, 21 November 2019

2 days old

Your jaw action has gone Super Saiyan on poor Mummy's boobies. The damage has left a sight that I can only describe as two miniature erupting volcanoes with molten magma pouring over the summits and flowing down the sides. In case you haven't made the link, the magma in the volcano image represents the blood you've drawn from Mummy. You've drawn so much of the stuff that you're now *throwing up* blood clots.

Imagine our fright when we witnessed that for the first time.

The breastfeeding specialist advises that we book you in to see a cranial osteopath. She says that the shape of your skull is causing your jaw to operate in the way that it is, and that a cranial osteopath may be able to do something about it. Just don't ask me what. She also says that, for the time being, we should accept feeding support from a bottle to allow Mummy time to heal. Mummy is gutted, but I tell her that it's all but physically impossible to continue this way. On a brighter note, I've managed to bring the correct-sized vests in for you today, so at least your clothes fit.

I'm still struggling to thread your little Arlo arms through the sleeves of your Babygros. While we're on the subject, I don't like working with hats or mittens either. They're so fucking fiddly, and it's stressing me out.

The Matriarch is supporting my anxiety by laughing uncontrollably – or *partially* uncontrollably – because of the pain she's still in from the surgery. Instead of suspending laugher altogether, she's changed her *style* of laughter to reduce the convulsions that so often accompany a good giggle. The result is that Mummy now laughs like Eddie Murphy, which then makes Daddy laugh.

Another nappy change for Daddy, Arlo, and it's my most challenging yet. I'm contending with the following variables: you being sick, you shitting, you pissing and you flailing both legs. Oh, and also crying. All of this is happening simultaneously.

This is frustrating because if you stop doing all these things at once or even some of these things, then these episodes will pass quickly and I can return you back into the loving arms of one of your parents.

But you're unable to grasp this. I guess that's understandable, considering you are only two days old.

The afternoon passes much the same as yesterday, with your parents smiling, cuddling you or watching you sleep. It would have been a perfect afternoon, save for Mummy receiving some blood-test results that were not what we wanted. In short, they're still indicating that her blood is 'deranged' (Mummy had pre-eclampsia before she gave birth to you). I have no idea how the NHS defines deranged blood, but I know that it means you and Mummy need to remain in the hospital again tonight.

For the third night in a row, I begrudgingly say goodbye and leave my family.

## Home Is Where The Heart Is
Friday, 22 November 2019

3 days old

*Please come home today.*

You're three days old, but I don't feel like we've properly begun parenting yet. We've changed nappies, clothed you, fed you and cuddled you *a lot*, but it doesn't feel authentic with all this taking place in the hospital.

Mummy tells me that you guys had a rough night and that she didn't have as much support from the midwives as she had the previous two nights, resulting in Mummy climbing in and out of bed to check on you on many occasions. No easy feat given her present condition.

During one stage, you *may* have urinated on your face. If you're proud of your accomplishment, then you are in good company.

Breastfeeding is still a no-go area. Even the specialist winced when she examined Mummy, telling her that she needs to rest for a few days before perhaps hand-expressing milk if she wants to continue on this route, which she does.

Mummy's empathy towards Daddy's ineptitude remains AWOL. She laughed so hard when you projectile-vomited over me that I had to ask a midwife to check Mummy's C-section stitches.

She's relentless.

Her stitches were fine, by the way, but I'll tell you something else: that Eddie Murphy laugh isn't as fucking funny as it was yesterday.

It's the afternoon, and the on-shift midwife arrives to check Mummy's blood pressure. We've been waiting all day for this. If the results are *normal* – or *non-deranged* – then Daddy can bring you and Mummy home.

*Please come home today.*

I worry how Mummy will handle having to stay another night in the hospital. Last night was tough on both of you.

The blood-pressure machine takes a few seconds to do what it needs to do before a beep signals completion.

The results are in ...

You're coming home.

*Yes!*

Two facts about Daddy and cars: I've never owned one, despite holding a licence since I was seventeen, and Mummy likes to do all the driving in our relationship. I only drive when I'm without Mummy. Keep those facts in mind as I place you in your car seat and then lower Mummy, who is wincing in pain, into the passenger side of the vehicle.

One of Mummy's many complaints about our car is that the 'suspension is shit' – a view I've always dismissed as 'it could be worse'.

Until now, when I realise I have to drive my three-days-post-op partner, along with my three-day-old baby, home. Suddenly, the suspension issue seems more of a pressing concern, especially as the hospital is overpopulated with speed bumps. I calculate the best possible route to limit the bumps and Mummy's discomfort.

*Almost home, Arlo.*

I don't recall ever taking a corner in first gear, but I count at least four on this journey. The drive is like an adult's version of the egg-and-spoon race, but with cars, newborn babies and an in-pain mummy. Luckily, we live close to the hospital, so it's a short trip, one I spend the entire duration of shitting myself. At least I can blame you for the smell.

The last time Mummy and I walked across the threshold of our house, it was as a two-person family, when we left to go to the hospital seven days ago. We return as a family of three.

Now our parenting adventure can truly begin.

And begin it does, as you wake up and use your lungs to tell us that you're hungry.

*SHHIIITTTT – we don't have any formula!*

I've been blindsided, Arlo. I thought Mummy was content with breastfeeding, but she can't breastfeed while substantial food-factory repair works are undertaken.

Luckily, it's Granny Feeder and Auntie Lisa to the rescue, who soon arrive with your first tub of formula. Auntie Lisa conducts a quick bottle-sterilisation training session for your clueless parents.

Crisis successfully averted. I fear there will be many more to come.

## Night Feeds
Saturday, 23 November 2019

4 days old

'Whhaaaa.'

It's midnight. Time for me to step up my dad game and commence my first night feed.

I drag myself downstairs, fill your bottle up with 2 oz of hot water, add two scoops of formula, and then I place the bottle into a jug of cold water to bring the formula temperature down.

'Whhaaaa.'

I return to our bedroom, gently scoop you out of your Moses basket and lay you down on our bed to change you.

You scream as soon as I remove the dirty nappy, but the pitch reduces once I dress you.

Bottle temperature check …

Hang on a sec, how do I check the temperature? How do I know if it's too hot still? *I don't have a fucking clue what I'm doing.*

'Here, squirt some on my wrist,' says Mummy, who's obviously awake as well.

I do as she says.

'It's fine.'

You and I get comfy, and I begin the feed.

You devour the two ounces.

Winding happens quickly as well. I barely sit you up before you release a great big belch. It's quite comical given your size.

Thirty minutes later, I put you down, and you immediately drift back off to sleep.

And now Mummy and I need to follow suit.

But I can't. I'm tense – unable to relax my shoulders into the mattress. Every sound you make prompts me to check on you, which entails crawling to the end of the bed where your Moses basket lives.

Eventually, I reach that place in between being asleep and awake.

'Whhaaaa.'

I check the time. It's 3 a.m.

I drag myself downstairs, fill your bottle up with 2 oz of hot water, add two scoops of formula ... you get the picture.

It plays out the same way: thirty minutes start to finish. Mummy tells me when the temperature has cooled enough, you gulp down the feed, burp immediately after, and you don't complain when I put you back in your Moses basket.

Once again, I flitter in and out of something that, at a stretch, could be described as sleep, while regularly checking on you to make sure you're OK.

'Whhaaaa.'

I check the time. It's 6 a.m.

'OK, buddy, Daddy's getting up.'

I'm shattered, but I'm pleased with how the night played out, all things considered. You fed, burped and went back to sleep – performing all three actions quickly.

Keep this behaviour up.

The quicker you feed, the quicker we can get back to bed and fall asleep. And the quicker we fall asleep means we sleep more, which then means we'll wake up in a better mood, replete with greater energy reserves that we can all draw on to aid us in piloting ourselves through the day.

Thankfully, it seems you've grasped that concept. For now.

*If only I could relax in between feeds.*

*Thud!*

Post has arrived.

I walk to the front door to find a brightly coloured parcel addressed to you. The sight of your name written in full on the label hits me in an unexpectedly emotional way.

Mummy insists that the wrapping paper be sedulously unfolded. 'It's his first present with his name on it, I want to keep it in his memory box.'

*Naturally.*

Next, we announce your arrival on social media. The response is swift. Everyone appears to like both your name and your appearance. I think they're telling the truth, though you never can tell. No one is going to write, 'Congrats guys! Shame it's an ugly munter of a rat, with a shit name to boot. Not exactly leading with your best foot, are you?'

But I don't care what other people think ... OK, I do a bit.

Mummy and I have agreed to open the doors to visitors this weekend, but then we're shutting them again for a week so we can have some downtime and get to know each other. Granny Smurf is staying in an Airbnb so it really will be the three of us.

But for now, visitors are welcome, and a steady stream of callers arrives throughout the day to admire you. The house is a mess, but no one gives a shit. They care only about meeting you and holding you. Mummy has a huge extended family. The number of cousins runs seemingly into the thousands. You are spoilt: people have brought you clothes, books, soft toys and keepsakes.

Mummy's spoilt as well: she's been brought alcohol and beauty products.

There's nothing for Daddy, though, which is fine. I mean, IT'S NOT LIKE HE DID ALL THE FUCKING NIGHT FEEDS LAST NIGHT, IS IT?

I'm often curious to know what goes through the mind of an adult when they gaze into the eyes of a newborn baby. What do they see? Is it beauty, possibility, potential, promise? Or perhaps there's envy. Envy that a baby's life is just starting out while theirs has been shaped, twisted, battered and scarred by their environment, their experiences, and by the choices they have made thus far. Perhaps there's regret: at opportunities not taken, expectations they held but were never realised, at easier roads they pursued instead of taking the harder path.

Maybe they find inspiration – a spark that alters the course of their destiny in a single brief encounter, one that ends with a promise, *'From this day onwards, I will ...'* Or maybe there's peace and love, and faith in the next generation who will inherit the earth and, hopefully, leave it in a better place than when they found it.

Who knows, but whatever they see when they stare into new eyes, I'd wager it's always poignancy that stares back.

What I do know is that the day passes at a rapid pace, and I'm shocked to look outside and see only darkness. In between making cups of tea, recounting the story of Mummy's labour to visitors, and feeding and changing you, time has raced by. But I've loved every second of it.

Now, I wonder what night two of night-feed duty has in store for us both.

# I Can't Keep ... My Eyes ... Op—
## Sunday, 24 November 2019

### 5 days old

I don't know what time it is, but it's dark outside, and I cannot get you back off to sleep. We've both been up for what feels like hours. I've done everything I can think of: feeding, cuddling, changing and winding. All of this falls into a new category that I've made up, called the 'Big Four'.

I've propped my pillows up in bed, and now I'm sitting gently bouncing you – desperately hoping your little eyelids will fall shut and your lungs quieten.

Finally ... you drift off to sleep.

I nervously shuffle to the edge of the bed. Then I stand, pause, creep towards your Moses basket, delicately lower you in, and then slowly back away from the biological wad of C4.

*Please don't let the bomb go off, please don't let the bomb go off, please don't let the bomb go off.*

It hasn't gone off. *Yes!*

Now, back to b—

'Whhaaaa.'

*KABOOM.*

OK, buddy, back into Daddy's bed we go.

*I wonder what the matter is?*

I strip you down so that you're wearing only a nappy, and then I place you on my chest so we can have some skin-to-skin cuddles.

I'm utterly drained of energy. I check the time: 2.59 a.m.

Must keep ... my eyes op–

My eyes snap open in panic. *I fell asleep*. But I'm in the same position, so I can only have been asleep for a few seconds. Once again, I check the time.

*Holy shit. Fuck.* Arlo, we've slept for three hours. It's almost 6 a.m.!

Shit, shit, shit – what if something happened to you?

I don't know much about the arguments for allowing babies to sleep in bed with their parents, but I know it's discouraged, in case a parent accidentally rolls on top of the baby. I also know that most recorded incidents occur when the parent is under the influence of alcohol or drugs. I had taken neither, but that doesn't get me off the hook. I need to be wary of this happening. It's hard, though, as I've never been at my best when I don't have enough sleep. I know most people aren't, but I am a lamentably pathetic example.

I confess my mistake to Mummy.

'It's OK. I was keeping an eye on you both, and you didn't move a muscle.'

She means well, but I'm a little shaken up. Again, I think to myself, what if something terrible had happened?

And why did you settle well the first night, but not the second?

After a while, we stumble upon what we think is the answer: heat. Or more to the point, we think the room was too hot. That's why skin-to-skin contact eventually settled you. Adults can regulate their own temperature, but babies can't. Skin-to-skin contact allows babies to regulate their temperature *through* the skin of their parents.

When I woke up from our danger nap, I put you back in your Moses basket, but with fewer layers of clothing. I also lowered the temperature.

You immediately went to sleep.

That's the thing with trying to settle a distressed baby in the middle of the night: you can work through the more common symptoms like hunger, wind and a dirty nappy on autopilot. I've already grasped that in the short time you have been home. But things get progressively trickier when it's none of those; when it's something that requires a bit of creative brainpower to solve. Because doing that while tired is really fucking tough.

It's another busy day for the visitors and I'm learning every minute: leave juice, biscuits and cups out on display for guests. Leave the bin out in clear sight rather than under the sink where it usually lives. Use dirty washing to clear up collateral baby piss instead of a clean muslin square. Use a portable basket with nappy-changing supplies that I can cart around the house. Move the outside bin to the back door so that shitty nappies can be hurled in easily. Fill your bottles up during the day with boiling water, so that when they're needed it's quicker to warm them up (we now have a bottle warmer) from room temperature than it is to cool them down from 98 degrees.

Get two dining-room chairs, put them together and wedge them between the party wall and our love seat. Then, get the buggy-bassinet attachment and place it on top of the dining chairs: we now have separate beds for you downstairs, and upstairs. Daddy no longer has to keep carrying the Moses basket up and down the stairs every day.

That's how we need to approach parenthood, Arlo, as one giant learning experience. Every day, we'll learn a little bit more and get a little bit better at it. *I hope.*

I've just realised that it's Sunday. When God was penning the finer details of his bestseller, I don't think he spent enough time focusing on individual circumstances for those expected to follow his resting-on-the-Sabbath-day protocol. It might work when you don't have kids, but not when you do.

But hang on a minute, God did have a kid, didn't he? Oh yeah, that's right, he gave him up for adoption and then had him sacrificed for the 'love and betterment of humanity'. I don't buy that for a minute, big G, more like you weren't stoked for night-feed duty – or having to pay your maintenance fees.

## Our First Difficult Decision
Monday, 25 November 2019

### 6 days old

The wonderful thing about forgetting to put the dishwasher on before bed is that – thanks to you, Arlo – I'm afforded several opportunities throughout the night to rectify the issue while preparing your bottle for a feed.

You slept much better last night. If it was the heat that kept you up the previous night, I'm relieved it only took us one night to figure out. From now on, the Gro-egg thermometer follows you around like an obsessive shadow. *I wonder what a non-obsessive shadow looks like? Maybe Peter Pan knows.*

We have no visitors scheduled today, and Mummy and I are looking forward to spending time with you, just the three of us. Unfortunately, you have other ideas. You've spent the entire day sleeping, waking only for feeds. I estimate we've had about fifteen minutes of your time when you were awake and alert, and not wanting one of the Big Four tending to. I make a joke about waking you up ... except it's not a joke. *WAKE UP, GOD DAMN IT!*

But you don't. So, Mummy uses the downtime to check in on her food-factory repairs, and see if they're ready to start production again.

It doesn't go well. Mummy has tried expressing manually and with a pump, but she's still in agony, and she's getting herself worked up about the whole situation. She's crying, and she keeps repeating that she's a failure. Which, of course, she's not.

Unfortunately, this is yet another component of the motherhood journey.

There's a lot at play here.

Mummy is still exhausted from giving birth to you, plus she's recovering from major surgery. She's also ridiculously stubborn, so she's putting undue pressure on herself to make breastfeeding work. To add to the pile of fun, she's also mindful of research I carried out while you were still Dory about the comparative risks and benefits of breastfeeding and formula-feeding. In short, I was hoping that Mummy would be able to breastfeed you to give you the best start at building up your immune system.

But that was a linear thought process, based on one variable: bottle-fed versus breastfed. It didn't take into account Mummy's mental well-being, nor did it consider the shape of your head, which causes you to clamp down and suck unusually strongly. And it also didn't account for Mummy's hormonal changes.

I don't understand why, from an evolutionary viewpoint, breastfeeding is difficult for women. Their bodies are insanely intelligent and intuitive when it comes to the entire baby-making process, apart from the breastfeeding element. Why does the female body time the rebalancing of its hormones, which is often responsible for the baby blues, to coincide with the mum's milk coming in, when she has to learn how to breastfeed – a process which is often painful, exhausting and emotionally demanding? That makes no sense to me, Arlo, but then I'm a bloke, and I'm hardly an authority on such matters, or any matters really – except maybe Marvel movies.

After a discussion, we both agree to move you on to formula permanently. This is a joint decision. It might be Mummy's body, but she needs my full support right now. Emotionally, she's in bits, and me taking 50 per cent accountability for a big decision like this will help shoulder some of the psychological pressure.

I explain to Mummy that we can start using probiotics in your formula, and we can regiment the shit out of weaning and the introduction of solids. This makes her feel better.

Parental guilt is real, and Mummy-guilt is among the most potent varieties of it.

## Week One Completed
Tuesday, 26 November 2019

7 days old

It's Mummy and Daddy's fifth anniversary. Five years since our first date. It starts a little differently from the previous four years. It starts with Daddy helping Mummy walk to the bathroom so that she can go for a wee, followed by – and I'm not exaggerating when I tell you this – a huge celebration because you've done a poo. It had been twenty hours, and Mummy was beginning to panic.

We follow up the assisted wee and poo celebration with a family selfie at 3 a.m. to celebrate you turning one week old.

'Can we take that again?' Mummy says.

'What, is our sleep-deprived-new-parent look not working for the camera? Maybe we just need to add in a bit more pouting.'

'No, cock, you can see the cabbage leaves that are sticking out from my bra.'

'Huh. You're not wrong.'

'So maybe shut up and take the fucking picture again.'

I retake it, but without the cabbage leaf infiltrating the *mise en scène.*

It's later in the day, and we're rounding off our fifth anniversary by heading to the last place Mummy and Daddy visited together before your birth. It's a little coffee shop down the road. While there, we experience our first instance of a stranger walking up to us to admire you, Arlo. It's sweet, and I don't mind people doing it, so long as they don't outstay their welcome.

I've been at Dadding Inc. for a whole week now, but I've not had a second to sit down and contemplate my new identity as a father. There just hasn't been time. But it has been a memorable first week on the job, and what I can say is that I definitely made the right decision in coming to work here.

## The Nights Take Their Toll
Wednesday, 27 November 2019

8 days old

I slept dreadfully last night, Arlo. It's not because of the night feeds, although – full disclaimer – they don't help. It stems from you stirring in your sleep. You're not necessarily waking up and needing something, but I never know that at the time. I'm on standby because I know I may need to go through the Big Four at any moment. Most of the time, your stirring amounts to nothing and you might only be dreaming or uncomfortable. I'm starting to learn the subtle differences in your movements and cries, but I'm hardly in a position to graduate with full honours in understanding newborn babies. And so sleep comes in an irregular and fleeting manner.

The silence is the toughest challenge because you become *too* silent. I've been up and down to the foot of the bed more times than I care to count to make sure you're OK, and by OK, I mean alive. I've followed this pattern for the last four nights.

Hopefully, things will become easier when Mummy recovers enough from her surgery to begin splitting night-shift duties with me. I don't know if I've mentioned this a million times before, Arlo, but Daddy does not cope well without sleep.

Despite a restless night, there is still much to be done. First on the list is to try you out on probiotics which come in a powder and are added to your bottle. I've checked with midwives and healthcare assistants, and they don't seem to know an awful lot about probiotics and babies. I expected this, but from the reading I've done I'm still confident it's the right decision. Giving you probiotics is the first decision I've pushed for as a parent. Hopefully, I've made the right call.

The next step on today's agenda is to register your birth so the government can document that you're a UK citizen / actual human. I contemplate asking Mummy if we're married to the name Arlo, because we have four formidably strong Ninja Turtle names to select from as backup, not to mention one extraordinarily agile rat.

We arrive fifteen minutes late for our appointment. The receptionist tells me late arrivals are common.

I believe her.

We're directed into a side room where we meet a kind, warm, smiling lady who's waiting patiently to register your existence. She writes down all of our details on your birth certificate before handing it to me. 'Please check the details very carefully because it's a hell of a faff to update them once I press enter.'

I do. I check the form thoroughly three times. For anyone that's counting, that's one more than Santa.

Next, we register you for your library card and in doing so you get a free book. Mummy and Daddy register as well, but we don't get a free book. I shrug when I learn this, but inside I'm gutted. Daddy loves his books, Arlo, and it all seems highly unfair because you can't even see yet, let alone read.

On the way out, we retrace our steps to find the exit, bypassing the stairs and opting for the ramp instead. It dawns on me that we've become people that seek out ramps.

## Changing Nappies? Easy!
Thursday, 28 November 2019

**9 days old**

I've just fucking crushed a nappy change, Arlo. I got everything ready as I always do, but this time my actions felt automatic instead of a conscious decision process: when to remove the old nappy from under you, what side to wipe first, when to replace the old wipe with a new one. These are all decisions, Arlo;

decisions that I agonise over every time I change you. I can usually drag out a sixty-second nappy change to the length of *Gone with the Wind.*

But no longer.

Something was different about this nappy change. It's like I had an extra hand assisting me. My movements were calm, collected and fluid. Even when you decided to piss mid-change, my instincts rose to meet the occasion and I calmly collected every drop of urine in the old nappy. Then I wiped you, switched out the old nappy for the new one, strapped it up, buttoned your vest and Babygro and then finally lifted you for a cuddle – celebrating my victory at the same time.

For my efforts, I receive twenty dad-experience points.

## And Rohan Will Answer!
Friday, 29 November 2019

10 days old

For the first time since you came home, Mummy says that she feels strong enough to tackle a night feed. I cannot express with words how welcoming this development is to my life. Picture a broken, sleep-deprived spectre of a man, who, after having his spirit bent and contorted in ways that seem unnatural (because they are), has glimpsed the shiny prospect of hope, and he's slowly reaching out with two shaky and desperate hands, wondering if it's real, and if he can grasp it firmly enough to mould it into reality. That's me.

'Are you sure you're up for it?'

'Yeah, I think—'

'That's great! Thank you so, so bloody much. You're so awesome. WHOOP WHOOP!' I practically shot-put the parenthood baton towards her from my side of the bed, before getting comfortable and shutting my eyes.

Arlo, I'm clocking off!

## Our New Names
Saturday, 30 November 2019

11 days old

Mummy and Daddy have many different names for each other. We have our first names, middle names, surnames, pet names, and names for when we piss each other off. Yet, these days, we don't use any of them.

Since becoming parents, we have only ever called each other Mummy and Daddy. It took me a few days to realise this, but we can't seem to stop it. Every day, mundane lines of dialogue such as 'Are you OK?' or 'Put the kettle on' become 'Is Mummy OK?' and 'Daddy, put the kettle on'. My favourite so far is Mummy saying, 'Does Daddy want to think about taking a day off from being a cunt?' It's madness, especially when she knows I'd never take a day off from that.

I don't know if this practice is unique to us, or if it's common among parents.

# December

## Exhaustion!
Sunday, 1 December 2019

**12 days old**

You've woken up at 1.30 a.m. for your bottle. It's my shift, and so I automatically follow the night-feed bottle protocols. Then I try to settle you back down to sleep. But I can't because it's now 4.30 a.m. ... and you haven't burped.

That's right, buddy, I've spent three fucking hours trying to get a single burp out of you. It's been so long that I think you must be due another feed soon.

I can barely function. I can hear sounds and distant snatches of conversation going on in my head, even though no one is talking; the effects of sleep deprivation, I suspect. I've exhausted every trick I know. I've rocked you back and forward, and side to side; I've patted you on the back; I've had you over both of my shoulders; I've walked you around the bedroom; I've put you on your front over my leg; I've even had you on your front resting on my forearm – a move I wouldn't have dreamt of attempting even a few days ago, but that's probably because dreaming requires sleep, and that's an activity that I've not been overindulging in of late.

This is shit for both of us. You're clearly in discomfort: squirming around in my arms, scrunching up your face, and punctuating the air with irregular piercing screams that slice through my eardrums. I assume you're in pain from wind, but as I said, you've been like this for three hours – it should have passed by now, shouldn't it?

I feel dizzy. Everything is swaying in and out of focus.

Finally, at 4.35 a.m., you burp. Its results are instantaneous: you stop moving your legs and crying because you're no longer in pain.

You fall asleep in my arms shortly afterwards.

Being tired is tough, but being tired because your baby is in pain and won't settle makes it a hundred times worse.


## Do Your Worst
Monday, 2 December 2019

13 days old

Reusable wipes are revolutionary, not to mention a breeze to set up and use. You have two buckets: one for clean wipes and one for dirty wipes. You fill each bucket with water, add a few drops of essential oils for odour-control purposes and then you place the wipes in the clean bin, allowing them to soak up the water. Then they're ready to use. The dirty bucket comes with a nylon drawstring bag so that, when it comes to washing, you lift it straight out of the bucket and into the washing machine. Easy.

My favourite thing about reusable wipes is how economical they are. I'm not talking in the money sense, although that's also a benefit, I'm talking about productivity. I can clear all of the excrement debris with one wipe, fold it over, and use the underside to finish the job. Before, I would have got through between four and eight disposable wipes per nappy change.

It's the little things in life, Arlo, unlike the poo you've done which is anything but little. It matters not, as I have a reusable wipe at the ready – come at me, bro.

## Week Two Complete
Tuesday, 3 December 2019

14 days old

'Do you think he's developed a case of the jowls?' I say.

'What do you mean?' Mummy asks, already prepping her hackles for immediate take-off.

'It's just ... He seems a bit jowly, that's all. Check out his cheeks – don't they scream "massive case of the droops"?'

Naturally, I give your cheeks a little wobble, just to demonstrate my point to Mummy. I also add sound effects, *wibble-wobble-wibble-wobble.*

'Absolutely fucking not, he does not have jowls, how dare you say that about my baby boy?'

'Not to split atoms but he's *our* baby boy. Don't worry, though, there's plenty of baby to go around – just look at his jowls!'

'HE DOES NOT HAVE JOWLS!'

You're two weeks old today. You've already changed so much. Jowl-joking aside, every day I see new facial expressions. Your weight has gone up, I can see it on your legs and your face. You're now on 4-oz bottles.

My favourite thing to do with you is to lie down on the sofa while you sleep on my chest. It's lovely. We've watched *E.T.* and a few *Star Wars* movies in this position.

My second-favourite thing to do is to pull faces and watch you copy me. I had no idea this sort of interaction would be possible at this stage. I thought we were months away from imitation.

My third-favourite thing is to read to you. You fall asleep almost every time. I don't know if that's an insult or a compliment, and I don't care.

In the UK at least, it's typical for dads to take two weeks of paternity leave to bond with their newborn baby, and then return to work. Having reached the end of the two-week mark myself, I cannot comprehend going back into the office so soon. It feels like I've been off for less than a day even though it's been almost a month. It is my humble opinion that two weeks off for dads is simply not long enough for them to bond with their babies and as a family.

When a friend or colleague returns home from holiday and you ask them how it was, you're all but guaranteed to hear a response like, 'It was nice, but it went too quickly.' Well, that same holiday is like a ten-year prison sentence in solitary confinement compared to the first two weeks of being at home with a newborn baby because it passes at light speed.

Luckily, I don't have to think about ironing a shirt for tomorrow because I've taken four months off to be at home with you and Mummy. This has been made possible by a new government scheme that came into play in 2015, enabling dads to share the mums' maternity leave. It's called Shared Parental Leave (SPL), and it's bloody great because it means we can add the *Back to The Future* trilogy to the must-watch-with-son movie list.

## Christmas Baubles And Pole-Vaulting
Wednesday, 4 December 2019

15 days old

Today, we're on a family outing to a nearby coffee shop, which is playing host to a baby hand-and-footprint keepsake company. Mummy is hoping there's an option for a personalised bauble for the Christmas tree.

Things don't get off to a great start as we're late, a term which I'm beginning to realise should be redefined as 'on time, but with a baby'. Our next hurdle is getting the buggy into the coffee shop. The entrance threshold step comes up just shy of my knees – hardly designed for pushchairs.

Once inside, I place the buggy in the corner and eject you from the bassinet, and then I begin removing the eighteen layers of blankets that Mummy has encased you in, before heading downstairs to where the keepsake company has set up shop. Luckily, it's not busy, so this shouldn't take long.

But apparently, it *will* take long because we didn't book. Mummy triple-checks the advertisement, which says nothing about booking.

Two lattes later, you're up. There's a lot of options to select from: plates, bowls, mugs and, luckily for the Matriarch, Christmas-tree baubles.

It doesn't go well. You refuse to open your hand and have it painted, and then placed delicately – but firmly – in position long enough for your print to transfer itself on to the glass ball. We try three times, but then you go from 'slightly irritable' to 'fuck off now and leave my hand alone', at which point I decide we should stop.

We do have something to show for our efforts, though. The nice woman who owns the business reveals a splodgy kinda-hand-shaped-if-you-squint bauble. It's more non-hand-shaped than it is hand-shaped, unless we pretend that you're a raccoon. To improve the bauble's appearance and make its semblance less raccoon-like, she's opted to fill in the gaps with fingerprints from your right little finger.

If you're looking at your bauble years from now, thinking, 'Hey, all my fingers look like they're made up of the tip of my little finger!' it's because they are. And yes, they're also upside down.

Still, it's nice that it's not perfect; a reminder that imperfection is its own kind of perfection if you adjust your perspective ... right?

At least we have something to hang on the tree.

'When will that be ready for collection?' I ask the woman.

'Well, I will try and have it ready for Christmas, but I can't promise. Is that OK?'

*Is that OK?*

Let me think this through for half a moment: is it OK that our son's first Christmas bauble, featuring something that – if I get jacked up on crack and mushrooms – could possibly resemble his handprint, might not be ready for his first Christmas, even though it says on the bauble 'My First Christmas'?

'Sure,' I say.

I know that's a complete lie, but what's the point? You weren't crazy about the whole process anyway, and the only ones who honestly give a shit are Mummy and me, and you know Mummy will acquire a million keepsakes over the years – that's in addition to the millions we have already. We could always invest in a bottle of Tipp-Ex and edit the bauble so that it says 'Second Christmas' if need be.

Now, let's get you strapped back in and see if we can't abseil down out of this coffee shop.

# Dear Santa
Thursday, 5 December 2019

16 days old

Arlo, in the last two weeks, I've gotten to know you well enough to understand everything you say. This is a wonderfully timed development as I can now go through your Santa list with you. And that's what we did together this morning while Daddy was dressing you in a cute little over-the-head koala outfit. I can't be 100 per cent certain on an exact translation from baby talk to English, but I'd bet my house on it being accurate enough.

This is what you wrote:

*Dear Santa,*

*This is my first-ever letter to you. I'm dictating the contents to my daddy as I'm only 16 days old and can't touch type yet (obviously – ha ha ha).*

*I don't want anything specific for my first Christmas: I have the love of my family, which if anything is a little too much to bear right now. But because I'm a brand-new, cute baby boy, people will want to spoil me – most people love newborn babies. It's sweet, and I'm comfortable receiving their gifts (especially cash).*

*But there is something* I don't *want to receive.* Ever.

*Please Santa, don't come anywhere near me with those stupid, annoying, fucking useless over-the-head Babygros. I fucking hate them, and they piss me off.*

*From an engineering standpoint, they make
no sense. Why complicate an issue that's already
been addressed with full-length poppers or a zip?
I mean, the poppers are even colour-coded.*

*I am willing to stake half of my next feed (that's
two ounces, Santa) that anyone on the planet who
has even remotely contributed to the existence of
an over-the-head Babygro does not have children.*

*Or, if they do, they're not very fond of them.*

*Yours sincerely*

~~*Arlo's daddy,*~~ *I mean just Arlo*

*PS: if you're short on staff this year, Santa,
I recommend hiring midwives. They're capable of
managing a heavy workload while maintaining
a sense of goodwill and Christmas spirit.*

## This Should Arouse You
Friday, 6 December 2019

17 days old

Mummy is going shopping with you, Auntie
Lisa and your cousin Haylee. They're taking one
car, and there's only enough space for one buggy
in the boot. You guys need two. Auntie Lisa has
a solution: she suggests that they take one for
Haylee, but use a sling for you. Auntie Lisa will
carry you in the sling because Mummy still has her
tummy ouchie, and Mummy will push Haylee in
the buggy. Lovely stuff.

The problem I have with all of this, and it's incredibly selfish, is that I wanted to be the first person to take you out for a test drive in a sling.

Luckily, it's Mummy to the rescue with a solution: she reminds me that we've been given a sling from a friend, and if I want to, I can test it out right this second around the house. I enthusiastically agree.

This was a mistake, Arlo.

The sling we have is called a wrap. Obviously, I had to google that. It's a little black number, and I look fucking ridiculous in it. A wrap sling is essentially a long piece of fabric, not unlike an extra-wide, and extra-long, scarf. Assembling it around my torso requires the fabric to be looped over my arms and crossed behind my back. It's threaded all around my body, and the leftover fabric is tied into a knot and left hanging from my waist, down to my knees. I look like I'm going to a *Mortal Kombat* fancy-dress party, having been given a budget of 60p and only ten minutes to get ready.

## I Was Never Trained For This
Saturday, 7 December 2019

18 days old

Sometimes, you want to feed at the perfect time because the bottles that I've prepped with boiling water have cooled down to room temperature, so I add the formula and away we go.

Right now is one of those instances. The bottle temperature is perfect, so I add the formula, and I'm about to screw the lid on and shake it when I notice an eyelash in the milk.

Now that's what I like to call a fucking curveball because I don't know what to do. My instincts tell me that this is not a problem. But I don't have the confidence to allow for instincts because a) I'm new to the job, and b) I've never come across this scenario before – or even considered it to be a possibility.

I could start the bottle again, but then I would have to wait another five minutes for it to cool down. It might even take longer as the water tank in the fridge is empty so I'll have to use water from the tap and that isn't as cold.

I say, 'Fuck it – you'll be fine.'

But instead of feeding you, I pour the contents down the sink and begin the process again. Fuck you, eyelash – you absolute bastard.

## Never, EVER Wake The Baby
### Sunday, 8 December 2019

19 days old

'Shit, babe, what time is it?' says Mummy.

'Five thirty a.m., my sweet.'

'Fuck, he's skipped a bottle. He's slept for six hours.'

'You say that like it's a bad thing.'

'But he's still asleep.'

'Again, you say that like it's a bad thing.'

'Is he OK?'

'He's fine.'

'How can you tell without looking?'

'I can hear him snoring.'

'Should we wake him?'

'That's a terrible, terrible idea. Never wake the baby.'

Thirty minutes later, you wake up for your bottle, none the wiser to your new personal-best record of sleeping for six hours, my darling boy. Six hours of uninterrupted sleep. You beautiful, special, wonderful little creature. Daddy is super proud of you. Keep up the good work. No, seriously, keep it up!

## Splish Splash
Tuesday, 10 December 2019

21 days old

Happy three-week birthday, son. To celebrate, we've decided to bath you for the first time in your life. I've prepared myself for a meltdown, along with arranging everything necessary to complete this activity inside sixty seconds.

But my preparation wasn't needed because you don't seem to mind the water at all. You appear content and happy. You're just chilling. Baths are the best, aren't they? Daddy loves his baths.

And then suddenly you're no longer chilling – you're crying. And you're squirming around in pain.

You've got trapped wind, but this isn't like the other night when it took me three hours to settle you back down that crying was irregular, brief and sharp. Now it's a constant, high-pitched wail. For the first time, I can see real pain in your eyes, and there is not an awful lot Mummy and I can do about it, apart from blaming ourselves for failing to wind you properly. And now Mummy is crying.

I'm trying to manoeuvre you into any position that will reduce your discomfort, but I'm not having much luck. Music is helping – a bit. We've recently taken to singing 'Mr Sandman' but replacing the 'Mr Sandman' lyric with 'Mr Arlo'. We add that to Frank Sinatra and constant body repositioning, and your suffering eventually passes.

Today's parenting lesson: make sure you get all the wind up and out through the top end, and not the bottom end. That was an unpleasant experience. But then parenthood can be like that: one minute you're transported to the most beautiful and profound emotional destinations where you're smiling, laughing and your heart is swelling to the size of a zeppelin; and then the next, it's like you've been possessed by a poltergeist and your entire body is being dragged, jerked and slammed into all four walls of the room you're standing in. When you emerge, all you want to do is sleep, except you can't because sleep is item number two on your list of priorities. Item one is a screaming baby who wants his suffering to end. You'd love to comply, but you don't know how. So you stumble forward, surviving on the fumes and the vapours from an almost empty petrol tank, until your baby's needs are met before your own.

Oh well, at least bath time was fun.

# Why Won't You Go Back To Sleep?
Thursday, 12 December 2019

23 days old

You will not settle.

You woke up at 3.15 a.m. for your bottle. I fed you the same way I always do: I allowed you to take two gigantic gulps, and then I pulled the bottle away from your mouth, to stop you devouring its contents in one go while also reducing the risk of trapped wind. Then I let you drink roughly an ounce before I stopped feeding and attempted to extract a burp. You and I *usually* make quick work of this winding lark.

This time, however, something was wrong. I came to the conclusion it was trapped wind, but, of course, that was just guesswork because, outside of crying and wriggling uncomfortably, you can't tell me what's up. It's like playing a game of charades with someone who doesn't know the rules or that they're even playing charades in the first place. So, at roughly 3.45 a.m., I drearily began my campaign in search of an elusive burp that might not even exist. I placed you over my shoulder and paced up and down the room.

Nothing.

I sat you up on my leg, holding you upright with one hand, and rubbing your back with the other.

Nothing. *Come on, buddy ...*

I stopped rubbing and started patting your back.

Nothing.

Next, I sat you up again, and I moved your entire body as if it were a gearstick in a car. I moved you up, down, left and right; a pattern I've not replicated since the last time I entered a *Sonic the Hedgehog* cheat[1] into my Sega Mega Drive console.

Still nothing.

It's now 4.45 a.m. I don't know what to do.

I've checked your nappy countless times, the room temperature is OK, I've tried dummies, I've attempted to lay you in bed next to me and I've called on Ewan the white-noise-emitting cuddly sheep to assist.

Again, nothing.

At this point, I'm getting fed up. I'm tired, I've gone through the Big Four, and I'm all out of ideas.

My frustration manifests itself in me swearing loudly enough to wake Mummy up, although I'm surprised she was asleep because you're hardly winning an Academy Award for Best Mime Act right now. Anyhow, frustrated at being woken up, Mummy suggests I lie you in the middle of the bed, give you a dummy and see if that settles you. I explain that I've done this several times already, but I don't have anything else up my sleeve so I might as well give it a try.

The change in behaviour is instantaneous. You're flat out asleep within thirty seconds. Mummy rolls over to go back to sleep without saying a word.

From the bottom of my heart – fuck you, Arlo.

---

1 The full *Sonic* cheat is up, down, left, right on the gamepad (you should hear the sound of a ring being collected). Then hold down A and press the Start button. If the sequence has been entered correctly, you can now select any level you want to play.

# An Argument Over Fucking Christmas Lights
Friday, 13 December 2019

24 days old

I'm rowing with your mother, who is currently sitting on the floor cross-legged, face in hands, sulking. This enchanting little episode in our lives is taking place in the Christmas-lights section of a local homeware store.

If we back up an hour, I'll explain why we're at an impasse. Someone had stolen the plug adapter from the box of lights that Mummy bought the other day, so we took them back to the store. However, the store had sold out of lights and could not offer us a replacement, so they gave us a refund instead.

That's when we travelled to the homeware store we're standing (or sitting) in right now. We came here intending to buy more lights, but this time, with a non-stolen adapter. This store is vastly different from the other one. Not only has this store not sold out of Christmas lights, but they also have a wide selection – we're talking numbers that rival King Kong's inside-leg measurement.

When we arrived, I knew what had to happen, so I stood back and let the Matriarch go to town on making her selection. She's in charge of Christmas because this time of year is exceptionally special to her. It's fun to see an adult display passion and ebullience over lights; overexcitement being one of your mother's most charming personality traits. I wouldn't dream of asking her to compromise.

That was until a few minutes ago, when she presented her choice to me: a box of *two thousand* LED lights.

'We don't need two thousand lights,' I said. I could already tell we were heading for a battle, Arlo.

'Yes, we do, plus you can use these lights outdoors,' she said, wide-eyed and beaming as if she had just got out of paying a late-fee charge on her gas bill.

*How do I get through to her?* I thought. 'We live in a terraced house. Where are you proposing to dangle these lights, on the pavement? Obviously not the back garden because not even Buddy the Elf decorates the back garden. Besides, all of this is irrelevant, as we don't need two thousand fucking lights. It's not Nakatomi Plaza!'

'OK, well, I'll use them on the tree.'

'Two thousand lights on a six-foot indoor Christmas tree?'

'Yes,' Mummy said, with a nod that implied it was settled.

Can you imagine the front page of the newspapers tomorrow? *Aeroplane mistakes terrace house for a landing strip at Heathrow airport.*

Anyway, I took a look at the box and read the specs on the back: the length of the lights was fifty metres. Fifty fucking metres, Arlo! The Rainbow Road track on *Mario Kart* doesn't have that many lights.

'No,' I said, taking a rare firm stance on the matter.

And that brings us to now: the Matriarch is sitting cross-legged on the floor of the aisle sulking. You're oblivious to all of this as you're asleep in the buggy next to us.

I try and subdue the mood by selecting a *smaller* box – one that contains an impressive five hundred lights. 'What about this one?' I say.

'It's not enough,' Mummy says, without even looking at the box.

'It's seventeen metres long. I promise you, it's big enough.'

'Fine, but we're buying two boxes in case it's not.'

'Sure – I wouldn't dare suggest otherwise.'

People are bizarre, Arlo – nearly a month ago, I watched your mother go through the unbelievable trauma that is giving birth to a baby. But whereas she pretty much shrugged at childbirth, tonight I've watched her allow herself to be negotiated down from two thousand lights to five hundred and the act has crushed her spirit. Unbelievable. She's looking at me like I've just kicked a sleeping homeless woman in the head. How is it I feel guilty over this?

Thirty minutes later and we've put the lights up, they look great and your mother is back to her cheerful, chirpy self. It goes without saying that we only needed one box, and the other is waiting by the front door to be returned to the store.

'Tis the season to be jolly, Arlo.

## Partying With A Newborn Baby
Saturday, 14 December 2019

25 days old

We have two social engagements to attend tonight. The first is at a friend of Mummy's. I know some of the attendees, but not most of them.

We arrive, and naturally you receive all the attention, which I don't mind. Well, a little bit of me does, because you're now being passed around by people I don't know, and it's a party, so alcohol is flowing. But it's still early (6 p.m.), and everyone handles you with care, ensuring your head is protected in their arms.

Still, I'm on edge.

I also don't like it that someone whom I've not met before tonight took a photo of you without asking permission. I'm all up for challenging the status quo in life, but walking up to someone of any age and invading their personal space to point a camera in their face without asking permission is universally unacceptable. The lens was about six inches away from your nose.

Fortunately, no one bats an eyelid when we say we need to feed you (which is true) and that we'd like to do so at home: one party down, one to go.

Our next engagement is a thirtieth birthday party for one of Mummy's cousins. The amount of people I know versus those I don't is vastly different from the last gathering. Another difference is that you will not be coming along.

We've made the admittedly difficult decision to leave you with Granny Smurf. She's still living at our house, so it makes sense. She feels privileged to be babysitting you for the first time. I've not even done that yet. This will be the first time that both of your parents have left you simultaneously.

To ease our guilt / anxiety / fill in the blank, we've told Granny Smurf that she has you for the night, but we've asked her not to be offended if we're back home in twenty minutes, wanting to relieve her of her babysitting duties. She agrees, and promises to send regular updates.

Begrudgingly, we leave.

It takes us a while, especially Mummy, but after a few drinks we both relax and start to embrace the atmosphere. Mummy hasn't enjoyed a proper drink since before she was pregnant.

Updates come through regularly: nothing exciting has happened, you've been asleep the whole time. It's reassuring to know you're OK.

At 1 a.m. I leave to go home while Mummy remains, carrying on to the after-party at one of the cousins' houses. I'm not going because I'm a lightweight, and the thought of getting a full night's sleep is more appealing to me than continuing to socialise.

I return home and check in with you and Granny Smurf. You're still asleep, and Granny Smurf is more than willing to continue babysitting for the night. I accept the support and disappear to my bed, where I plan to have the longest sleep I've had in nearly a month.

## Wakey Wakey, Baby
Sunday, 15 December 2019

26 days old

That long sleep lasted until 5 a.m. (four hours total), when I was woken – not by you, or by Granny

Smurf – but by the Matriarch, who disturbed my slumber to tell me how she wasn't even drunk and that we had made a beautiful, perfect little boy.

I agree with one of those statements.

## Say Cheese!
Tuesday, 17 December 2019

### 28 days old

Granny Smurf is convinced you've smiled for the first time. I'm not on board: certain conditions need to have been met before I'll be satisfied that you have pulled your first social smile.

For starters, you've been threatening to smile all week, we've had half-smiles and smirks, and you've even produced a noise that sounds like laughing, but I think that happens when you have wind and make this strange inhalation. It's cute, but it's not a social reaction.

Also, Granny Smurf has contracted conjunctivgrannyitis – a condition of the eyes where grandmothers see whatever they want to see in their grandchildren. If I believed everything about what she claimed you could do at under a month old, I'd be disappointed you weren't the newly appointed CEO of Microsoft, or at the very least, someone capable of understanding the rules to Connect 4.

For me to be convinced, I would like to see the following: both sides of your mouth curled up into a smiling position that you hold for at least two seconds, and for that to happen outside of feeding and winding time. Once those conditions are met, and either Mummy or I witness the event, we will officially record it as your first social smile.

It turns out I only have to wait twenty minutes for those conditions to be satisfied. I've taken you and Mummy to see a nice lady named Marie who does something – don't ask me what – to Mummy's eyebrows. The girls get started, and I busy myself with extricating you from your car seat. Once you're liberated, I move on to removing a few layers of clothing. I get one sleeve off when you hit me with an unmistakeable social smile. My heart changes from solid to liquid in a nanosecond.

Perhaps I imagined it?

Nope, that's another smile right there, and now another one. Even Marie caught a glimpse of that last one.

These are your first confirmed social smiles. Annoyingly, this development adds credibility to Granny Smurf's version of events from this morning, meaning she can, and most definitely will, claim the first confirmed sighting.

As charming as this development is, Mummy didn't see it. She missed all of your smiles because she was on the operating table having her eyebrows ... can I say threaded?

Now I feel guilty.

Once the girls conclude their eyebrow business, we drive home.

You're now lying on the bed, naked, looking at your parents like we're from another planet, and for good reason: we have spent the last twenty minutes performing an array of movements, faces and noises – even a combination of all three simultaneously – just to elicit a smile from you in front of Mummy. If I keep my face in the same smiling position any longer, I think I'll have a seizure.

But try as we might, the most you have surrendered so far is a half-smirk. Damn it! Would you please perform for Mummy? I think she deserves a smile.

You must hear my thoughts because you perform – although not in the way I was hoping. We got so distracted trying to make you smile that we've forgotten you are still naked ... and so you piss all over your mother.

Way to add salt to a hormonal new parent's open wound!

## Cinemas And A Sensitivity To Altitude
Wednesday, 18 December 2019

29 days old

Mummy didn't have to wait long for her first smile. It's morning, and you've just given her a beautiful smile, one that's full of glowing, emanating energy. She is smitten. Good boy – very good boy!

Can you maintain your good behaviour for the rest of the morning? I hope so, because we're on our way to the cinema and you're coming with us. The cinema we go to has one screening a week where babies can attend.

We arrive to find only three other small humans in attendance. We park the buggy at the front and take our seats, ready for *Knives Out*.

You behave extraordinarily well. Mummy feeds you forty minutes into the film, and we have to stand and pace up and down with you every so often, but that's the extent of it.

The film ends without any baby drama. I'm proud of you. Does this mean this can be a regular thing?

You're no longer a good boy. You're a bad boy. You've developed something I'm calling UAS. It stands for Ultra Altitude Sensitivity. What happens is this: I sit down with you in my arms with the aspiration to relax for a few minutes, and you respond by wailing. So, I stand up and hold you in the same position, and you stop wailing.

Why is this, Arlo? Why?

I could understand it if you were uncomfortable and you wanted me to reposition you, but all I'm doing is standing up or sitting down.

I readjust you again and again: on my legs, on your front, in my arms and over my shoulder, yet you cry when I sit down and settle when I stand up. It's not like it's the view that's infringing upon your delicate sensibilities because the walls don't change colour when I stand up.

I'm asking for five minutes to drink my coffee, that's all. I'll remember this when you're a teenager about to set out on your first date. I'll be like, 'Arlokins, have you packed your pink Power Rangers handkerchief? You know how you get the sniffles when you're around girls.' I mean it. I'll go there if you don't simmer the fuck down and let me drink my coffee.

Mummy thinks this is hilarious – you being an arsehole, not my Power Rangers joke. She tells me not to call you a bad boy. She thinks you're the best-behaved boy on the planet.

Mummy has reversed her position: she's just called you a very bad boy – FYI, I never went as low as using the word 'very' – and she's accusing you of showing her up in public.

We're at an NCT[2] reunion with all the babies from our class, and, within five minutes of us arriving, you've thrown up over your new Christmas jumper and refused to settle, and now you're kicking out your legs and causing a right scene.

*Lad.*

I see this as karma, Arlo – balance restored.

'I can't believe you used the word "very",' I say to Mummy, with an expression of exaggerated shock and horror.

---

2 National Childbirth Trust (NCT) is the UK's largest parent charity. Among other things, they run courses for groups of new parents who are expecting their first child around the same time. I covered our NCT experience in *Dear Dory*.

# One Month Old
Thursday, 19 December 2019

### 30 days old

You're one month old today. I've learnt so much I don't know where to start. There have been things Mummy and I predicted right, things we got wrong, and some things that we sort of knew, but woefully underestimated. Let's take a look.

Your temperament is one of the factors that has helped get the three of us out of the gates and off to a good start on our parenthood journey because, minor mishaps aside, you're sleeping wonderfully for a newborn baby. It's got to a point where we find ourselves having to apologise to other parents because you only wake up two or three times in the night for a feed. We daren't tell them about that time when we logged six glorious hours of uninterrupted slumber.

But you still need to be fed, and both parents are up multiple times a night, so we're always tired. But it's not the same feeling of tiredness as not being able to keep your eyes open when you stay up late – that night I fell asleep with you on me being a one-off. It's more like when you go to sleep, but then you have to get up in the middle of the night to catch a flight to go on holiday. A parent's tiredness is like that, but it's there 24/7. Still, I'm coping better than I expected.

According to the internet, you're going through your first development leap where your body and mind adjust to new sensations and feelings. It's said to be a difficult time for a baby and we were prepared for a stormy patch. The science appears to correlate with your behaviour as you've become unsettled over the last few days, but that could be a coincidence, and honestly, it's not that bad.

This has to make a world of difference to a new parent's experience.

Everyone keeps telling us that your calm temperament will disappear, that we have no idea what we're about to face. I detect resentment.

'Just you wait,' they say, or, 'Don't get used to that.'

But until your temperament changes, we'll continue being grateful for what we've got today, which is a baby who feeds well, sleeps wellish, and who is happy and chilled 90 per cent of the time.

That doesn't mean we have it easy, though. Outside of cuddles and staring into your eyes (or eyelids), there are a ton of chores that need completing daily, which is something we expected, but woefully underestimated. Let's start with washing: bottles need washing and sterilising each day; the reusable wipes need washing and replacing; and the washing load in general is without a shred of mercy.

Taking inventory of your changing bag and changing caddies requires regular attention. Feeding you takes longer than expected: by the time you've had 4 oz, been winded and had your nappy changed, forty minutes have elapsed.

It's true what other parents say: you struggle to get much done. Mummy and I find ourselves regularly skipping meals, forgetting to shower or even brush our teeth. Before you were born, I was reading my fifty-sixth book of the year. Since you were born, I'm still on my fifty-sixth book. Ironically, I've learnt more in the last month than I have all year, which illustrates that no amount of reading or time in a classroom can replace experience.

As a man who has taken time off work to be a hands-on parent, I will be offended if I ever hear another of my fellow species comment on how stay-at-home mums have it easy – 'All they do is watch television all day.' That's bullshit. I've now done both the full-time-working and the stay-at-home-parent gigs, and I can tell you that babies are hard work. Let me reiterate that you're a well-behaved baby, you're our only child and you have both of us looking after you full-time. Yet it's still tough.

I'll always respect any parent that stays at home to look after a baby.

You do not like having your nappy changed. It's the one time where we can guarantee you will start crying. To make the process drag out a little longer, we've learnt that it's foolish to fasten a fresh nappy on immediately after removing the dirty one. Genital exposure to the fresh air all but guarantees you'll wee again, which is especially frustrating at night when you're performing your impression of a siren at sea who's had her arm hacked off.

It took me a while to get used to the fact you have a willy. I know that sounds strange given I possess one myself, but it's only my own that I've had to look after before. It took both Mummy and me a few nappies and being pissed on to get used to it.

Speaking of your micturition habits, I no longer flinch if you export any type of bodily fluid over me. It doesn't bother me any more. As long as you're safe and content, then so am I.

All the various check-ups you've undergone from healthcare workers and community midwives have been fine. I keep pointing out the cloudy film over your left eye, but every medically trained person dismisses it as 'probably nothing'. I'm good with the 'nothing' part of that phrase but not the word 'probably'. What does that even mean? But then I remember when you were born, and the eye specialist had no concerns, so I guess they're right, and it is probably nothing. Still, if a pilot said, 'I'll probably nail the landing,' or a prostate doctor said, 'I'm probably in the right hole,' you wouldn't just shrug it off.

Mummy has lived up to the admittedly high expectations of motherhood that everyone and their dogs (and cats and rabbits) had. She's truly unbelievable. She's patient, she's loving and she's caring. She excels in every element. I get untold amounts of pleasure listening to her talk and sing to you. Especially at night when, every time you burp, she makes an impression of Jafar from *Aladdin* and says, 'Excellent, Iago.'

She's phenomenal.

And so are you.

Thank you for everything you have taught me, and thank you for enriching my life.

## 'Hi Ho Silver'
Friday, 20 December 2019

31 days old

I like to output a ton of bullshit from my mouth when trying to entertain or wind you. I tell stories, ask stupid questions and make up songs. I have to make the songs up because I don't know the lyrics to any of the nursery rhymes yet and I have a terrible memory in general, so I don't even know the words to songs I love that aren't nursery rhymes.

This morning, for instance, you would not burp for me, so I found myself singing a song that consisted entirely of the lyric 'Do a burp' to the theme tune of *The Lone Ranger*. It went something like this:

*Verse*
Do a burp, do a burp, do a burp, burp, burp
Do a burp, do a burp, do a burp, burp, burp
Do a burp, do a burp, do a burp, burp, burp
Burp, burp – burp, burp, burp, burp
(repeat verse twice)

*Chorus*
BURP, BURP, BURP, BURP, BURP, BURP, BURP,
BURP, BURP, BURP, BURP, BURP, BURP
(repeat chorus four times)

Repeat above as many times as it takes until the burp appears or until you cannot be fucked to continue and you need to offload to Mummy.

# The Fatherhood Trials
Saturday, 21 December 2019

32 days old

'It will only be for a few hours. Are you sure you're going to be OK?' Mummy says.

'Of course I'm going to be OK. I don't know why you're making such a big deal out of it,' I say. My body language is that of a stoned teenager reading a magazine: chilled out to the max.

But my body language, and my words, are a ruse. Because I'm not sure if I am going to be OK.

'In that case, I'll see you guys later.' Mummy leaves the house to go to a hair appointment, leaving you and me to have some father-and-son bonding time. This marks the first time I've been in charge of you alone for a period longer than an hour, which might explain why my chest is thumping like it's the main speaker at an underground rave, and my heart rate has just landed a new personal best of a thousand beats per minute.

*Gulp!* I won't lie, I feel a million miles outside of my comfort zone.

But at the same time, I'm determined. Not only do I need to be able to look after you by myself, I want to. So, I've decided to use this as an opportunity to test out my new parenting skills.

First, I feed you. This one's easy as I've done it countless times before, but what I've not had to do is prepare your bottle while holding you in my arms.

I can't do both at once, so I put you down and distract you by teaching you about my favourite *Star Wars* characters.

Simple.

Next, I bath you. This is something I've never done by myself either. Come to think of it, this will be only your third bath. I take the temperature more times than I need, and I triple-check everything I need on the list – two items: a towel and a baby.

You cry when I get you naked, but settle as soon as you're in the bath. We have a bit of kit that you sit in, so I don't need to worry about you drowning – something we refer to as a positive.

That's feeding and bathing successful.

Next up is baby pampering. I lie you on your changing mat and pat you dry with your towel. You piss on the towel, but I wanted you to have a bit of naked time, so I had mentally factored in a pissy towel. Once you're clean and dry, I apply some coconut oil to your body and put a fresh nappy on.

Now comes the final test and it's the hardest of all. When selecting your outfit, I *purposely* select a cunting, dreaded full-length over-the-head Babygro. But then I immediately regret my decision because you've decided you've had enough pampering and you would now like a cuddle – a desire you express by crying and shaking your limbs.

I open the wardrobe, about to reach for an easier outfit, when a voice in my head causes me to halt.

*Come on – you can do this.*

I can do this, Arlo.

I get the hardest part out of the way first – the arms. But it's not as hard as I was expecting. It's ... easy. You're crying, and flailing all four limbs around. You look like a professional yo-yo performer who's midway through a complicated manoeuvre. But none of this fazes me.

*Huh?*

I thread your arms and legs in, do up the poppers and pick you up for a cuddle. You settle instantly – it feels like you're congratulating me on how far I've come on my parenthood journey.

Ten minutes later and you're asleep, and you don't wake up as I put you down. I celebrate by making myself some victory porridge.

Today is a win for dadding. I accept my award on behalf of all the other new dads around the world.

## It's Finally Happened
Monday, 23 December 2019

34 days old

*I suppose it was only a matter of time before this day came.*

I'm looking at the results of your first up-the-back shit. The poop has breached the sides of each leg, crept around to the front and is in touching distance of your belly button – like a mole peeking out of his molehill. And then finally, as per the headline, it's commuted up your back.

Your outfit, which happens to be another over-the-head job, is steeped in the stuff.

Fortunately, we're at home with Mummy. She'll know what to do, Arlo – she always knows.

Mummy tells me that the over-the-head outfits have been engineered to account for up-the-back shits. I'm suspicious, but I needn't be. There are poppers on the shoulder so I can pull the outfit *down* your waist as opposed to over the head where you're almost certainly guaranteed to acquire at least one shitty eye.

Because we're at home and we have the option, we plonk you straight in the bath. Do not ask me what protocol we will default to when we're at the local Starbucks.

Mummy takes care of bathing duties, and I take care of the clean-up, which I fail before I've even begun because I don't know what to do. Where do I even start? With your outfit? I don't want to chuck it in the washing machine because your clothes are covered in shit, and it might clog the machine up, causing a blockage. But washing machines are bloody good bits of kit these days, so perhaps that's exactly what I need to do.

I don't want to risk guesswork so I ask my guiding star, Mummy, who tells me to handwash it in the bath once you're out of it, to remove the debris, and then to put it in the washing machine at 60 degrees.

Fine.

But I immediately stumble again. I don't know what to clean your changing mat with. Do I need warm water and a cloth, or something stronger? I'm not sure I *can* use anything stronger because you're brand new, and you might have sensitive skin. Once clean, it's back upstairs to seek counsel from the oracle.

'You're overthinking it,' Mummy says. 'Use surface spray with some tissue.'

Again, fine.

What would I have done if we had been out in public without Mummy, Arlo? Tried to bath you in the sink and thrown away your outfit? Or, perhaps, triple-bagged it and dealt with it at home?

I guess we'll find out one day.

## No Peeking ... Or He Won't Come
Tuesday, 24 December 2019

35 days old

It's Christmas Eve, and I've put food out for Santa and his reindeers. I know this is stupid, and that we're a few years off from getting the full value out of this exercise, but I wanted to do it for myself.

Santa got a cookie and a Baileys, and Rudolph got a carrot. I assume Santa was still hungry and thirsty, but Rudolph and the others weren't, because the cookie and Baileys were gone, but the carrot remained.

It's time to get ready for bed, and we're all wearing matching pyjamas.

*Who would have thought it?*

Arlo, I remember a time when I was eighteen at university and 'had' to drink a pint of my mate's piss for a lacrosse court-session punishment. And now I'm posing for selfies with you and Mummy wearing matching pyjamas.

*Curious how life operates.*

Anyway, sleep well, son. No, seriously – sleep well, otherwise Santa won't come!

## Christmas Day
**Wednesday, 25 December 2019**

**36 days old**

Christmas 2014: your mother and I had just started dating. She bought me a Nerf gun, and I got her theatre tickets to see *Peter Pan Goes Wrong* – her first-ever theatre show. It had been a tough year for me, Arlo, but it had more than improved towards the end.

Christmas 2015: we celebrated a wonderful first year that saw us going on six holidays, enjoying countless days out and meeting each other's friends and family. We had a blast.

Christmas 2016: despite now being homeowners, Mummy and I stayed in the smallest room in our house (now your nursery) so we could rent out the larger rooms to lodgers to help save up for travelling.

Christmas 2017: we celebrated Christmas Day in Australia, having spent a phenomenal seven months backpacking. We were swimming in the sea, when all of a sudden everyone in the water jumped to attention. I thought someone had sighted a great white shark, but it was a pair of dolphins.

Christmas 2018: we were living at Grandad Tools and Granny Feeder's house because our house was a building site undergoing extensive renovation work. It was tough, the work was slow and we didn't have the money to pay for everything we wanted. The worst part was that we had spent fourteen months trying to start our family without success. A few weeks later, doctors told us that it was unlikely that we would ever conceive naturally.

Christmas 2019: today I have everything. Christmas in my home with my family, memories of all the adventures I've had with your mother, and a vast blank canvas waiting for the three of us to fill with a million more.

And what a Christmas it's started out to be. Why? Because you slept for not five, not six, but seven and a half hours, my boy.

Merry Christmas, Santa, you sly old dog. I still believe!

We're spending the day at Grandad Tools and Granny Feeder's house. As I walk through the threshold of their living room, I'm confronted by an ocean of colour. There are presents everywhere. I'm about to vocalise my awe when Granny Feeder steps in and says, 'Look, I know there aren't that many presents, but I didn't want to overwhelm the babies, and so I left all of my presents upstairs. I'll go and get them in a sec.'

At first, I think she's joking, but then I see the look on her face that tells me she's genuinely worried that she's fucked Christmas up. Seriously, there's half of fucking Hamleys here! And as for the *babies*, there's you who still can't see clearly beyond 12 inches, and your cousin Haylee who had her first birthday two days ago and has already amassed a generous stock of new toys.

Somehow, I think we'll be OK.

It takes us over an hour to open presents.

I've been given several clichéd dad-presents: nose-hair trimmer, socks, and slippers, but my favourite is a framed black-and-white photo of you asleep on my chest, skin-to-skin. Great job, Mummy.

I was adamant that we didn't need to get you anything because you won't remember today, but Mummy insisted you get something. In the end, you receive three presents from your parents: a book with faces in it, a play mat and finally (my pick) a pack of copper-coloured paper. I chose this because you love to stare at our copper lampshade at home so I figured we could do something with it. My favourite part was writing 'To Arlo. Love, Daddy' on your gift tag.

I've had such a blast with your mother over the past five years, but I've been transported to another reality in the last five weeks.

Happy first Christmas, son.

## Your First Cold
Saturday, 28 December 2019

39 days old

I think you're sick, Arlo. You're snuffly and needy, and you won't let either of us put you down while you're awake. And if you fall asleep in our arms and we put you down, you wake within a few minutes and demand, by crying, that one of us pick you up again.

Your temperature hasn't spiked, but that doesn't stop your parents from going online and spending an hour researching the symptoms. This is the stupidest thing we could have done, because – if our internet diagnosis is to be trusted, which it isn't – you've either got African horse sickness or you're midway through the menopause.

The other day I saw a meme that made me laugh. It was a pile of boxes being delivered by Amazon Prime, with this tag line: 'The day after your baby shows any signs of illness', mocking parents for overreacting about nothing. I don't find that meme funny any more.

Seeing your newborn baby in a helpless state is hard going. It might only be a cold but you're a little over five weeks old. You're still brand new.

I wonder if the probiotics are working. Should you be sicker, but you're not because the probiotics have equipped your immune system with the heavy weaponry needed to repel unwanted bugs? Or perhaps they're not working, and you're sick when you wouldn't have got sick if you were breastfed? Or is it none of these things and you've just picked up a bug? It's as I said – impossible to tell, but I'm wondering about all of the above.

Today sees us tackle yet another module on the parenthood curriculum. Get well soon.

## Mummy, The White-Noise Machine
Sunday, 29 December 2019

### 40 days old

It's 7 a.m., and I've woken to the most bizarre of scenarios, a pattern of sorts.

First, you're stirring, which is right on schedule for your morning feed. Mummy wakes, but I tell her to go back to sleep. For once, she does as I say, while I prepare your bottle and leave it on the side.

Nothing out of the ordinary so far.

But then Mummy starts snoring, and you stop stirring.

A coincidence, perhaps?

Mummy then wakes herself up from snoring, which in and of itself is already a highlight of my day. She asks where you are, and I somehow refrain from saying that you've popped out to get bread. Instead, I explain that you went back to sleep. But now you've started stirring again. Mummy slurs some sort of acknowledgement and once again shuts her eyes.

I leave it another minute, and then I creep to the end of the bed to collect you when the same thing happens again. Mummy starts snoring, and you go silent. It's incredible.

Again, I wonder if this is a coincidence?

No, it happens two more times. Is this a thing? Is snoring a type of white noise? I know white noise is a thing, so could this be linked?

Regardless, it's comical to watch.

# January

## An Open Plea To The World
Wednesday, 1 January 2020

43 days old

Happy New Year, everyone – or should that be Happy New Decade? I'd love to be out celebrating, but I don't get to do that any more, because I have a newborn baby, and even if I did have the option, I'd much rather go to bed early. So, on behalf of parents around the globe, particularly those with newborn babies or children who are light sleepers, may I ask you to do us all a favour and LAY OFF THE FIREWORKS! Thanks.

## Only A Mum Understands
Thursday, 2 January 2020

44 days old

The Matriarch is showering so I guess it falls to me to select what you'll be wearing today, which is fine, but Mummy never lets me pick out your clothes. She probably doesn't want me to pick now, but she's in the shower and you need changing so ... I guess I'm in play.

With you in my arms, I march towards your nursery, imbued with excitement. *I wonder what adventures lie in store.*

But then, in a scary but impressive move, your mother appears by my side like she's just fucking teleported.

'What are you doing?' she demands.

'I'm getting Arlo dressed, is that OK?'

'What are you picking out for him?'

*Hmm, what an excellent question.* Let's take a look. I open your wardrobe doors and begin rifling through our options.

*Not this one ... Not this one ... Definitely not this one ... Aha! This one.*

I present my selection to the Matriarch.

'No, I want him to wear something else.'

*Rude.* Before I can tell her to fuck off, Mummy selects another outfit for you: a jumper and a pair of trousers.

'I want him to wear this, but I need to iron the jumper.'

'Iron the jumper? For a six-week-old baby?'

'He can't go out with a creased jumper.'

'Of course he can't. How silly of me.'

At this point, Arlo, Mummy notices that you have nothing on, and are almost certainly getting cold. 'If you dress him how you were going to dress him, I'll iron his jumper, and change him again,' she says.

I'm desperately searching for a crumb of logic, but it's like standing on the deck of a fishing trawler in rough seas, staring into the ocean, trying to find a grain of sand on the ocean bed. Oh, it's also night-time. And I'm blind.

But before I can respond with what we all know will be more sarcasm (always play to your strengths, Arlo), Mummy chimes in with: 'Look, you're a dad, this is something only a mum would understand.'

Well, at least that's one thing we can agree on this morning.

## Thou Shalt Not ...
Friday, 3 January 2020

45 days old

There are unspoken truths when dealing with babies – commandments, if you will, that a new parent knows, even if other parents don't tell you about them. For instance:

1. Thou shalt never remove a dirty nappy without having a fresh one ready to hand.

2. Thou shalt never leave the house without packing three times as many spares of everything as you think you need.

They're pretty standard. I learnt those in week one. But recently, I've discovered another:

3. Thou shalt not utter a single syllable, make eye contact, or perform any move that could distract another parent from counting out formula scoops.

If you hinder a parent from counting, then you can consider yourself among the most execrable individuals that inhabit the planet, and you should prepare to be damned to a place worse than hell when you die.

## Yes, Yogi!
Saturday, 4 January 2020

46 days old

It's the middle of the night, and you won't settle down to sleep. You've been crying for hours, though neither of your parents knows why. Mummy decides to change your nappy to see if that helps. She switches your spaceship light projector on to accompany the changing ritual. The projector plays music, and it's playing a melody that I recognise, but for the life of me, I can't remember its name.[3]

'What's this song called?' I ask.

'I think it's ... Nope, it's not coming to me,' Mummy says.

But ... I'm sure ... That's it! I know a version of this song where the lyrics are about Yogi Bear, and they're – how shall I put it? – not age-appropriate for a forty-five-day-old baby. There's a verse in it about Suzie Bear being into whips and chains. I used to

---

3  I had to resort to googling it in the end. The song is 'Camptown Races', written by Stephen Foster. It was written for minstrel-show performances, where white people wore black make-up. Basically, it's incredibly racist. Good to learn that I've taken to using racism as a way to get my baby boy to sleep. Perhaps next time, I can look to use misogyny to settle you in the bath.

sing this song at uni with my mates. We'd make up verses, it was all jolly good fun.

So, while Mummy is softly humming as she re-dresses you, I'm on my phone searching to see if a recording of the Yogi Bear version exists.

It does.

Your crying intensifies, reaching new heights of auditory unpleasantness, like a set of large robotic arms shearing sheet metal apart in a factory.

But through the noise and despair, a beacon of hope appears, like a calming glow of pulsing white light giving off hypnotic hues. It's me, it's your daddy. And, like the hero I am, I bounce you in my arms, while playing ... let's call it 'The Yogi Bear Sex Song':

Yogi likes it all day long, horny, horny.
Yogi likes it all day long, he's a horny bear.
He's a horny bear! He's a horny bear!
Yogi likes it all day long, he's a horny bear.[4]

Your mother is mortified.

'What on earth is that you're playing to him?'

'Shhh, Mummy, can't you see I'm dadding?'

Much to her horror and my delight, your discomfort simmers down from volcanic anger to placidity. You even throw us a smile.

I can't describe the possibilities that this discovery opens up. I'm going to play this song in as many public places as I can. I will be judged, and it will be brilliant.

---

4  If you're familiar with the song but don't recognise the lyrics, there's a reason: I wrote new verses for the purposes of this book, just to be certain that no one could sue me.

I voice my optimism at the possible mileage this song will have for our family to Mummy. She smiles, the same smile she pulls when she's humouring me. Poor woman, Arlo. She thinks I'm joking.

## HA HA HA, That's Hilarious
Sunday, 5 January 2020

47 days old

If you burp, shit, piss or vomit in the company of anyone who isn't Mummy, I guarantee I'll hear the same response: 'Just like his dad.'

Fucking hilarious.

I got it the first few times but you're almost fifty days old now, son. Why can't people get a better cliché or a better joke?

Another thing that annoys me – and I'm looking at your Granny Smurf, although she is by no means the only offender – is how upset people get when I say certain things to you in a certain way. For example, when I change your nappy, I'll lay you down and I'll ask you if your name is Arlo Pissy Pants or Arlo Shitty Pants, as a precursor to finding out what damage you've done in your nappy – and, for the record, I've never changed a nappy where it's not been one of the two. But despite me saying this in a smiley, playful manner, which you decode as such, and despite you having no clue what I'm saying, the behaviour offends other people.

I've thought about how to respond to my critics, and I'm now doubling down on how many times I can call you Arlo Pissy Pants. Don't take it personally, son, but people need to find something a bit more tangible to take offence at.

## Someone Call Robert Langdon
Monday, 6 January 2020

48 days old

I'm soaked in piss, but for the life of me, I don't know how. It's obviously yours, but how it went from your willy to spraying up the side of my torso without my awareness is a puzzle. Let me take you through the steps and see if we can solve this mystery together as father and son.

Our story begins roughly ten minutes ago when I began changing you. Now, forgive the pun, but I was 'pissing around' with this particular nappy change because I was trying to make you smile, meaning you had more naked time than usual.

I'll admit that screams perfect pissing-on-a-parent conditions, but I was all too aware of that fact, and I was watching the danger zone with a level of focus equal to that of a brain surgeon.

Eventually, I put your clean nappy on, triple-checked the fastenings and scooped you up. And that's when I felt it: a damp, soggy patch on my right side. And that brings us to where we are now.

It's gone through my hoodie and my T-shirt. A quick sniff confirms it's definitely piss flavoured.

As part of my root cause analysis, I check the clean nappy to see if I fucked up on the assembly, but I haven't – it's bone dry, which means it hasn't leaked.

You must have somehow pissed on me while enjoying the freedom that naked time provides, but I'm still baffled: given the distance I was standing at when trying to make you smile, you would have needed some serious firepower; firepower that at your age you can't have developed yet. Also, you generally notice when someone's pissing on you, at least if you're sober. I can say I've learnt that much in life.

So, what gives?

# Sabotage
Tuesday, 7 January 2020

## 49 days old

Just when I'm starting to build up my confidence with apparelling you, the Matriarch races in to dismantle it with the efficiency of an assassin disassembling his sniper rifle after a successful hit. Needless to say, I don't like her very much today, and I've silently called her a prick at least two times. I'm even contemplating a third.

Why am I upset, you ask? I'll tell you why, Arlo. Your mother gave me today's outfit and asked me to get you changed. Fine, that's my pleasure. But one of the items was a vest, and it wasn't your typical standard vest. It was the vest equivalent of a Babygro. I needed to lay it out flat like a boneless chicken carcass, put you on top of it, fold it *around* your body and pop the poppers up to fasten it.

On paper – straightforward.

Yet it's anything but straightforward. There are more poppers on the thing than a ten-metre roll of bubble wrap and, to make matters worse, this particular garment is designed to overlap. So, you tuck one side in first, attach it to the correct poppers at the back and then repeat the process for the other side. You need to know how to fold it the right way, otherwise you run into trouble.

If my description doesn't paint a clear picture of what you have to do then that's because it's not clear what you have to do.

After what feels like hours I begrudgingly accept that I need to call in the Matriarch for air support.

At this point, Arlo, I want it on record that, when I called your mother, she shouldn't have had a clue what I wanted.

'Mummy,' I say, without any frustration or tears or concern in my voice. It is entirely neutral.

Yet Mummy's response is to burst out laughing, Arlo. How can she do this before I've told her what I'm calling her for? I'll tell you how. She knew this would happen, Arlo. She knew the poppers would confuse your poor father to the point where he would get frustrated, and that he would have to call her in.

And that's why I've called her a prick for the third time, but on this occasion ... it was to her face.


## Hallelujah
Wednesday, 8 January 2020

50 days old

Last night, you didn't wake once.

That's right, son, you slept through the night.

*Oh my god isn't this just the greatest day EVER!* The profound joy I feel is almost as wonderful as when I held you in my arms for the first time.

You know that feeling that I've had since you came home? The one where I feel got-up-at-4.00-a.m.-to-catch-a-flight tired all the time? It could soon be a distant memory.

Let's all take a second to appreciate how much of a wonderful, special, kind, sacred, smart little thing you are.

Let's hope we can add 'consistent' to that list.

*God, I feel so refreshed right now.*

## Core Resentment
Thursday, 9 January 2020

51 days old

You did it again.

You slept through the night.

A baby sleeping through the night twice in a row at seven weeks old has to be comparable to six winning numbers on a lottery ticket, right?

You can have anything you want forever so long as you keep this behaviour up.

It's now evening, and I'm at a Pilates class that's predominantly attended by women – all of whom have children. While contorted in one particular pose, the instructor asks me how I'm getting on with being a dad. I announce that you've slept through for *two* nights in a row and that Granny Smurf is looking after you tonight, so I'll be getting a third full night's sleep.

Silence, Arlo. Stone-cold silence.

'I'm happy for you,' says the instructor through gritted teeth.

She's not happy, Arlo – no one in the room is. 'Just you wait until the four-month sleep regression,' says one of the other ladies. Green mist permeates the air, and through the envy, I hear another say, 'It will never last.'

*We'll see.*

## A Fun Day Out
Friday, 10 January 2020

52 days old

Mummy has suggested I take you to a rhyme-time music session at the local library. Personally, a week of night feeds sounds more fun than *rhyme time*, but I do want to spend some one-on-one time with you, so I commit to going.

Instead of heading directly to the library, we're first going into town, on foot, to stock up on formula. We don't have much time, so we'll have to hop to it.

One of my pet hates in life is people that walk slowly. I would even go as far as to say that slow-moving people frustrate me as much as other road users annoy your mother. It's not that I'm in a hurry to get from A to B, but I'd like to take the opportunity to visit C and D and sometimes even E every once in a while – all of which is accomplishable if you pick up the fucking pace.

As we begin our journey into town, I notice that I'm not the only one with an errand to run. It seems every man, woman and child in the UK has business in Northampton this morning, business that requires them regularly transiting into my sphere of personal space. To add to the fun, they're moving at speeds that *might* give a post box a run for its money – but not much else. In short, their presence is hampering my ability to move through town quickly.

Before I had you, the slowest creatures in the world could be avoided by a quick, course-correcting sidestep, but with a buggy – not so.

After a *lot* of zigzagging, we make it to Boots, where I in due course realise that I'm on the ground floor, and the formula is on the first floor.

I steer us towards the lift. There's a queue comprising two mums with two buggies. A quick look at the watch confirms I don't have time for dilly-dallying. Hopefully, this lift is big enough for the three adults and three buggies—

The lift doors ping open to reveal ample space. Perfect.

What's not perfect is the geometric positioning choices that the dumb twats in front of us have selected. There isn't room for us, Arlo, not with how they're standing. It's not like they can't see me either. I'm formulating a response to address their lack of brainpower when the doors close.

*Absolute cun—*

No matter. I'll wait for the lift to return.

While I wait, my attention is drawn five metres to the right where the escalators loom – daring me to attempt an ascension with the buggy. I haven't thought of escalators as menacing sentient beings since I was a child, but that's what comes to mind as I'm looking at them right now, with their monstrously large, grime-stained, rotating silver teeth, ready to make light work of a novice buggy operator.

I daren't attempt them, Arlo. I'm just not qualified – not without your mother.

But the fucking lift hasn't returned and time is ticking. Why didn't those twats readjust themselves and make room?

Right, fuck it. We're taking the escalator.

As we approach, I weigh up one choice: Option A or Option B. Option A: I wheel you on and *then* apply the buggy brake. The problem I have here is having to faff with the brake once we've mounted the escalator. What if the required cognitive action of applying the break causes me to roll the buggy back? The margin for error is small, even a few millimetres could prove fatal. Option B: I wheel you on and hold on to you for dear life, not moving a single muscle, thus reducing the risk of any onboard mishaps.

I choose Option B.

I approach, take a deep breath, and move forward.

We're on, Arlo, and I haven't fallen backwards.

By the way, you've been asleep since we left the house and you have no idea what's going on.

We disembark. I'm a lot prouder of myself than I should probably admit, and I can't wait to tell

Mummy of my achievement. We reach the formula section unscathed. Once the transaction is complete, I begin a hasty exit. We only have three minutes to get to the library. Tight, but doable. I think about the escalators again. Ascending is one thing, but descending? Nope, not today. Another day ... perhaps.

Fortune smiles on us, Arlo – the lift doors ping open upon our arrival, and there is no queue. We enter the lift, and I begin mentally rehearsing: '*The wheels on the bus go round and round and round.*'

We make it to the library on time, but you're still fast asleep, and a glance at the other rhyme-time participants confirms there aren't any babies your age here. They're a lot older. I now need to weigh up the cost of waking you up to participate in something I don't think you can participate in, or letting you sleep and waiting around like a weirdo who looks like he wants to get involved but doesn't have the confidence to join in without an invitation from one of the 'big kids'.

In the end, I wait until five minutes before the end and surmise that, even if you were to wake up, by the time I removed the eighteen layers that Mummy insisted you wear, the session would be over, and there wouldn't be any point.

So, after all that, I leave.

Still, it's nice to get out of the house. Plus, I have my escalator accomplishment to warrant the trip.

# Haven't We Been Here Before?
Sunday, 12 January 2020

### 54 days old

I'm suspicious of how today is turning out already, and it's not even 10 a.m. yet.

We've all been invited to the christening of a young chap named Eddie. He's son number two to one of Daddy's closest friends, Ian. Ian and his wife have asked me to be Eddie's godfather.

The reason I'm suspicious is that we've had to travel from Northampton to Broxbourne, which is eighty-five minutes away, and somehow, not only are we on time, but we made it to the church early. We even had time to stop at the petrol station, buy croissants and then park up and eat them. I didn't think this was possible with children. Are we getting better at this, or is this a fluke that we shouldn't get used to? I guess time will tell.

You already know I don't go in for religion. I've made my thoughts on the subject quite clear in *Dear Dory,* and witnessing the miracle of childbirth hasn't seen me budging from atheism. That's just my opinion; everybody has a right to one. I certainly don't look down on anyone else who chooses to believe something I do not. And I also need to play along to support Eddie and receive my role as godfather in an official capacity – at least in the eyes of the church.

The ceremony proceeds without event. Eddie now has, in his corner, two sets of godparents that he can lean on any time he needs them.

Shortly after the ceremony, I find myself watching the children of my closest friends playing together and I think how it won't be long before you're doing the same thing. It's as close to a perfect moment as you could wish for ... until your mother comes along and announces that she wants you christened.

Let me remind you that this is the opposite of what we decided last year when we attended the christening of your cousin Haylee.

My first question is: 'Why?'

Mummy gives me a comprehensive response. 'It's important for Granny Feeder and other members of the family, Arlo won't remember it, it's an excuse to have a party and invite all of our friends and family and get lots of presents, and it's just nice. You've had a nice time today, haven't you?' At no point does Mummy use 'avoiding eternal damnation' to bolster her argument.

But, try as I might, I can't find an opening to disagree with any of her arguments. I'm even warming up to the idea, but then I'm told that I would need to attend several meetings with a priest *before* the ceremony, and openly discuss my commitment to God. I may also be required to attend a few church services.

No!

Absolutely no fucking way. Forcing me to go to church will be a disaster for everyone. I won't be able to keep my mouth shut, which means I'll offend people, I'll get angry and your mother will get pissed off. Why can't we stick to something like a naming ceremony? We can still select godparents, we can still have a party, and Daddy doesn't have to go through thirty rounds of prayers before he can have a beer and relax with his friends.

I'm against wasting my time discussing theology which I believe to be all nonsense. I've spent this week watching a documentary on planets, and I'm sorry, but Brian Cox talks more sense than the hymn I've been mumbling through.

To be continued.

## Fuck Off, Dawn
Monday, 13 January 2020

55 days old

We've arrived at the drop-in clinic to have you weighed. As we're walking through, you decide that now's as good a time as any to have a full-on meltdown. This is your first explosive public display of displeasure.

I don't understand why. I've fed you, Mummy has changed you, you're not too cold or too hot; yet you sound like a woolly mammoth who's had his trunk sawn off. You're the loudest baby in the room, which is saying something given we're at a weigh-in clinic for babies and, let me tell you, it's a busy day.

'Shhh, shhh, Arlo. What's wrong?' Mummy says.

I can tell Mummy's anxious about the impression this scene is casting on those around us. I'm sure this is known as a 'parent thing'.

But I'm not anxious.

I'm calm and relaxed.

Because I know what I have to do.

Yes, your crying tells me you're in distress, but it also ignites my neurons with electricity for another reason: signalling that I need to step up and act, and be the hero that everyone needs, especially Mummy.

I have to play the NFF card. NFF stands for 'never fucking fails'. It's a card that I have tucked away for emergencies, and I believe this scenario qualifies as an emergency. After all, it's the health visitors who carry out the weighing and they're probably already raising eyebrows, judging us, jotting notes down ahead of a Social Services referral, for being those parents who lack the necessary skills to look after a baby.

Laying the NFF card is not a course of action your mother condones, but like I said, this is an emergency. So, I mentally say 'Fuck it', take out my phone and hit play on 'The Yogi Bear Sex Song':

Boo Boo rocks up with his pals, orgy, orgy.
Boo Boo rocks up with his pals, he's an orgy bear.
He's an orgy bear! He's an orgy bear!
Boo Boo rocks up with his pals, he's an orgy bear.

First, let's pause for one moment to imagine the amount of matted fur at such a scene – the necessary post-coital hair brushing must be one hell of a sting fest.

Back to our present situation, and your mother is fucking furious.

She shoots me a death stare that's 80 per cent gorgon.

I lower the volume so only you and I can hear it.

You've stopped crying – immediately!

It's worked, it's fucking worked, Arlo! And now, you've shut your eyes, and you're starting to drift off to sleep. Am I a superdad or what?

I'm not.

Despite me lowering the volume, Mummy can now hear that Yogi's knob is green and sore, and that he's 'an unwell bear'.

'Turn that off. Now!'

I comply, and you start stirring immediately, which in my vocabulary is a win! I'm about to deliver a smug response to Mummy, but we're called over for the weigh-in.

We meet ... let's call her 'Dawn'.

Dawn kicks thing off by offering Mummy some parenting advice. Not once does she look in my direction. 'Now, it should be for the baby to tell you when he's hungry. You shouldn't dictate feeding times.'

'We don't, and never have.'

The temperature drops 30 degrees and Mummy's eyes narrow to half the height of a breadcrumb. I conclude that she probably doesn't want to add Dawn as a friend on Facebook.

'And you might need to monitor how much you're feeding him, sometimes he might want less and sometimes he might want more.'

'Uh-huh,' manages Mummy, but really what she wants to say is: 'What the fuck do you think we do, force-feed him like he's the gluttony victim in the movie *Seven*?'

Dawn moves on swiftly to the weighing. Smart decision, Dawn.

You are 11 lb 11 oz.

Dawn asks if we have any questions and, once again, I raise my concerns about the cloudy film over your left eye. Dawn conducts an investigation that lasts under three seconds.

'I can't see anything ... I'm sure it's nothing to worry about ...' she says, although her smile says, 'Aww, poor ickle first-time parents.'

Cheers, Dawn. Don't be sending your CV to 221B Baker Street any time soon, you fucking prick. Honestly, why does everyone treat us this way when we're voicing a genuine parental concern?

## Spluttering And Splurting
Wednesday, 15 January 2020

57 days old

Mummy has gone with you to see Granny Feeder. But she was due back a while ago now.

*Ring ring.* It's Mummy.

'Hello, Mummy.'

'I put Arlo in his snowsuit, and we were ready to leave, but then I noticed he smelt a bit, and so I undressed him, and I could see poo coming out the side of his nappy, so I went to change him, but he hadn't finished.'

'Oh ...'

'It went all in my hand. It was like water running from the tap but with more consistency and a slower flow. It sort of spluttered and splurted out and it made a sort of soft, long drawn-out pat-pat-splat sound. You know what I mean?'

'With that description, how could I not?'

'I know, I'm not gonna bother putting his dungarees back on as they're covered in shit.'

'Sounds logical.'

## Injections
Thursday, 16 January 2020

58 days old

Today is something your mother and I have been dreading for weeks. It's your first round of injections. It doesn't help that you've had a virus over the last few days and you're a bit out of sorts. Listening to you struggle to breathe, and knowing you're about to be in pain from needles, is not fun for Mummy and me.

We're in the doctor's surgery, and you're fast asleep. I'm trying to weigh the pros and cons of waking you up now. If I wake you, you'll have a few minutes to orient yourself and properly wake up before the not-fun begins. If I leave you sleeping, you'll be afforded a few more minutes of peaceful ignorance, but then you'll be woken up to have your injections immediately.

I'm not sure what's best, so I bring the decision to an independent committee, Mummy, who says we should let you sleep.

We can hear another baby having her injections, and she is screaming the surgery down. By now, we know the subtleties of baby cries – that was 100 per cent a pain cry. *Are they using needles or Calpol syringes?*

Before we can think about leaving, we're called in and welcomed by a lovely nurse named Sue.

'Is this the first time your baby is having injections, and is this your first child?' Sue says.

'Yes, on both counts,' I say.

Sue gives us a warm smile that tells me we're in safe hands. 'Right, well this is likely to be very scary, but it really doesn't need to be. I can see Arlo is asleep so we'll gradually start getting him undressed, but there's no need to rush at all, we'll give him a few minutes to wake up.'

Our anxiety softens.

'Now, let me ask you, how does it feel when you have an injection?'

Hmm. How does it feel? To be honest, Arlo, injections don't bother me in the slightest. They never have. Mummy doesn't mind them either. I explain this to Sue.

'Exactly, and it will be the same for Arlo. The reason it's scary is that Arlo will feel a short sting and he'll use the only communication mechanism he has, which is to cry. It's the same one he uses if he's hungry, bored, or if he wants his nappy changed. Yes, it will sting a little bit, but nowhere near as much as you think it does.'

That ... actually makes a lot of sense. I didn't think of it that way. A sideways glance at your mother confirms she's registered the same 'Aha!' moment.

We're big fans of Sue, Arlo. She can do all your jabs going forward – and mine.

Next up, she tells us about the injections she'll be giving you. Today, you're receiving immunisation against the following: diphtheria, tetanus, pertussis (whooping cough), polio, haemophilus influenzae type b (Hib), hepatitis B, meningococcal group B disease (MenB), pneumococcal disease and rotavirus.

It's time.

I lift you up and sit you on my lap while Mummy rubs your feet. Sue administers the first injection. She's quick. She's pulled the needle out before you register any pain. But then it does start to hurt, and the tears invariably follow. I won't lie: despite Sue's reassurance, it's not pleasant, and we're not done yet. I turn you around on my lap so Sue can access your other leg and she administers the final two injections. Again, she does this quickly.

There's a bit of blood. Again, it's not pleasant.

But as soon as we get you dressed and into the arms of Mummy, you stop crying and you even manage a half-smile.

That wasn't even half as terrifying as I'd made it out to be in my head.

## Date Night
Friday, 17 January 2020

59 days old

Despite being a little more unsettled in the night than usual because of your injections, you're in good spirits, which means we don't need to cancel the babysitter.

Thanks, Granny Feeder and Grandad Tools. Why are they babysitting? Because Mummy and Daddy are going on a date.

It will be our first official date night since before you were born. We've been out for beers with the family, I know, but tonight is just Mummy and Daddy. We're going to the cinema.

'Did you book the cinema?' Mummy says.

'No, you told me not to, you made it very clear that you wanted to do it yourself.'

'Shit, I haven't booked it. What are we going to see, again?'

'You said you wanted to see *Bad Boys 3*.'

'Oh yeah, that's right.'

I take charge and open the cinema app to book tickets, but I'm immediately faced with a problem: unless we want to sit in the front row, we can't sit together.

'Why are there no seats together?' says a disgusted and horrified Mummy.

'Erm, probably because it's the opening night of a new film and *we* left it to the last minute to book.'

'Fuck it. We'll sit in the front.'

We don't drive straight to the cinema because we have a short side mission to pick up a second-hand bookcase. Not great timing, I'll admit, but it's the only opportunity we'll get where you're not with us, which means we can lower the back seats to fit it in.

Mummy disapproves of the acquisition. She says that we shouldn't be spending money on non-essentials. The bookcase is £5. I had a ream of excuses ready to counter her argument, but I selected only one: 'Anything related to books is classified as essential – never non-essential.'

'Where are we going to pick this stupid bookcase up from?'

'How can you call something that houses knowledge stupid? It's in Kettering.'

'You said Wellingborough before.'

*Well, if you know the answer, why are you springing a fucking quiz on me, you dickhead?*

'It seems I was mistaken, my queen. I will spill four quarts of my blood in penance for such a blunder. Don't worry, we have enough time to collect the *stupid* bookcase and make it to the cinema.' That's what Google Maps tells us anyway.

We are a *go*, Arlo!

The traffic is less than ideal, but we're making good progress, nonetheless. As long as we load the bookcase into the car quickly and then leave immediately, we'll make the film and have date night—

'Fuck, I didn't take the buggy out of the boot,' Mummy says.

That too is less than ideal, Arlo. We don't exactly drive an artic lorry. Instead, we have our Peugeot 306 named Phoebe, whom Mummy loathes. No matter. As long as we remove the Isofix base (the bulky bit of kit that your car seat sits on) we can lower the back seats, load the bookcase in and then squash the buggy and folded-up Isofix in by the sides. It will be tight, but workable.

'Do you know how to remove the Isofix?' I say.

'Of course I do. It will take me two seconds,' Mummy replies, with the confidence and annoyance of someone who's been asked what one plus one equals.

Fast-forward twenty minutes, and I'm shining my phone torch over the Isofix while the Matriarch sets about making good on her statement by removing it in two seconds. Except she doesn't make good, and two seconds gradually turns into two minutes.

The tension is mounting. I offer to help but, full disclaimer, I don't know how to remove the thing either. Although I also never claimed I could.

It's no use. We need to make a decision: bookcase or movie.

We select movie.

I apologise to the seller, and we agree to reschedule once we've discovered how our baby equipment works, and when we're not in a rush to get to the cinema.

It's 7 p.m. The film starts at 7.30 p.m.

Google is telling me it's going to take us forty minutes to get back, which is OK because adverts and film trailers usually last for twenty-five minutes. Assuming that's the case, and assuming we can park up quickly, we should be able to get in and sit down just as the film begins.

*It's going to be tight.*

Ten minutes into our voyage and a recalculation of the route, cross-referenced with the time, tells me we've already made up a couple of minutes. I don't know how that has happened as Mummy *never* speeds ... ever!

In my head, the mission is accomplished already and I'm singing the *Bad Boys* song. I'd quote the lyrics here, Arlo, but I think I'd get sued. The general gist of the song is that there are these individuals known as Bad Boys, and the singer of the song would very much like to know our plans should the Bad Boys come for us.

I've already mentally ordered the popcorn when we arrive at a roundabout only to discover a broken-down lorry that's being winched up by a recovery vehicle. Between them, both vehicles block every exit on the roundabout.

Mummy gives me this look, a look that I'll admit I want to eradicate with a big, jagged stick, a look that says: 'This is all your fault because you wanted to collect that stupid bookcase.'

I throw her one back that says: 'How many fucking times do I need to repeat myself, it's not a stupid bookcase and I'm not a clairvoyant, and I'm not responsible for the lorry breaking down!'

Once the congestion eventually clears, we bypass the cinema and drive straight to Grandad Tools and Granny Feeder's house.

So much for date night!

## That'll Never Hold Up In Court
Saturday, 18 January 2020

**60 days old**

I've teamed up with Mummy to change your nappy. I like it when we do this together: like bath time, it's a little moment to enjoy some quality family time.

Today's nappy change is in two sections; two conversations, if you will. In the first, Mummy explains how she *can* remove the Isofix from the car in under two seconds, and campaigns for last night's efforts to be forgotten. She cites poor lighting and being under pressure as the reasons for her failure.

The second part is me dismantling her arguments and concluding that she's a lot like the contents of your nappy.

## Two Months Old
19th January 2020

61 days old

Two months old today. It feels like we've settled into parenthood a little more. It's a nice stage because the novelty of having a newborn baby remains, but everything involved in looking after a baby is starting to feel normal and ingrained in our daily routines.

Your personality is developing. You get agitated as soon as we take your bottle away so we can wind you. It's funny. You've begun showing an interest in certain toys, although I'll admit Daddy is getting a bit bored with hearing 'I'm a friendly light-up bear' from one such toy, which, if you couldn't guess, is a bear. I think his name is Alfie.

You love being in the bath, and you love white noise. Hoovering soothes you. So does being in the buggy and the car seat.

It pleases me no end to report that when you are in a state of displeasure, 'The Yogi Bear Sex Song' does wonders to soothe you. It boasts a 100-per-cent success rate and, as much as your mother hates to admit it, she can't deny that it works.

You're talking more. Every day you make new sounds and new facial expressions. Outside of smiling, my favourite expressions are when you're stretching, or when you're listening to us talk to you, taking it all in with a hint of a frown and a side-eye glance. It's as if you're saying, 'Look, I'm not sure I fully trust you guys yet, but I'm gonna stay and listen to what you've got to say.' And then you smile as if to say, 'Who am I kidding, of course I trust you. I love you guys.'

Visitors have dried up quicker than a Serengeti watering hole in midsummer, but again, this is a reflection of our lives returning to 'normal'.

Outside of trapped wind and injections, you've had your first experience of dealing with pain. The other day, your cousin Haylee whacked you over the head with your bottle. She did this because she was frustrated to learn that the bottle was yours and not hers. You responded with equal frustration, but yours was one of physical pain – you cried. I wasn't there but I was surprised to find myself stiffen up when Mummy recounted the story to be. *How dare anyone cause my boy any harm?* Apparently, that includes my one-year-old niece.

I'll admit something I'm not proud of: I've completely forgotten about you twice. The first was in the supermarket. I was pushing the trolley and Mummy was pushing the buggy. We had just picked up some fruit. Mummy took over the trolley duties, and I followed her without taking the reins of the buggy.

'Aren't you forgetting something?' Mummy said.

'Oh, fuck – Arlo!'

The second time was in the car. It was just you and me. I was driving, and you sneezed, which shit me right up as I'd forgotten you were there. I've heard parents recall similar experiences, and I never understood how something like that was possible. Now I do.

The other day we were at the christening, and my mate Ian turned to me as we were both picking up the changing bags and said, 'Do you remember when we used to carry Osprey bags instead of nappy-changing bags?'

I think Osprey is missing a trick, because parenthood is the ultimate adventure, and a baby-changing bag would slot in well to their brand.

Keep up the good work, buddy, you're doing great.

## It Must Be Wonderful, Right?

Monday, 20 January 2020

62 days old

I can't help but feel jealous of babies and the experience they have every day lying on their backs in the buggy. It must be wonderful. It's a tragedy that such experiences are forgotten.

Essentially, you're lying in bed while your bed is in motion. The bumps in the road send vibrations up through the wheels, through the chassis, and right up into your body, soothing and massaging you. No wonder you fall asleep every time.

And if you're not sleeping, then you're gazing up at the sky and its ever-changing conditions: the light of the sun, the shadows of the clouds; the clouds themselves a permanently evolving tapestry of whites and greys.

And then there's the rain. I love watching the rain, Arlo. Everything about it calms me: the sound, the smell, the sight. Water is life.

Every day, you experience the views of the sky from a place of comfort while the motion of being pushed and massaged relaxes you. And you get to enjoy these views without straining your neck looking up from a standing position like us grown-ups do.

Have I stumbled on a new business venture? I wonder if there's a demand for adult buggy rides. 'Guaranteed to send you to sleep within twenty minutes, or your money back!'

## First-Hand Versus Second-Hand
Tuesday, 21 January 2020

63 days old

Yesterday, Mummy purchased a brand-new outfit for friends of ours who have recently had a baby girl. The outfit cost £14. If you're anything to go by, it will only last a few weeks, and *might* be worn a handful of times.

Today, Mummy, having responded to an advert on Facebook, has walked through the door carrying a bag of thirty-six second-hand items: six Babygros, one coat, two pairs of pyjamas (one set by Blade & Rose, a company that gives Mummy a wide-on), five top-and-trouser sets, one velour dinosaur tracksuit, four long-sleeved vests, three short-sleeved vests, one pair of jeggings and three sleepsuits. And more.

The advert only lists what I've described above, and I can't be bothered to go through the bag, but rest assured, there are thirty-six items. How much for all of that? £10, Arlo. This is another example that illustrates the lunacy of buying baby clothes brand new.

Also, why don't we have velour dinosaur tracksuits for adults?

## Who's Gonna Know?
Wednesday, 22 January 2020

64 days old

Fuck! We forgot to take a picture of you on your mat when you were two months old. No one will know if it's a few days late, right? I bet this happens all the time. This has to be a 'thing'.

## Stay Away, Witch
Thursday, 23 January 2020

65 days old

I'm at the point where the novelty of strangers telling me how lovely you are is not only boring, it's annoying.

I'm sitting in a waiting area with you and Mummy for your final cranial osteopath appointment. There's a woman, early fifties, lurking on the other side of the room, smiling in our direction and attempting to make eye contact. I think that she thinks if I make eye contact, it's an invitation to come over and strike up a conversation.

It's not.

I'm so done with reciting your age, weight at birth, sleep reports and labour reports like it's the final round of 'I went to the market and bought' ... Especially to someone we're never likely to see again.

Oh God, she's now begun slowly shuffling towards us, looking to improve her odds.

In my experience, strangers that want to talk about you always outstay their welcome, Arlo. It's never a quick smile and move on, they stay forever. What's worse, just because we have a baby and they had a baby at some point in their lives, or they know someone who knows someone else who once thought about having a baby, they assume this makes us blood relatives, and that we're desperate to hear the intricacies of their life story.

She's still approaching, but now she's bobbing her head up and down like some species of birds do when they want to attract a mate. Her behaviour definitely belongs in the creepy-and-fucking-weird category. I think she wants to eat you, Arlo. Don't worry, Daddy will protect you.

'What if we turn our backs to her?' I mumble to Mummy.

Mummy turns, immediately acting on my suggestion. I follow suit, completing the manoeuvre.

Our backs are now facing the demon. It might appear rude, but I shouldn't be labelled an impertinent miscreant because I don't want to converse with a stranger.

Anyway, I think that's done the trick, Arlo, she's abandoned—

'How old is your baby?'

*Ah, fuck!*

The woman has the most whiny and annoying voice I've ever come across. My eardrums have immediately logged on to the dark web to order three ampoules of cyanide, paying a premium rate for instant delivery. Beat that, Mr Bezos. It's like listening to a tone-deaf cat meowing while simultaneously playing an out-of-tune violin. This is the last time we turn up to an appointment early!

## Piss Hard
Saturday, 25 January 2020

67 days old

I unfasten the straps of your dirty nappy and take a look under the hood, making my usual damage inspection.

Just piss.

I reach for a clean nappy while still holding the front of the dirty nappy upright (just like I was taught) to contain a follow-up wee. Holding up the front of your nappy reminds me of a wall of sorts, like the one you would see on a football pitch, with defenders lining up to block a free kick.

Historically, this method has worked well to contain any follow-up wee-wees.

But no longer.

The wall fails to do its job.

Somehow, you skilfully aim above the front nappy flap and fire out a streak of urine with such force and ferocity that the trajectory arcs over the dirty nappy, spraying all over the side panelling of your wardrobe.

*What the—*

The piss is now dripping slowly all the way down to the floor and on to our less-than-a-year-old carpet.

There's nothing I can do. Your changing station is tight up against the wardrobe, and my hands aren't small or agile enough to fit through the gap to halt any runaway piss drips in their tracks.

I look at you as if to say: 'Not cool.'

You respond by projectile-vomiting all over my arm.

## Bittersweet
Sunday, 26 January 2020

68 days old

Three things have happened today to reinforce a sad truth – you're getting bigger. This is besides the incremental micro-growth adjustments you make every day.

Firstly, you've graduated in nappy size. You're still too small to wear the reusable ones, so we're continuing to rely on the eco-disposables, but we now need the next size up.

Secondly, I looked at two photos of you asleep in your crib: one was taken a month ago, and the other today. I couldn't believe the difference in size after only four weeks.

Thirdly, and most telling, I held another baby today who was at least 2 lbs lighter than you are. Holding her felt like I was holding a small balloon filled with air. It's been two months, yet I cannot for the life of me fathom how you were ever that light.

## Teething
Monday, 27 January 2020

### 69 days old

Mummy thinks you're teething, even though most babies don't start teething until around six months. She thinks you're teething because you're constantly dribbling and chewing your hands a lot, and today you presented us with five shitty nappies, which Mummy says is also a sign of teething. That's a personal best – you've never produced such quantities in your entire life, despite your feeding habits remaining the same as ever.

I might start calling you Arlo Five Shits. Mummy will think I'm taking the piss out of you and get defensive, but every dad on the planet knows a name like Arlo Five Shits is something bestowed with pride.

I'm trying to think if I've ever achieved that level of success. I don't believe I have. Not unless you count my trip to India, but the less said about that the better.

# Piss Hard 2: Piss Harder

Tuesday, 28 January 2020

70 days old

I don't believe this, Arlo. You've lobbed me again with another explosive high-arc piss while I was changing your nappy. Like last time, you've sprayed piss all down the wardrobe side panel that has then dripped down, seeping through a gap that's too small for my wet-wipe-wielding hand to follow.

Also like last time, it's dripped down and landed on our less-than-a-year-old carpet, replenishing that wonderful smell of ammonia that had just begun to fade.

It's not as if I didn't learn my lesson either, although there's strong evidence to the contrary. You're now in size-two nappies, which means I have a taller dam / wall / blockade – whatever the fuck you want to call it – at my disposal. I also brought it forward, so it was closer to you, reducing the odds even more!

Yet you still managed to triumph against me.

I will not be beaten a third time; do you hear me?

By the way, you're ten weeks old today. No need to thank us for keeping you alive for that long, just carry on doing what you're doing and pissing all over the furniture.

# February

## The First Night By Myself
### Saturday, 1 February 2020

*74 days old*

Tonight, Mummy is going out to wet the baby's head. I don't know the origins of this tradition, but I know it's an excuse to go out and get pissed without having to worry about parenting for the night.

This means it's just you and me, kiddo, and it's likely to last a little longer than *the night* because I've told Mummy not to return home until tomorrow afternoon at the earliest. You might be thinking I'm overgenerous, but there are many reasons why this is a good idea.

I've never looked after you overnight by myself and I want a good run at it to see how well I manage. I don't *rely* on Mummy as such, but she's so bloody wonderful at the job that everything baby-related is a lot easier when she's around.

Next, if Mummy comes home drunk, I don't foresee any scenario where she doesn't want to wake you up for a cuddle. And I know for a fact she won't listen to me if I tell her not to. She's not renowned for listening to me when she's sober, let alone drunk.

Also, I'm buying time for next week when it's my turn to wet your head. If I'm an arsehole and tell Mummy she needs to get up first thing and feed you, then I'm begging for the same treatment next week. If I allow her space and time to recover, she'll have to grant me the same courtesy. It's an investment, Arlo.

Finally, and most importantly, she deserves it. She takes such good care of us, and in my opinion, she hasn't put a foot wrong in her motherhood journey.

Besides, it will be fun, just the two of us ... right? I'm not the least bit worried. How can you be worried about a human who spends his days sleeping, dribbling or feeding?

4 p.m. Mummy kisses us goodbye and leaves. The natural light coming into our house fades, and I conclude that a dark cloud must be passing in front of the sun, and that it's not any sort of foreshadowing.

4.45 p.m. I carry you up the road in the wrong direction for 200 metres in search of the car. A quick call to Mummy confirms she *may* have miscommunicated its location to us.

5 p.m. All the coffee shops are closing up, and it's getting too dark to take you to the park, so I walk you up and down the street a few times to get you off to sleep.

5.30 p.m. We return home in time for you to have a nuclear meltdown. You're not hungry because you fed ninety minutes ago. I check everything else and try to discover why you sound like the mating call of an aggressive, deranged alpha-male parrot. But I have no idea: your nappy is dry and you don't have wind, but you don't like being cuddled, no matter what position I hold you in.

I'm more upset than frustrated, and I can't help but think that you want your mummy and not your daddy. But Mummy's not here, so we need to figure this shit out. In the end, I revert to the one thing I know I can call upon in great times of need: the NFF card.

Suzie swallows every drop, nom-nom, nom-nom.
Suzie swallows every drop, she's a nom-nom bear.
She's a nom-nom bear! She's a nom-nom bear!
Suzie swallows every drop, she's a nom-nom bear.

Within ten seconds you stop crying.

6.07 p.m. We've spent the last half an hour on your play mat having conversations with a red dog and a blue elephant with pink polka dots tattooed on its belly. You've transitioned into a different baby from the one you were forty minutes ago.

6.15 p.m. I exchange a few text messages with Mummy. She wants me to set the baby monitor up so that she can watch you from her phone app. I know for a fact that she'll get drunk and start talking to you through it, so I agree to set it up but turn the sound off.

6.30 p.m. Bath time with 'Pure Imagination', from *Willy Wonka & the Chocolate Factory*, playing on repeat in the background. There's no particular reason for the song selection, I just thought you'd appreciate the melody.

7.10 p.m. I read you a *Star Wars* story about princesses. Princesses are good people, Arlo.

7.20 p.m. You break out into your second meltdown performance of the evening, but this one is easier to fix because you're hungry. We watch some of *The Good Dinosaur* together while you have your bottle.

8 p.m. I put you down, and you go straight to sleep. I spend ten minutes staring at you.

10 p.m. I fall asleep watching *Archer.*

# Piss Hard 3: Piss Hard With A Vengeance
Sunday, 2 February 2020

75 days old

Five days ago, I vowed that I wouldn't allow you to blindside Daddy again with a mid-nappy-change spray-piss. That commitment echoes in the back of my mind as I lay you down on your changing station to begin what I hope is a routine nappy change.

Mummy has shuffled your nursery furniture around, and the layout means I can stand in front, and to the side, of your changing station. The wardrobe isn't tight up against it any more so, hopefully, we can wave goodbye to ammonia-smelling carpets.

I position everything I need within reach, take a deep breath, and begin.

I start by taking a quick peek inside. No poo-poo, only pee-pee. I unfasten the straps and unfold the front flap. As I do this, I'm greeted by a baby erection. I'm not kidding you; this thing is fully erect. Someone once told me that baby boys couldn't get erections, but I beg to differ.

You've had these before. When you get a baby erection, it's usually a precursor to a follow-up piss, so I put the front flap of the nappy back over you. I've learnt from the last two accidents that holding the front flap upright isn't enough. I need to smother your piss-producing implement to avoid damage to the surrounding area.

*I will not be beaten.*

I chance a quick peek every few seconds, but four of these quick-peek inspections reveal nothing, only that your erection has gone. I think we're good to go.

I get ready to swap out the old nappy and slide a fresh nappy in.

Three, two, one ... I begin the transition.

At which point, two things happen: first, your baby erection returns so that your willy is pointing towards the ceiling; and then, you lift both of your legs up and over until your feet are pointing towards your shoulders like you're midway through a yoga class. Your erect baby willy is now pointing *directly* at your face – specifically, the mouth area of your face.

And, of course, it comes as no surprise when I tell you it's at this exact moment that you start pissing – the stream of urine arriving with a backstage pass to the back of your throat.

Fortunately, dad-reflexes exist, and I somehow manage to get my left hand between your face and willy, preventing your face and mouth from onboarding a large volume of the yellow stuff. Your upper torso is not so lucky, but that's the lesser of two evils.

Staying on dad-reflexes, the thing about them is that they are amazingly intuitive for one action at a time. Once that one action is spent, the dad-reflex energy bar needs to recharge. This isn't a problem for, say, catching a falling baby, as once the baby is caught, it's held on to for dear life while the reflex meter charges back up and dad thanks whomever that he's not on his way to the hospital.

I've used up all of my reflex energy on stopping you from pissing in your mouth, and it's depleted the power bar and it needs to recharge. As I realise this, your baby erection softens, and you lower your legs. Of course, this all happens while you're still pissing, so the stream arcs, continuing to cover more of your body in piss while soaking the fresh nappy, which I drop, and finally sending its last remnants up the walls.

I now find myself in a position where you're covered in piss, the changing mat is covered in piss, my hands are covered in piss and there are streaks of piss running down the wall.

I'm unsure of my next move. I can't put a third nappy on you yet because I need to clear up the aftermath, but I don't want to risk further damage. You're unlikely to piss again, but I don't trust you – not one bloody bit.

So, I place a muslin square over the bane of my life, remove your clothes, clean up the damage and retrieve nappy number three. I start to slide it under ...

You start pissing AGAIN!

There's no erection or flailing legs this time. You bypass your face and torso and go straight for the walls, the carpet and your old man.

Fuck you, Arlo, and fuck these stupid, expensive eco-friendly nappies, and fuck everything else in life.

I'm a broken man.

And now the Matriarch has arrived on the scene. She's wearing the biggest smile I've ever seen on her face – it's like looking at a U-bend pipe under the sink.

I want to drop kick both of you in the face.

'What happened?' she says.

'What's happened is I've gone through three nappies, and he's pissed over himself, me, the walls and the carpet.'

'How many times? You need to keep the old nappy in place right up until you replace it with the new one.'

*ARRRRRGGGGHHHHHH!*

I want to respond and tell her the full story, Arlo. But, honestly, what's the fucking point? Who is going to believe that I've been fucked over again by a baby erection and an overextension of your legs?

# Rehearsing For Panto
Monday, 3 February 2020

76 days old

'Don't move a muscle!' I say.
    'Why?' Mummy asks.
    'You were right.'
    'He's shit?'

'Everywhere. It's on your hand, and it's now all over my hands.'

Mummy can't see the severity of the current situation because of how she's sitting on the bed, and how she's holding you, but take it from me – Houston, we have a problem.

'What shall I do?' she says.

'We need to get him to the nursery and then strip him down. I've got most of the debris contained, but we'll need to move as one unit.'

Try and picture the scene: your mother is creeping slowly down the hallway holding you over her left shoulder. She's supporting you with her left hand only. She leaves her right hand free because it's covered in shit. I'm walking backwards, but bent over forward cradling your bum.

A few seconds ago, I pulled your pyjama bottoms down, only to be rewarded with a handful of the smelly stuff. Now, if I move my hands, then a healthy percentage of the nappy contents could well end up on the carpet.

We move from the bedroom to your nursery as one, looking like a reversing horse from a pantomime show, but one with spina bifida and without the horse costume.

Once we're in the nursery, I remove your trousers and dump them straight in the bath. Next, Mummy holds your arms while I remove your vest and dirty nappy so that I can think about beginning the clean-up operation. It doesn't take long for you to slam your foot into the centre of the open nappy; the effect being akin to a mortar shell landing in the earth, spattering a crowd of mushy specks that careen through the air in multiple directions. Some crash-land unceremoniously on my T-shirt and forearm.

You talk and smile at us the whole time, and I'm left wondering why I didn't have kids years ago.

## Shit Day To Be A Parent
Tuesday, 4 February 2020

77 days old

Last year, when you were Dory, I taught you about those times in life where you learn a truth that disappoints you: that feelings of love and affection don't have to be reciprocated, that we all must die someday, and that Santa isn't real (metaphysical debates notwithstanding). I told you that Daddy even calls these times 'Santa isn't real' moments.

I think Mummy and I are about to experience one of them now.

What sucks is that it's our first parental 'Santa isn't real' moment.

After finally tiring of reporting the cloudy film over your left eye to every medically trained professional we encounter, we have decided to take matters into our own hands. Guided by a friend of ours who's an optician, we *demanded* a referral by our GP to see another doctor from the eye clinic.

And that's where we are right now. The doctor has finished carrying out some tests on you, which you hated, and he's about to deliver his diagnosis.

I can read it on his face – something isn't right.

'He has a congenital cataract in his left eye.'

My mind reacts instantly, pulling all available records from my memory banks. From the information it retrieves, I know, or at least I think I know, that cataracts can be fixed, and that it's not uncommon for the elderly to develop them.

'The problem,' the doctor continues, 'is that he's got this from birth. Arlo is at a stage of his life where his eyes are rapidly developing, and if we don't act immediately, then he may suffer poor vision in that eye for the rest of his life.'

My arms and legs have turned to stone. My entire body feels heavy and there is a tight knot forming in the pit of my stomach.

The doctor continues to talk while I try and digest the information, quantifying the impact to your quality of life. I won't lie, I'm finding it hard to take all this in.

Mummy starts crying as soon as the doctor mentions eyepatches.

The takeaway from this is that your eyesight will never be optimal, at least not in one eye.

The doctor presents us with two options. For the sake of clarity, I'm going to refer to your eyes as the 'weaker eye' (left) and the 'normal eye' (right).

Option one: you undergo surgery to remove the lens with the cataract, and a contact lens is then inserted so that your eye maintains focusing power. The contact lens will stay in place until your eye is fully developed (usually after a year from birth) before another operation is performed, this time, to insert an artificial lens that will remain in place for the rest of your life. You'll need to wear glasses to fine-tune your vision.

For this, you would need to be under a general anaesthetic.

Over time, the artificial lens will function less effectively because of the reasons I mentioned above: you're a baby, and your eye is still developing and changing.

I don't know how we define 'function less effectively'. My eyes don't function as well as they used to and I have glasses, but the impairment to my eyes and the quality of my life is minimal. I couldn't even tell you where my glasses are at the moment.

Anyway, that's option one.

Option two: we forgo the surgery and rely instead on an eyepatch to strengthen the weaker eye in order to prevent further degradation, and hopefully prevent it from becoming 'lazy' and developing a squint, which, according to the doc, will happen quickly if we do nothing. You live with one normal eye and one weaker eye, but both of them will, hopefully, move together in unison.

I don't like either of those options, but it's hard to make any headway when we're hearing this for the first time. If you have the surgery, you will still need a lot of 'patching' – the term the doctor uses to describe wearing an eyepatch – to help with the recovery. You're eleven weeks old today. I have no idea what wearing an eyepatch at your age will be like for you, but I do know you get pissy if your hat falls over your eyes. The thought of having to watch you go under general anaesthetic does not make for a blissful image either, but we'll do whatever is in your best interest.

'How has this happened?' I ask.

'I can't say for sure,' the doctor says, 'but it could be genetic, or it could be a blip in his development during the first half of the pregnancy.'

Mummy looks up and I can tell without looking at her that she's somehow holding herself accountable.

'Listen, I am going to refer you to a colleague of mine for a second opinion and to help you make an informed decision. I'm also going to send you to a geneticist for genetic counselling' – *whatever that is* – 'and a paediatrician. If it is genetics, then you can see if that needs to be factored in when deciding whether to have more children.'

*Great.*

My brain is racing at a million miles an hour. I have so much I want to ask, but I cannot process what I'm learning fast enough to ask the right questions.

'How soon until we see your colleague for the second opinion?' I manage.

'About three weeks.'

Three weeks, Arlo. We've got three weeks to read up on your condition and learn as much as we can so we can ask the right questions and find a way forward.

The doc ends the appointment on a low note – so low it's practically touching the floor.

'This is tough, I know. I'm sorry I've had to deliver this news to you. The tricky problem is that we can't know for sure if whatever option we select is the right one until after it's been implemented. But I'm afraid that, ultimately, the decision rests with you as Arlo's parents.'

I shake the doctor's hand and make for the exit.

We've barely set foot outside the office when Mummy asks, 'Is this my fault?'

'One hundred per cent no, this isn't your fault. Don't go down that road.'

She nods, but she's understandably upset that the thing she loves more than anything in the world is having to go through his first medical hiccup at such a young age.

As we walk through the hospital and head home, my mind continues to operate more commands and queries than it has the processing power to handle. After a few minutes, it subsides enough for me to begin working through the pros and cons of our situation.

'He's got this from the beginning of his life,' I say out loud, more to myself than Mummy. 'He'll never know any different. He's not blind – he's not even blind in one eye. We still don't know what we're dealing with, we haven't begun to read up on any of this yet and doctors aren't exactly known for their bedside manner. Don't get me wrong, this is a shit day to be a parent, but it could be worse. He could have cancer or some other horrible disease. Plus, we were told Arlo would never happen naturally. If a genie had appeared after we heard that news, and said he would give us Arlo, but with a cataract in his left eye, we would have agreed hands down to that condition.'

'I know. We're lucky to have him.'

'And also, who won't find Baby White Nick Fury ridiculously attractive?'

She smiles, but it soon dissipates. 'What if he's bullied at school for wearing an eyepatch?'

The same thought did occur to me. 'We'll figure everything out.'

As I sit down to write to you about today, I'm reminded of 'Maybe', the Taoist story that I recounted in *Dear Dory*. The story teaches us that if we interpret a situation as something negative, then it paves the way for how we respond to it emotionally, even though we can't know for sure that the outcome will, in fact, be negative. So let's see how this one plays out, son. In the meantime, I want you to know that if your eyesight is permanently impacted, I will not be going easy on you during our lightsabre duels. If anything, I'll be taking advantage. I'll purposely attack you from your left side to win.

I love you, buddy. So bloody much.

## You Will Never Drive A Bus
Wednesday, 5 February 2020

78 days old

Yesterday was a shit day to be a parent. Today isn't much better, but we've begun to let the news sink in, and we've started researching your condition. We've spoken to an optician friend of ours who happens to be one of the mums from our NCT group, Maeesha. She's the one who recommended that we demand the referral in the first place.

Maeesha reiterates the positives: it's unilateral, meaning you will have one good eye (please don't fuck that one up), you'll go to a mainstream school and play sports, and you will legally be able to hold a driving licence.

It's your 3D vision that will be affected, which means certain professions are out. So, while you will be able to hold a UK driving licence, you won't be able to become a bus driver. I shrug this off at first, but then I get upset that choices are being taken away from you.

For its vision to develop, a baby has to have the ability to see in the first place. If an eye isn't getting any stimulation, then the brain eventually relinquishes interest and control in that eye. This is what leads to further deterioration, resulting in a squint, or worse, the eye going blind.

If we proceed with the surgery, there are best-case and worst-case outcomes. Best case: your vision improves significantly, and you'll be only two or three lines worse off. By 'lines' I mean the lines on the chart you have to read when you go for an eye test. You will still need to wear an eyepatch, though I'm unsure for how long, and you'll probably need glasses with a custom-made lens for any close-up activities like reading. Again, we can't say for sure, because we don't know how successful the surgery will be until after the fact. That's even if we go ahead with it. And if we get the best possible outcome, we won't know how long it will remain that way. The doctor confirmed that your eyes would continue to develop as you grow, which could reduce the effectiveness of the artificial lens. Maeesha corroborates this as well.

At least we have something to ask at the follow-up appointment.

A worst-case scenario is that the eye doesn't improve at all, and it may continue to deteriorate.

Last night, Mummy and I carried out some tests. First, we covered your normal eye with a bib to see your reaction. You immediately got pissed off and started shaking your head. We repeated the experiment with your weaker eye, and you barely reacted, suggesting that your vision in that eye is indeed poor.

Maeesha ended on a high note. She said that she has never come across a child who's had a congenital cataract and been bothered by it. This is comforting to hear, as it validates what we discussed yesterday about you not knowing any different.

She said the worst thing about this would be having to deal with any tantrums if you can't have the design of eyepatch or glasses you want. That's something we can all live with.

# Your Great-Grandad
Monday, 10 February 2020

83 days old

Today, you're meeting your great-grandad, Mike (Granny Smurf's dad), and your great-granny, Hazel, who's not Granny Smurf's mum – my grandparents separated and remarried.

Sentimentality isn't wildly abundant on my side of the family. Life has scattered us around the country, and our blood ties alone don't bring us together all that often. Plus, we're missing that one family component (or member) who's able, willing and motivated to choreograph family functions and events. It's been an open position for as long as I can remember, but no one's applied for the job, and if they did, I'm not sure how impressive their CV would be.

Because of that, over time, the belief that blood ties alone don't command or warrant my time has formed. In my opinion, the phrase 'blood is thicker than water' is nonsense. A better way to approach relationships is to surround yourself with only people that add value to your life in some way, whether they be your immediate family, a distant cousin in Fiji (we don't have any of those, as far as I know) or a homeless Chinese man you met while backpacking. No one should tell you who you can and can't spend your time with. Only you should decide that. This includes your parents, your childhood years notwithstanding. It's the gig we've signed up to.

On the surface, this may seem negative and depressing. It's not. It's liberating to promise yourself only to spend time with those you want to be with. It also makes saying no a lot easier as well – which is an underrated and under-learnt skill in life.

Despite my general lack of family ties, I am close to my grandad, and seeing you and him meet for the first time is poignant and emotionally rewarding. He asks you questions, he holds you close, and he smiles a lot. The sight is a snapshot in time: the journey of life, handed down like a baton from old to new. There's a lesson there, Arlo. Life is transient. And the rarity and scarcity of these moments make them all the more special, especially when you projectile-vomit on Grandad's cardigan.

## My Twilight Years
Tuesday, 11 February 2020

84 days old

Mummy has taken to calling your great-grandad GG (and calling Hazel GG Hazel). GG is seventy-eight, and he's enjoying your company a great deal.

I rarely think about my own mortality. This might be because I believe I've made peace with it, or it might be because I'm hopefully still in the first half of my life, and it's such a long way off that I don't need to think about it yet. I suspect it's the latter, and I guess it's something I'll dwell on more and more as I age. But for now, I don't.

Something I do think about now, though, is my quality of life once I reach GG's age – if I'm lucky enough to do so. Aside from a recent hip-replacement operation slowing him down on his feet, he's fit and able-bodied. He's also extremely intelligent, acutely observant and highly amusing. I watch my grandad, and he looks like he has years left ahead of him. I hope that's true, but I also hope it's on his terms. He might not be able to run a marathon, but at least he can still refer to his mind as an ally.

I want that for you, Mummy, Granny Smurf and any other children we have. It's also something I want for myself and anyone else I care about. A lot of my daily routines such as exercise and nutrition are driven not by my quality of life today, but the quality of life in my twilight years. If Disney is still making *Star Wars* and Marvel movies when I reach ninety, then I want to be able to watch, understand and enjoy them without worrying about a loss of bladder control.

I would encourage you to give this some thought. The old adage that prevention is better than cure could not be more true.

## Everyone's An Artist
Wednesday, 12 February 2020

85 days old

Today was great; I was wearing a black T-shirt when you projectile-vomited all over me. Mummy took one look, laughed and told me I looked like a Jackson Pollock painting.

## Giggles And A Piss Hard Spin-Off Movie
Thursday, 13 February 2020

86 days old

You're in the bath when something makes me laugh, which in turn sees you produce your first ever baby-giggle. The sound is a melody composed entirely of spellbinding beauty.

You've been producing half-giggles for weeks now, but that was a fully fledged baby-laugh. Furthermore, both Mummy and I were there to witness it, and its sound has made the commendable number-two spot on my all-time-greatest-sounds-ever-heard list. Hearing you cry for the first time when you were born claims the top spot.

Fast-forward an hour. I've returned home from a Pilates class, to find an entirely different atmosphere from the one I left behind. I walk into our bedroom to find you asleep in Mummy's arms. It's 9.30 p.m., so you should be sleeping in your cot.

'He won't let me put him down without waking up,' Mummy says. 'He's spent over an hour crying uncontrollably. He's never done that before. I don't know what to do.'

There could be a few reasons why you're not settling this evening: you've had your second round of injections; we've changed your formula brand; you could be teething.

But you were fine during the first round of injections and you've been on the new formula for a few days now.

'It's got to be his teeth, right?' I say.

'I don't think it is.'

The reason I'm voting teeth is because of how red your cheeks are. Moreover, you're chewing anything you can get hold of, and dribble has been gushing from your mouth in torrents.

But I know that a mother's intuition is real.

'He smells like he's done a poo, but there's nothing in his nappy,' Mummy says, before trying to put you down yet again.

You wake up instantly and begin crying.

This is unlike you, buddy.

'I'm going to change him and see if that makes a difference.'

Two minutes later I hear: 'Daddy'.

I leg it into your nursery to find a bizarre situation unfolding. You're crying, but Mummy is laughing.

*Eh?*

A closer inspection reveals you've pissed everywhere; it's all over the changing mat, your legs, your torso, your neck and, finally, your face.

'How has he pissed on his face?'

After the giggles subside, Mummy recounts the story to me.

What happened was that Mummy changed your nappy and found the source of your frustration: you had pooed, but it somehow went only up your back. Mummy referred to it as a 'cheeky, up-the-back, explosive shart'. The positioning of this poo meant that every time Mummy checked your nappy, it appeared empty. When Mummy realised what had happened, she immediately removed the dirty nappy, lifted your legs upright and began cleaning your back. It was at this point you decided to start pissing.

I'm overcome with a lot of emotions as I hear this. The root cause of your annoyance is now understood. Good. But what's not good is that you've pissed on your face, and you're crying. But at the same time, I'm ... I'd go so far as to say euphoric that this happened on Mummy's watch. After my recent trauma of you besting me on three consecutive nappy-changes, this couldn't come at a better time.

'I thought you knew that you needed to keep his willy covered at all times when changing his nappy?' I say. 'You know that, don't you? I know you know that because you quote the same thing at me every time he has an accident when I'm changing him. Do you remember those times? When you blamed me for letting him piss all over his mat, up the side panelling of the wardrobe and on the wall. Remember? Do you also remember how you said you'd never let that happen? But now his face is covered in piss, and I wasn't the one responsible, so what you said previously must have been a lie, right?'

Look, Arlo, if your mummy were a bit more understanding and supportive about my recent mishaps, then I'd reciprocate. She wasn't, so I won't. I let her have everything I've got!

'That's not even the worst bit,' Mummy continues.

*Oh God, Arlo, what has she done?*

'I think some of it went in his mouth,' she says.

Today will forever be remembered for two things: the first time you laughed, and the first time you pissed in your mouth.

## Three Months Old
Wednesday, 19 February 2020

92 days old

We've successfully kept you alive for three months, and I've made it 25 per cent of the way through my first year of being a dad.

I'm still learning every day. So is Mummy. We've learnt to seek out four-seater table booths whenever we go out in public, even if we only need two chairs. Table booths often come equipped with a soft-covered seating bench which is excellent for changing babies and essential if the place we're at has substandard facilities, a queue for the changing facilities or no changing facilities at all.

No one ever says anything.

You love to look around more than ever. Your eyes are inquisitive and searching. They've developed into gorgeous shades of dark blue and grey. There's a slight colour variation between your normal eye and the one with the cataract, but every shade of colour they contain is stunning. It's like looking down on a pile of lightly charred sapphires or a deep section of the ocean.

If I pull back ever so slightly from your eyes, then your face comes into view. Every expression, every smile and every cry elicits an emotional response from everyone who sees you. You are the ultimate distraction.

When you were Dory, I reflected on why we have children. One of the reasons I believed was that procreation is a biological device to ensure we have someone to take care of us as we grow old; an evolutionary remnant of the past. I still believe that's true, but I also believe a different element of survival is served by having children. When you smile at your baby, and your baby smiles back, it gives you something that no doctor's prescription or illegal substance could ever deliver.

Your strength continues to develop. Sometimes you can stand, with us holding you by your forearms only. You hardly need your head supporting any more. We've started sitting you in your Bumbo seat and then positioning it up on the table with us while we eat. We have a good natter.

Your speech is also coming along. You've progressed past *awwaaa* and *goooobla* to *ahslkhfhgf, ayyejhohsd* and *ayehhsk*. Granny Smurf said it wasn't until I was five months old that I learnt to say *ayehhsk*. The tricky bit must be the *-sk* sound at the end of the word.

A fun pastime is to hold your bottle out in front of you first, before sticking it in your mouth. The reason we do this is that you can now recognise what your bottle is, and you make these amusing little lurch actions with your body reaching for it, and we never miss an opportunity to cash in on the fun at your expense.

The cataract thing was a shock. I have no idea how challenging the initial adjustment period will be as we get you used to wearing an eyepatch. Whatever happens, we'll tackle it together as a family.

Your mummy remains overqualified for the role of motherhood. She pours all of her love and energy into your well-being, and she gets everything right. It's wonderful to see and even better to be a part of, especially as it makes life easier for me.

I never watch the news. I figure if it's that important, then it will eventually reach my ears somehow. And that's what's happened now. There's been a virus outbreak in China (a coronavirus strain). I think it started in December. Truthfully, I've not paid much attention, because China is far away from Northampton and, as tragic as it sounds, these things do happen from time to time, and there isn't anything I can personally do about it. But now the virus has reached Italy, and people are dying. This wouldn't have captured my attention pre-dad-life until zombies came knocking. But that was pre-dad. Now I'm wondering if I need to do anything. I don't know. I guess I need to keep a closer eye on the news.

Next month will be challenging as I return to the workforce. I'll level with you now, I'm dreading it. I love my routine at the moment, but that is about to come to an end. I won't get to feed you and play with you as much in the morning, I won't see you in the day during the week, and when I return home from work, it will only be for an hour or two before you go to bed. It will be sad, but I'm grateful for having as much time off as I've had during these early stages of your life.

Well done for reaching three months.

## Old MacDonald Had A Farm
Friday, 21 February 2020

94 days old

'I just think it will make a really lovely memory and he'll love it,' Mummy says. She wholeheartedly believes in the voluminous amount of bullshit that's tumbling out of her mouth like when you empty a sack of marbles on the floor.

'He's asleep. He won't know it's even happening,' I respond, having equal faith in the validity of my own words – except that mine are correct, and Mummy's are, as I said, of the smelly variety.

'He's waking up. See? He wants to go on the ride with Daddy.'

Let me bring you up to speed, Arlo. We're at the farm with Auntie Lisa, cousin Claire and six children, including you. We're in the queue for a barrel-ride, which is essentially a ride on a train. The 'carriages' are constructed from plastic barrels and have been haphazardly engineered to allow small children to sit in them. Notice how I said 'small children' and not six-foot adult males who have a history of lower-back problems.

It's also rather chilly. I'm wearing a long-sleeved base layer, a T-shirt, a jumper, a down jacket, a waterproof jacket, a buff and a hat. I'm still cold.

Mummy is right, you have begun to stir, but I'm confident in two things: you will not *love* the ride, and you definitely won't remember it.

But all these facts and figures are irrelevant, and unless I want to be a massive spoilsport and ruin the lovely day we're having, I'd better hop into my designated barrel and smile and wave for pictures as we make our way around not one but *two* laps of the circuit.

You're not crazy about being snatched away from the warmth and comfort of your buggy. But before you complain too much, I ungracefully clamber into our carriage and take our seat.

*Ouch!*

I was expecting discomfort, but this is next-level. I feel like I'm sitting on a pile of broken, discarded Rubik's cubes.

You endure the duration of the barrel ride with one eye closed and the other squinting enough to also be classified as closed. As predicted, you don't smile once. The only expression you give me is one of disdain because I've moved you from a warm, cosy environment into the cold, hostile conditions of an open-top barrel-ride that's under a merciless assault from the wind on all fronts.

It's not that I don't like farms, I do ... I mean, they're OK ... but I'm not too fond of farms in sub-zero temperatures, especially when I'm forced with the guilt-gun to ride something designed for beings a third of my size, along with my three-month-old son, who I'm pretty sure doesn't want to be out in the cold either.

Still, at least we have a picture to capture this delightful memory. If I'm ever on trial for neglect, I'll wave the Polaroid in the face of any judge, juror or journalist – just to prove how much of a fucking good dad I am.

## Is It A Bird?
Sunday, 23 February 2020

### 96 days old

Since you've developed enough strength and control in your neck, I can now lie down and hold you up in the air for some baby-Superman action.

I like this game because we each get something out of it. You get to fly like Superman, albeit with a limited range that matches the length of my arms, and I get to hum the *Superman* theme tune to you.

But that's not the only value I get from this activity: I also get a spike in my adrenaline levels, never knowing if my face is seconds away from becoming a safety net to capture falling baby vomit – like it did a few seconds ago.

I barely had time to shut my mouth before a plateful of the white stuff came hurtling down from above, splattering all over my face, chin and neck.

It was the complete opposite of up, up and away.

## Swimming
Monday, 24 February 2020

97 days old

Today is going very well. First, we left you in the morning for a couple of hours with your Auntie Lisa, where you unleashed such a large amount of waste that it penetrated every layer of clothing you were wearing. The outside layer was a light-grey Babygro made of wool. Auntie Lisa described the scene as 'Play-Doh coming out the other side of a spaghetti machine'.

After escaping the nappy drama, Mummy collected you, and now the three of us are on our way to the local pool to take you swimming for the first time. We're having a debate about the pool's stance on photography. I'm adamant that it will not be allowed.

'They won't let you,' I say.

'Well, I'm going to take my phone in anyway. There is no way we're not capturing this. The staff can fuck off.'

We arrive, pay the admission fee and make our way through to the changing rooms. We've got a Superman baby swimming costume for you to wear. If I were at a high-stakes poker table and I had to bet on the most adorable baby outfit you've worn so far, I'd go all-in right now.

Because of your age, there are specific swim times for babies, and the water has to be heated to a minimum of 32 degrees, which means we can't swim in the main pool – we have to make do with a smaller one. That's fine by me because we're the only family here, we have the pool to ourselves.

Perfect. We might even get away with taking a few pictures, after all.

You're a content baby in the bath so I'm anticipating little or no resistance from you.

'Ready, Arlo? Three, two, one ... and *in* we go.'

As expected, you don't mind the water. You seem to like it.

*I bloody love being a dad.*

There is no one else in the pool and only one member of staff around, but she's busy sorting out some equipment, so Mummy begins snapping pictures quicker than a professional touch-typist.

After we've taken plenty, and we've each had a few turns at pulling you through the water, we focus our attention on an ability that babies are born with, called the mammalian dive response. It ensures that if babies are submerged in water, they will naturally hold their breath. The decision to test this isn't one we've taken likely and I've got the biggest muscles in my body clenched up tighter than a bungee cord knot. The reason we are testing it is because we've seen the mammalian dive response tried and tested on holiday a few years ago, with a chap named Harry. Harry is the son of my mate Ian, and he was about your age at the time of the test. He also happens to be the former owner of the Superman outfit you're wearing.

So we're confident …

Are you ready?

Once again, but slower: 'Three, two, one …'

This time, it's *under* we go.

You emerge a few seconds later, to the tune of … success! Judging by your reaction, it's caused a bit of a shock, but you recover quickly.

Don't worry, I got that bad boy on camera as well.

After another ten minutes, we think about getting out. But not before capturing one last family selfie—

'Oi. You're not allowed to take photos in here,' says a lifeguard who's appeared. His name badge says 'Manager'.

'Oh, I'm terribly sorry,' says Mummy, who, I can tell you, is not even a little bit sorry, let alone *terribly* sorry. 'I didn't realise that it wasn't allowed.'

He doesn't buy it at all. 'There's a sign right there that isn't exactly difficult to miss.'

'Oh yes, so there is.' Her acting at this moment is dreadful, Arlo. 'Honestly, I didn't see it. I'll put my phone away immediately.'

He's still not buying it, but he can't exactly demand we delete any of the pictures. So he skulks off.

Mummy turns to me with a look on her face like she's just won all five golden tickets to Wonka's chocolate factory. 'Fucking told you I'd get those pictures, didn't I?'

## Reusable Nappies
Tuesday, 25 February 2020

98 days old

Today is our third attempt at trialling reusable nappies. The first two trials failed before they could start because the nappies we bought were too big. They caused your legs to bow out, and we worried about them affecting your hip development.

Not this time, though. After adjusting the poppers, you stand (supported) with your midsection fully encased in a nappy, one that you will wear more than once.

Now, we need to wait for you to do your worst and see how they hold up. I will report back at the end of the day.

Lots to unpack (pun intended) on day one of our reusable-nappy journey. Firstly, the system is almost identical to the reusable wipes, which is easy-peasy and one we've been using since you were ten days old.

The nappy operator adds an insert the size of a small towel into the nappy, and then lines the top with a disposable liner. That makes up the nappy. When it comes to changing the nappy, the liner is flushed down the toilet along with the bulk of any debris, and the rest of the nappy is thrown in a soak bucket, where it remains until it's ready to be washed in the machine. Once washed and dried, the insert is replaced and a new liner is added and, bingo, you're ready to go again. Only one extra washing load a day, and no more disposable nappies going into landfill.

Reusables aren't without their challenges, though. The nappies are bulkier than their disposable counterparts. Mummy is worried about how to replicate the system when we're out and about. We usually pack six to eight nappies in your changing bag. Carrying that many reusables in the changing bag along with everything else will be a tight fit. We may need to get a bigger bag.

Then there are the dirty nappies. We need an out-and-about containment method. I have a 5-litre dry bag that should do the trick, but we need to test this out. For now, we have agreed to only use reusables at home for a couple of weeks while we adjust.

Of the two brands that we have, one of them leaked. It doesn't necessarily mean it's a dud because sometimes the eco-disposable nappies leak as well (mainly the ones I put on). It means we'll need to carry on testing, and if need be, adjust the poppers to amend the size.

In the meantime, if you could reduce the instances of shitting out your body weight every time you do a number two, that would be swell.

# Anyone Got A Bottle Opener?
Wednesday, 26 February 2020

99 days old

Today, I'm taking Mummy to London to go and see *Harry Potter and the Cursed Child*. Granny Smurf is on babysitting duty. It will be the longest period of time that we've left you alone.

Mummy has admitted that she's nervous about leaving you for what will probably amount to over twelve hours.

'You didn't get this nervous the last two times we left him to go out drinking.'

'Exactly!'

'Touché.'

So, I pack a few trip-beers to enjoy on the train ride down to settle Mummy's nerves. We kiss you goodbye, ask you not to hate us for leaving you for the day, and then we make our way to the train station.

Mummy's patience holds out forty minutes before she texts Granny Smurf to see if you're OK. Granny responds with a picture of you all wrapped up and ready to go out on a walk.

'He's got too many layers on. I'm going to tell her not to put any blankets on him.'

'You need to put your phone away right now. He's fine. Now have a cider.'

Ninety minutes later and we're sitting in a burger restaurant. Mummy has one cider left to drink, but this one is in a bottle, not a can, and I've forgotten to pack a bottle opener.

'Give it here, and I'll open it with my teeth,' she says.

'That's a terrible idea.' By the way, the restaurant we're at is not one where you can bring your own alcohol, so we've having to go about the whole thing incognito.

'I do it all the time.'

'That's because you have terrible ideas all the time.'

She snatches the bottle out my hand and makes to rid the bottle of its top, applying the appropriate amount of pressure and leverage. But then time slows down as I watch, not the bottle top, but a chunk of Mummy's tooth *ping* out of her mouth.

The transition from confidence to self-pity happens quicker than a lightning flash. She drops her chin to her chest and her expression is that of a child who's been knocked out in the first round of pass the parcel.

'I don't understand, Arlo must have weakened my teeth during the labour.'

Not for a minute do I buy that, Arlo.

'Does it hurt?'

'No, but it has made me a little bit upset.'

I'm trying to keep a straight face. 'What can I do?'

'You could go and find a me a bottle opener?'

We square the bill, leave the restaurant and spend a few minutes looking for a bottle-top remover. I find one in the form of a scaffolding pipe. It in no way looks odd that two adults in their mid-thirties are doing this in broad daylight. Mummy is still beside herself. Her bottom lip could rival yours. I'm laughing as much as I was ten minutes ago when the tooth-chipping occurred.

The show is outstanding, and we have a blast. Me especially, as all my teeth are intact. I'm happy we were able to take this time out. But it has been strange being without you. Even though you're still only three months old, we've fully adjusted to life as a three. You have occupied 80 per cent of our conversations, we spent time on the train watching videos of you and looking at photos of you, and Mummy couldn't go long without checking in with Granny Smurf to see if you were still alive.

I now understand why parents, particularly mothers, never, or rarely, leave their babies unless they have to, like for work. It does take a bit of getting used to. This lesson completes a reflection exercise I undertook in *Dear Dory*, where you and I examined the rules for parents going away without their children. I still stand by what I said last year – parents need time away from their children and vice versa – but I'm humbled by putting that theory into practice.

We have a fantastic support network available to us, and everyone deserves a day off, Arlo.

Let's just hope we remember to bring a bottle opener with us next time.

## The Soundest Logic You Will Ever Hear
Thursday, 27 February 2020

100 days old

'I knew I was right. My teeth have weakened because of giving birth to Arlo. I've had it confirmed online,' says Mummy, or should that be Hercule Poirot?

'But you gave birth over three months ago,' I counter.

'Well, obviously my calcium count is still low, and I need to eat more cheese. So go and get me some cheese and crackers!'

## Skiing, Baby!
Saturday, 29 February 2020

102 days old

Next week, specifically Thursday, is looming in the auditorium wings. It's the date I return to the workforce. Fortunately, it will remain in the wings until then. Taking centre stage in my life right now is a trip to the airport. I'm going skiing for a few days in the French Alps.

Somehow, Mummy has allowed me to go on this trip without her. The reasons are twofold: we haven't got round to applying for your passport yet and Mummy can't ski, which means that Mummy will stay at home and look after you while I'm off enjoying myself.

At one point, it was touch and go if the green light to go skiing would change to red, all because of a selection of words I used that weren't ... how do you say it? ... 100 per cent accurate.

I told Mummy I would be skiing for 'a few days', which she interpreted as 'three days'. I confirmed this to be correct. But what I forgot to remind her was that those few days *obviously* didn't include the day either side to account for travelling to and from our destination.

'So you're not going for three days, you're going for five?'

'Well, I'm skiing for three days, but it will take me one day to get there and one day to get back.'

'So why not say five days?'

'Well, because you're such a seasoned traveller, I assumed you would automatically add the travel time to the three days that I'm skiing.'

'Do you want to go skiing or not?'

'I absolutely do. I'm so grateful you're allowing me to do this. I love you so, so much. We have a baby. Life is perfect.'

'Hmmm.'

As an insurance policy, I bought Mummy a spa-day voucher so that she couldn't change her mind.

By the way, Arlo, this nasty virus business is still occupying headlines. It's reached Italy, and it's causing all sorts of chaos. I haven't heard anything about France, or the UK, so I'm still going skiing.

# March

## The Follow-Up Appointment
### Monday, 2 March 2020

104 days old

Today is your follow-up appointment with the ophthalmologist. The goal is for Mummy and me to come away with a clear idea of how we approach your diagnosis, and in particular your surgery.

The previous doctor's words echo in the back of my mind. He said our chances of making the right decision for you are fifty-fifty, and that we won't know if we made the right decision until after the fact. Any decision we make cannot be undone, but it ultimately rests with us as your parents to make that decision. I'd love to come away from today with a little more optimism.

I can't be there in person today because I'm selfishly skiing, so I'll be dialling in.

I'm sitting in Courchevel 1850 village watching blue skies contrast with white peaks. I see these views every year and never tire of them. Mountains are like poetry to me, and I can't wait to share them with you.

But I can't start enjoying them yet.

*Ring ring.*

The line is clear and I can hear everyone in the room: Mummy, Granny Feeder, you and the ophthalmologist, Louise.

'Hi, Dad, can you hear me?' Louise says.

'I can.'

'Right then, let's get started.'

It doesn't take long for Louise to provide a second diagnosis that matches the first: you have a *severe* congenital cataract in your left eye. She recommends surgery to remove the cataract as soon as possible.

'I'm used to performing this type of surgery on babies who are as young as six weeks old. I'm surprised Arlo doesn't have a squint.'

No one knows how to respond to that. Is that a good thing? No squint sounds better than a squint to me, Arlo.

'The good news is that because he's that bit older,' (I'm struggling to accept you being 'older') 'there is less chance that he will develop scar-tissue complications from the surgery, which isn't uncommon with the newborns. Sometimes they require additional corrective surgery.'

'What happens after the surgery?' Mummy asks.

'He'll need specialist contact lenses that we'll need to change every couple of months. You'll have to come to Cambridge to have that done and extra visits may be needed if his contact lens falls out or his eye looks sore. Once Arlo is over a year old, his eye will have fully grown, and I can insert an artificial lens, which will remain in place for the rest of his life. He will need glasses throughout childhood, and he'll need to wear an eyepatch on his right eye every day to force him to use his left eye so that the vision can develop.'

'How does the eyepatching work?' I ask.

'Start him on three hours a day. He has to be awake for those three hours. Move up to four hours when he's four months, five hours when he's five months and then to six. He won't need to wear a patch for any longer than six hours a day.'

*I bet you're gonna love life the first time we slap one of those on you.*

We ask a few follow-up questions, but the appointment lasts no more than fifteen minutes. Louise comes across as confident, warm and caring the whole time.

I'm feeling positive, Arlo. Let's see how this one pans out. In the meantime, you are scheduled for surgery on 21 April.

Mummy rings me again to update me on your first eyepatch experience. In short, it didn't faze you at all.

Does anything?

I end the call with Mummy and take a moment to regard the glistening white mountains: unshakeable, defiant and resilient to the end. They weather and absorb everything that Mother Nature throws at them with a silent shrug and a calm, quiet acceptance.

You remind me of every single one of them.

# Something's ... Different
Tuesday, 3 March 2020

105 days old

I'm noticing a reluctance in myself to pursue challenging ski routes. I'm hesitant about going off-piste, and I'm skiing slower than I typically would. There are a few possible explanations. My boots feel loose. I own a set, but they didn't accompany me this year because I had only hand luggage to take on board my flight.

Loose ski boots are one possibility.

Maybe it's because I'm getting older. I've noticed that as each year passes me by, a fact of life solidifies and reinforces itself – that I'm not immortal or infallible.

That's another possibility.

Or is it because I'm now a dad? I'm accountable to you and Mummy for every choice I make. A decision to take on a dangerous ski route isn't just a decision to put myself in danger for the chance to capture a thrill, it's rolling the dice on breaking a leg and not being able to perform my share of parental duties and having to rely on Mummy instead. It's a choice of risking having to say no to throwing you up in the air while I recover.

Once, while skiing about ten years ago, I messed up a move, which resulted in me free-falling from a height of twelve feet and landing directly on my back. Luckily, I landed on a fresh mound of soft snow that cushioned my fall. Somehow, I wasn't injured at all.

But what if next time it's not a fresh mound of soft snow I fall on. What if it's ice? That doesn't bode well for soft-play adventures, does it?

So it looks like I'm taking things slow this year. *From now on – every year.*

## My Return To The Workforce
Thursday, 5 March 2020

107 days old

One of the many splendid things about having a baby is that when you need to set your alarm to get up for work after having four months off, it's easy to get up on time.

But that's where easy begins and ends for me.

Having to hand you back to Mummy after feeding you for less than five minutes because I need to get ready for work is not easy. Saying goodbye to my family as I shuffle my feet out the door is not easy. Accessing the building where I work is physically not easy; my access is revoked because I've been away for so long. It's the same story when trying to log into my laptop.

I knew this day would come, so why am I not prepared? I've had four months at home with you and Mummy, and it's been a gift. But it's a gift that always had an expiry date, and I've reached it. I wish I had a pair of scissors so I could snip the expiry-date label out and continue the routines that we've established since you were born.

But it can't be so, because Santa isn't real, and bills need paying. We need to eat, we need to stay warm and dry, and, more importantly, we need access to all the streaming platforms we subscribe to.

Wednesdays used to be my favourite day: cinema in the morning and baby sensory class in the afternoon. I don't know the next time I'll be able to do that with you. I have twenty-seven days a year to take as annual leave, but I'm reluctant to start booking time off because, now I'm a dad, I don't know when I'll need to use them for you. What I do know is that the calendar isn't exactly shy of baby medical appointments.

On paper, and in reality – at least my reality – going to work is easier than staying at home and looking after a baby. At work, I control where my time is spent, and I'm doing something I've done for several years. At home it's different. Parenthood is a job Mummy and I have had only for a few months. It's harder.

And it changes every day.

If I have a problem at work, I have a long list of people I can approach to help me resolve it. The world of work, typically for me, is consigned to the hours of 9 a.m. to 5 p.m. Monday to Friday. It's structured, which I'll confess is something I crave.

Why then is today difficult? I have the easy part to play. It's Mummy who doesn't. The adjustment will be hardest on her because she's doing a job that requires 50 per cent more effort today than it did yesterday.

If someone gave me the opportunity to trade my position for Mummy's, would I honestly take it? Today I would. Tomorrow? Almost certainly. But any longer? Hard to say. I know what it's like to stay at home every day and look after a baby when there's two of us, but not one.

Today isn't easy, but the photos Mummy sends me of you 'saying' that you miss me make it easier.

We all commit to things in life that aren't always easy, Arlo. Today, going to work and providing for my family is one of mine.

At least I have the opportunity to provide for my family. That's more than some people get.

## Eyepatches
Saturday, 7 March 2020

109 days old

'Please keep your head still, Arlo. Otherwise, Daddy is going to poke you in your good eye, and we really don't want that, do we?'

This is me trying to reason with you so I can apply your eyepatch, something I've not personally done before.

I figured it would be attached to a headband, but it's not. I guess that makes sense, as anything that you could remove easily is unlikely to stay in place for long. The eyepatches we have are essentially plasters, so precise and careful application is required – unless you fancy having the sticky part of the plaster coming into contact with your eyeball.

But eyepatch application is fucking tricky when you, Arlo, keep turning your head quicker than an enthusiastic tennis spectator sitting midcourt watching a rally.

Eventually, I succeed.

The experience reminds me of the first time I put an over-the-head Babygro on you. I didn't enjoy that either.

I feel out of practice at dadding this morning. I know it's because I've been away for three – sorry – *five* days' skiing, followed by two days of working. That's only a week, yet my nappy- and outfit-changing abilities have dipped, and I don't feel like I'm in control. It's a bit like when you go round someone else's house and offer to make the tea: you know what you're doing, but it takes you a while to find where everything is. Your task-completion time is slower and you feel that little bit more awkward.

I feel like that.

Thankfully, you and Mummy have taken pity on me, and you're both working to help me regain my confidence: you by dropping a category-one in your nappy that wrought more pain and desolation upon my senses than three canisters of mustard gas, and Mummy by allowing me to change it. I'm enraptured by the level of support you guys give me.

If I told you I didn't get any shit on my hands, then I would be lying, but who cares, right?

One thorough hand-wash later, and I'm ready to address today's main focus: helping Granny Smurf move out. She's been with us for ten months, but now it's time for her to have her own space. She's not going far, so I'm hoping that means that Daddy still gets to go to the cinema ... Oh, and that you get to maintain the grandmother-grandson relationship that you've built.

But mainly the cinema.

## They've Been Wrong Before
Sunday, 8 March 2020

110 days old

I'm unconvinced that your cataract is as severe as the medical community claims. Right now, you're wearing your eyepatch, which, I'll remind you, covers your normal eye. I'm waving your bottle in front of you, and you're lunging forward to get at it like you're a king cobra striking a rodent. After your bottle, I carry out another test: I sit you down and then leave the room for a few seconds. I then creep back in and advance towards you without making any sound. As soon as I get close, you reward me with one of your gigantic loving smiles, and if I get closer still, I can see your pupil adjust its size as if it's refocusing.

What does this mean?

I know I'm not a doctor, optician, or any sort of medical specialist, but you do have sight in that eye that's working well enough to recognise both your bottle and Daddy, as long as they're close enough. Does this mean your long-range vision only is impaired by a cataract? I thought a cataract impaired sight in the affected eye regardless of distance.

I might not be medically trained, but I do believe I'm well within my rights to order myself a deerstalker hat. If your eyesight isn't as bad as doctors claim, does this explain why both your eyes follow in tandem and why your left eye hasn't developed into a squint? It's hardly the first time a medical diagnosis concerning our family was wrong.

The game is afoot, my dear boy.

## Rushing To Get Home On Time
Monday, 9 March 2020

III days old

I'm beginning to accept my return to work. Last week was hard but I've told myself there's no use directing energy and focus towards something that isn't. It's better to invest in what is. One change I've noticed already is that I don't clock-watch to anticipate the end of the working day, I clock-watch to see when I can go home to my family. Same clock, different narrative.

At 5 p.m. I shut my laptop down, pack my bag, descend the three flights of stairs and exit the building, the same building that gives me the opportunity each day to provide for my family. *I must never forget that.*

Outside, I march valiantly to the bus stop, striving to beat the competition and ensure I'm one of the first passengers on board. I do this so I can sit at the front and be one of the first passengers off.

You never know how the traffic will play out. Sometimes my bus journey takes fifteen minutes, other times it takes forty. I used to cherish the heavy traffic and long bus rides as it meant I could read for longer without interruption. Not today, though, and not any day from now on.

The traffic gods take pity on a first-time dad who's missed his little boy today. They don't commit to making every journey this easy, but they give me this one. I arrive at the bus depot at 5.30 p.m. Next, I have a fifteen-minute walk from the bus station to the front door.

At 5.45 p.m. I walk across the threshold of our home, and I find you lying down playing with Mummy. It takes you all of three seconds to begin smiling. You are a performer who cannot comprehend missing a cue. You start talking, telling me about your day and asking me about mine. My day was fine, but it's just got a whole lot better.

We play: with toys, and in the bath (which we call 'splish splash').

You smile the entire time.

At 8 p.m. I put you down for bed. We've spent two hours and fifteen minutes of quality time together. I don't for one minute expect every evening to be so enjoyable, but this one certainly has been.

## Working From Home
Wednesday, 11 March 2020

113 days old

I'm working from home today. I've explained to Mummy that I need to concentrate and that working from home doesn't mean we can go back to how things were when I was on shared parental leave. I can't do a lot of dadding. Mummy tells me that she not only understands this but that she's also fully supportive.

I'm not on board with her sincerity. I'll explain why.

It's 11.22 a.m. I'm on a work call about a big project that I need to begin leading on next week, and I have no fucking clue about any of it. To turn 'not having a fucking clue' into having 'a little bit of a clue' requires me to listen attentively to everyone speaking on the call, to take notes and ask questions. But I'm struggling to concentrate because I've got you on my lap babbling away while the Matriarch is upstairs hoovering. What's more, you find the wires on my earphones either interesting or offensive. I don't know which one it is, but I do know you're ruthlessly tugging away at them.

I've learnt two things from this experience, Arlo: I need to set clear working-from-home boundaries that are bulldozer-proof, and I need to get some wireless headphones.

## Covid-19
Thursday, 12 March 2020

114 days old

Arlo, this virus business has rapidly developed from a problem that's making headlines on the other side of the world to a potential global pandemic that will claim countless lives.

The virus is a corona strain (Covid-19).

It's surreal to be writing to you about this as an event that is happening right before me. And because of my ignorance I've arrived late to the party, only now recognising the gravity and magnitude of what's happening.

Many parts of the planet are on lockdown. Global sweetheart Tom Hanks has contracted the virus. Expos and sporting events are being cancelled. Countries have restricted travel and closed schools and shops, and employees of large organisations are being asked to work from home.

And worst of all – people are dying.

I'm still in the office at the moment, but it could change at any second.

To reduce the likelihood of us contracting the virus, we (and by 'we' I mean humanity) are being advised to wash our hands often, cough into a tissue, or the crook of our elbows if we don't have a tissue available, and limit how often we touch our eyes, nose and mouth – something that face masks will help with.

What's not on any of the literature (that I've read at least) is how you get a four-month-old teething baby who's recently had croup (something I forgot to write to you about) to apply those measures.

Arlo ... I don't know what to say ... this is fucking nuts! I spent much of last year envisioning every possible scenario that could threaten us.

It seems I missed one.

## Panic Buying Toilet Rolls
Friday, 13 March 2020

115 days old

Covid-19 is now officially a pandemic: the World Health Organisation declared it as such two days ago, and it continues to escalate at a frightening pace. More and more events with large groups of people are being delayed, postponed or cancelled outright. Film releases are being impacted too. I was looking forward to *No Time To Die*.

People are responding to the coronavirus in a big way, Arlo. They're panicking, bulk-buying supplies in case of state-imposed or self-imposed periods of home quarantine. The most sought-after product is toilet rolls.

Certain food items are also being snapped up, namely dry goods: pasta, rice, cereals, etc. One of the mums at my Pilates class last night said she couldn't buy flour to bake cakes. The supermarket had sold out and the shelves were barren. Eggs were another scarce item. And you can forget buying handwash gel, unless you pay through the nose for it on the black market. As an aside, I'd be curious to understand what everyone's hand-washing habits looked like before all of this.

Babies are affected too: parents are stocking up on nappies, formula and anything else they feel they need to survive the times ahead. This is where my opinions become distorted and unclear. I'm happy to claim that bulk-buying toilet roll is stupid, but I'm slower to offer my view on buying baby products, as I have a baby and he is my number-one priority.

I don't know if it's Western culture or global culture, but when something like the Covid-19 virus arises, we default, as a species, to survival mode, and much of that means acting selfishly and often unintentionally impacting others in the process.

I don't know how to approach our personal stockpiling agenda. Especially baby formula. You consume five 7-oz bottles a day. That's 35 oz a day, 245 oz a week and over 1,000 oz a month. I estimate with our current stock we have enough for the next ten days. But if everyone is panic buying, then it increases the odds of formula selling out, so we should probably stock up, right? But if we stock up, how much should we get? Surely it's better to be overcautious, in case Covid-19 requires us to take a longer-term view. After all, running out of toilet roll is one thing, but a baby running out of formula milk is another.

But how do I define what a longer-term view looks like? One month, two months, six? Is a month's worth of formula sensible? At least we wouldn't be adding to the frenzy of panic buying. But if we buy two months' worth, do we join the ranks of people buying as much loo roll as their wallets and available stock will allow for?

We don't know all the facts, Arlo. The media is in the business of selling drama and catastrophe, but most people rely on the news. If they're misinformed on the gravity of the situation, they'll respond accordingly, and that might indirectly impact us – or, more importantly, you.

After a few messages back and forth with Mummy, we decide to buy formula for the month. If the situation continues to escalate, we'll revisit this decision.

Once again, I cannot wrap my head around any of this.

## The Threat Is Real
Sunday, 15 March 2020

117 days old

Today, I saw the Covid-19 impacts first-hand at several of our local supermarkets. A lot of the shelves were bare, and it was impossible to buy many of our regular items.

Supermarkets, which are first and foremost competitors, have joined forces and issued an open letter to the public, encouraging them to slow down on the panic buying, desperately attempting to reassure us all that they're responding to the situation appropriately.

While we couldn't get hold of many food items, we were able to add several tins of formula to a friend's online order.

I find myself regularly checking the news. Politicians are warning the nation to prepare for measures that aren't normally observed during peacetime. I can't fathom the breadth and depth of the impacts, but I fear we're in for a rough ride. I've certainly never come close to experiencing anything like this in my lifetime.

The government is asking for things, particularly from the NHS, that are unprecedented – a word I hear hourly. They're asking for hotel chains to make empty rooms available for patients, for private hospitals to follow suit and for car factories to explore switching some of their manufacturing capabilities to help supply much-needed ventilator machines. Apparently, there are about 5,000 available across the UK, but people are predicting we are going to need many more. Retired doctors could be recalled to the workforce, with additional thought being given to how quickly they can be trained up to use the ventilation equipment.

Finally, the government is asking hospitals to convert operating theatres into wards, as many non-urgent surgeries are being cancelled.

*Cancelled?*

This last point has alarming implications for your upcoming eye surgery (scheduled for 21 April). I should probably contact the surgeon and ask how she is classifying your surgery.

*Urgent, surely?*

The stakes are noticeably higher than running out of toilet roll and knowing how much baby formula to buy. Operations are being cancelled because the Covid-19 virus is life-threatening, people are dying and we have a global pandemic. Yet my little boy might not get his operation, and I honestly don't know what that means. If you put it into perspective, one boy potentially losing his sight in one eye versus people dying isn't something that needs to go before a committee to debate.

But still, it's my little boy. The rationalist in me gets it, but it's not the only part of me speaking up to be heard.

Toilet roll might be in short supply, but they're doing buy-one-get-one-free on 'Santa isn't real' moments.

# Be Careful What You Wish For
Monday, 16 March 2020

118 days old

My first job this morning has been to email your surgeon, Louise, to ascertain the likelihood of your surgery not going ahead, and to ask if it's possible to bring your appointment forward. I also ask what we can expect to happen to your eye if you don't have the surgery, and for her not to shy away from honesty. I'd like to know what we're dealing with upfront.

It doesn't take long for Louise to respond with some reassurance. She says that it's 'extremely unlikely' that your op will be cancelled, especially given the time-sensitive nature of the procedure. She also says that she can't bring the date forward because her theatre is full tomorrow, and she's off on annual leave for a few weeks after that.

At first, I'm relieved.

But then I'm not.

'Extremely unlikely' isn't a guarantee, what's happening is unprecedented and no one can possibly fully understand the knock-on impacts yet. I'm reading many predictions of how the crisis will unfold, and what this will mean for the UK – and the planet. They all paint a grim picture of rough times ahead.

But it's the media's job to tease out these headlines, making threats appear more severe than they are, because when that happens people turn on their televisions and buy newspapers. Everyone knows the media overhypes these things.

But it's not as if the government isn't taking any action. They have advised people in their seventies and older to begin self-isolating (staying at home) to limit their chances of infection.

Things are moving rapidly.

What if the government's next announcement is to cancel any surgeries that aren't life-threatening?

Like I said yesterday, the rationalist in me accepts that death outranks *potential* loss of sight in one eye every time, but the father in me cannot reconcile the possibility that his little boy could go blind in one eye. I'm desperate for you to have this operation.

Before I can dwell on the uncertainty any more, I receive another email from Louise:

Hi Tom

Just had a cancellation for theatre tomorrow afternoon – are you all up for that?

Fuck, fuck and double fuck. Talk about being careful what you wish for, Arlo.

Are we all up for that? I don't see how we can't be, especially after everything I've just blurted out.

I call Mummy and explain that we have a decision to make.

179

'Fuck, I'm not mentally ready for this. What do you think?' Mummy says.

'I honestly believe they'll cancel the op if we wait.'

'Let's take him in.'

Now we've made the decision, we need to prepare because a lot needs doing. First, I need to make sure work are comfortable with me taking time off so soon after returning.

Fortunately, they are. I can take tomorrow off as emergency carer's leave and then work from home on Wednesday. Next, we need to fill the car up with petrol and fix the rear seat belt (it's stuck under the seat), as I imagine one of us will be accompanying you in the back for our return trip home. You're not expected to need to stay in, but it's a possibility, so it's probably worth us packing overnight bags just in case.

Once I confirm to Louise that we're on for tomorrow, her assistant sends me the details. We need to be there for 11 a.m. and you need to fast from 6 a.m. That's a minimum fasting period of five hours. You won't like that, but you'll probably sleep for most of the journey. The challenge will be when we're at hospital waiting for you to be called in for surgery, and you start getting a bit peckish.

The more I think about it, the more I'm dreading it. It's not unreasonable to assume that we will be handing over a hungry and distraught baby to the medical team, to then watch them put you under general anaesthesia. Mummy and I will be a mess.

I keep telling myself how lucky I am. Did you know that exactly one year ago today, Mummy and I found out we were going to be your parents?

# For Old Times' Sake
Tuesday, 17 March 2020

## 119 days old

5 a.m. The alarm goes off. Mummy and I get up and begin getting ready.

5.20 a.m. Mummy summons me to the bathroom to have an emergency meeting about towel protocol. Apparently, I keep using her towel, and she doesn't like it. She says, 'The top rung on the radiator is for Baby Bear, the bottom one is for Mummy Bear, and Daddy Bear has the middle one, as it has the most space.'

5.55 a.m. We wake you up. I feed you your bottle while Mummy triple-checks we have everything we need.

6.30 a.m. Before our sudden change of plans, Mummy had a full day's worth of St Patrick's Day celebrations lined up. As a consolation, Mummy has decreed that you will still wear your St Patrick's Day outfit. Therefore, you will be travelling to Cambridge hospital dressed as a leprechaun.

Shortly afterwards, we hit the road.

8.18 a.m. 'If Arlo goes in for surgery at 11 a.m. then it will be the best possible time,' Mummy says.

'How so?'

'Louise will be at her optimum performance, she will have woken up, got her first couple of surgeries out of the way, had her first couple of coffees. It's early enough for her not to be thinking about lunch, and she won't feel sluggish from the carb downer that most people get in the afternoon.'[5]

*Wow!*

Mummy has thought this one through, hasn't she, Arlo?

9.05 a.m. We arrive at one of the reception desks at Addenbrooke's Hospital, to find a member of staff in outrage because someone has stolen a hand-sanitiser unit off the wall. 'Why?' she says.

Covid-19 is the answer.

9.15 a.m. Mummy and I eat breakfast in the food court. The last time I had breakfast at the hospital was in Northampton on the day of your birth. Today's plate of grease is marginally better than last time, but that's nothing to boast about. The lesson here is that I should probably stop eating in hospitals.

9.45 a.m. We check you into Ward G, bed five. I'm momentarily unsettled as I realise you've not been allocated a standard bed; you've got a cot trolley and it's tiny. *What was I expecting?* The bars on the cot are blue and green.

Other than that, it's your typical-looking ward, except it's friendlier than other wards I've visited. Art hangs from the walls, there's a kitchen-room for parents and a playroom for children. The staff wear a voluntary perma-smile.

10 a.m. It's been four hours since your last bottle. Other than at night, you rarely go this long. You're in high spirits, though, and we're logging some solid

---

5  I sent these chapters to Louise so that she could fact-check all the medical terminology. One of her notes back to me was, 'No surgeon ever has coffee before microsurgery!'

play time. If you do start getting hangry, we have only an hour to kill before your surgery.

10.15 a.m. Slight error in our understanding of today's timetable: you don't go in for surgery at 11 a.m., you just have to be checked in by that time, which is frustrating to learn because Mummy rang up to double-check last night, and the nurse was adamant that it was 11 a.m. for surgery.

We're now told that surgery is *likely* to be around 1 p.m. Right on cue, you decide it's about time for a bottle, and you enact the feeding protocol that to date has boasted a 100 per cent success rate: you start crying.

Fuck! We somehow need to keep you distracted for approximately three hours.

All aboard the Hoot-Hoot Express.

10.25 a.m. 'Fucking feed me now, Mummy or Daddy! I never have to wait this long, what is going on?' you say in baby talk.

10.37 a.m. Sarah, the nurse looking after you today, explains that there have been changes to the nil-by-mouth rules and that you can have a small amount of water every hour, as long as it's consumed within ten minutes. Don't ask me why. Sarah weighs you and quickly determines that you can have 30 ml of water. You consume it in under sixty seconds.

The water has done nothing to soothe, so Mummy takes you for a walk to try and get you off to sleep.

10.47 a.m. Supermummy to the rescue – you're fast asleep. Mummy puts you in your temporary cot, and you don't stir. Sarah then checks your heart rate and oxygen levels to assess that you're fit for surgery.

Next, she checks your blood pressure – all fine. Sarah clears you for your procedure.

Now, how long do you fancy napping for? *Please lord, let it be for at least two hours.*

11.50 a.m. You've woken up, and you are one unhappy leprechaun. I give you another 30 ml of water, and then Mummy takes you for another walk while I stay by your bed, in case the medical team arrives to collect you.

12.32 p.m. We meet the anaesthesiologist. I can't place his accent, but I find his voice calm and hypnotic. An irony, given his job title. He explains that Mummy and I will not be present when they put you under. I quickly run the numbers through my mind and conclude that that's a good thing. Your resolve will be stronger than ours in that moment.

12.34 p.m. Sarah administers several sets of eye drops before leaving us with a parting gift: 'I don't think Arlo will go in until 2.30 p.m. now.'

Wonderful stuff, Sarah – thank you!

1.20 p.m. The afternoon surgeries begin. First up is a six-week-old baby who needs *extensive* surgery on both eyes.

Things can always be worse, Arlo.

2.30 p.m. No sign of anyone arriving to take you into theatre, Arlo.

You've now gone over eight hours without a bottle.

2.50 p.m. The children from this morning's surgeries begin coming round. It doesn't take them long to ask their parents for food, drink and toys. *Such hardiness in children.* This moment serves as a brief positive beat in an otherwise anxiety-ridden day.

3.30 p.m. Sarah appears with a porter. It's time for you to go down to theatre to have the cataract in your left eye removed. Mummy strips your leprechaun outfit off and re-dresses you in a baby-sized hospital gown that the hospital has provided. You look like an unmasked baby kendo warrior.

*My brave little warrior.*

Despite the hunger and everything else going on today, you manage a smile, and I find myself fighting back a few tears.

The porter pushes your cot, but it's empty. Instead, I walk the length of the short trip cradling you in my arms. I've trekked up mountains, volcanoes and sand dunes, yet they're a walk to the shops to pick up a loaf of bread compared to walking down to theatre with my four-month baby boy in my arms. I am not enjoying being a parent at the moment, Arlo.

I'm scared shitless.

We arrive at a holding room that leads into the theatre. This is where the anaesthesiologist will employ drugs and a hypnotic, soft-sounding European voice to put you under. In fact, he's here now, as are other members of the medical team. They introduce themselves. I don't register anyone's name, except one: Louise, your surgeon. She's as friendly in person as she is over the phone and on email.

'You made the right call pushing for a cancellation. The government has announced they're cancelling all elective surgeries from the fifteenth of April – for at least three months,' she says.

Your surgery was originally scheduled for the twenty-first.

Louise explains what she'll be doing today, and what the next twelve months look like. I don't take much of it in, but needless to say we'll be making many trips to Cambridge.

Soon after, we're asked to lay you down in your cot and say goodbye. This is hands-down fucking torture. I hate it.

I've not asked you to do this in a while, but for old times' sake, just keep swimming, buddy.

Mummy kisses you on your forehead and tells you that everything will be OK and that we'll see you shortly.

We leave you in the hands of the medical team and allow the porter to escort us back to Ward G and to bed five, which looks exactly the same as it did before, minus the blue-and-green-barred hospital trolley cot – and you.

The porter leaves and Mummy and I find ourselves alone. We comfort each other as best we can.

We're given a pager like the ones you get in posh restaurants where the staff judge you if you swig from a wine glass while chewing gum. It will ring when you're out of surgery and we can go and see you.

3.45 p.m. We head down to the food court and order a Burger King. The food is dry and tasteless, but I'm not holding Burger King accountable for that today.

4.10 p.m. I bury my head in my phone to distract me and check the latest on the Covid-19 pandemic. I also read a message from my manager, who says that, effective immediately, our entire team is to begin working from home until further notice.

4.25 p.m. Mummy is on the phone to your Auntie Lisa, updating her with how things are going, when all of a sudden: 'Oh-my-fucking-God-there's-a-Starbucks-cup-over-there-and-I-need-it,' Mummy says, before coming up for a much-needed intake of oxygen.

I turn my head around, following her eyeline towards a freestanding dirty-tray trolley. And on one of the trays stands, as Mummy rightly observed, a Starbucks cup. I can see why she's excited. The cup is on the large side without being too tall. You might think of it as a girthy mug, Arlo. Perfect for those times when you need that little bit extra. Either way, your mother wants it. We have one at home that's exactly the same. It arrived in our possession the same way as this one is about to: it was stolen, just not by Mummy.

Let's pause for a second and observe how wonderfully complicated our species is, and how our minds operate. Your mummy is almost inconsolable right now, yet she's temporarily distracted from the seriousness of your surgery by the prospect of bolstering our Starbucks-mug inventory by one. If that doesn't give you an insight into the wackiness of humanity, I don't know what will.

Mummy takes the brown paper Burger King bag that our meals came in and does the most uninspiring piece of acting you've ever witnessed. She pretends she's clearing her rubbish, placing it on the same tray where the mug sits, but really, she deposits the goods in the bag, and then she stands up in the middle of the food court and yells to absolutely no one in particular: 'Oops, I won't put my rubbish on this tray after all, I'll put it in the bin instead.' She then walks back to our table with the newly liberated Starbucks mug, wearing a smile that says she's pulled off a job that Danny Ocean couldn't manage.

The whole thing is a farce, but it's wonderfully entertaining, not to mention distracting. By the way, Mummy didn't damage any property when stealing this, so she's nothing like the scumbag that stole the hand-sanitiser unit off the wall ... OK?

4.40 p.m. We're back on your ward playing Dobble – another noble effort by your mummy to make light of the situation. Mummy gets off to a storming start, but then I settle into my rhythm and begin my comeback.

4.46 p.m. I'm about to claim my first scalp of the day when the pager goes off. Mummy ejects herself off her seat as if it suddenly heated up to 1,000 degrees and sets off at a run. I hurry after her.

A few minutes later, we meet Louise, who takes us into a side room to see you.

You're already awake ... and you're smiling. You're not wearing any bandages or eyepatches of any description – heck, there's not even a plaster in sight.

*What the fuck is going on?*

'Now you might be thinking that Arlo doesn't look like he's had surgery, and that's because, well, he hasn't,' Louise says.

'Right ...' I say.

'We put him to sleep and I had a closer look at his eye, and I realised that we've misdiagnosed him. He doesn't have a congenital cataract.'

My mind erupts. I have a million questions, but I don't know where to begin.

Louise takes the time to explain, but this is the second conversation that I've had with her today where barely anything sinks in.

But some bits do.

You still have a congenital abnormality in your eye, but it's one that affects the corneal endothelium; it's not a cataract. That means you won't ever have to have surgery or contact lenses.

Let me repeat that – you won't *ever* have to have surgery!

You will still need to wear an eyepatch, but only for three and a half hours a day. And you will still need to wear glasses until you're around eight years old, but if we do everything we've been instructed to do, we should be able to get your weaker eye to the point where it's strong enough to read the middle line of an eye-test chart.

In short, this is phenomenal news, and a much better outlook than the one we were facing before. It means the bus-driving career is officially back on the table.

You have two exhausted but utterly relieved and happy parents.

*What a day.*

5.05 p.m. Mummy feeds you your first bottle in a little under eleven hours.

7 p.m. As we leave the hospital, I glance at a plaque on a wall. It contains a quote by the alphabetarian, David Kindersley, that says:

*It will pass, whatever it is.*

What an apt way to end the day.

# Four Months Old
Thursday, 19 March 2020

121 days old

The good news is that, last night, Mummy managed to stock up on an emergency stash of ciders for our self-isolation period. She calls it mummy juice. The bad news is that, today, we have no emergency ciders in the house.

You're four months old today, Arlo. As of Monday, you weighed 14 lbs and 14 oz, which is 4 oz shy of double your birth weight.

This has been your toughest month to date, yet you continue to amaze me with how you respond to, and overcome, the many challenges that life hurls in your path. You've been prodded with hands, poked with needles and examined – against your will – by strangers. And you've had to adjust to wearing an eyepatch. To top it off, you went without food for eleven hours while spending most of that time awake.

While most of the population are stockpiling toilet rolls, you're stockpiling resilience.

In terms of development, you were steadily growing until last week when everything changed, seemingly overnight. The curve went from gradual incline to straight-up vertical because your awareness of your surroundings has exploded. Feeding you a bottle used to be such a pleasure, but now it's more of a chore because you won't keep your head still. You want to look everywhere, and your curiosity has caused you to develop a bald patch on the back of your head because of your constant head-turning while lying down.

Can you guess how many times I've heard the 'just like his dad' remark? I'll give you a clue – fucking tons!

You've learnt to take your dummy out and put it back in your mouth the other way, so that you can chew on the harder surfaces to help your teeth, which appear to be giving you grief. No actual teeth have appeared yet, but all the signs point to them arriving soon.

The other night, Granny Smurf taught you how to fake cough. It was hilarious, but then you got a bit carried away and threw up everywhere. You've started crying when Mummy leaves the room. You love standing. You plant both legs firmly as soon as you're held up. Mummy doesn't think you will be a late walker.

We now have a way to make you laugh which never fails. Mummy discovered it. She blows kisses in your face while, at the same time, she places a hand behind your head to support it and brings it forward towards her every time she blows a kiss – think of it as a gentle shake while kissing you. It kills me – your temperament is textbook perfect.

The reality we now find ourselves in is difficult for me to carve out in words. None of the changes thus far have impacted us greatly. I can work from home, we have enough money to cover the bills and you no longer need to make short-term hospital trips. You're also not old enough to have your education impacted. It was announced last night that schools would close tomorrow.

And what about contracting the virus itself? If the early research is to go by, then we don't stand a strong chance of developing any life-threatening or even major symptoms should we get it – you especially. That's not to say it's not possible, but the odds appear very much in our favour because we're young, and without any underlying health conditions. That doesn't mean we won't be following the guidelines, or I'm not concerned, it just means I'm taking some comfort in the early research, and I'm not up all night in a panic-induced frenzy about the prospect of us catching the virus.

The last time measures of this sort were put in place was during the London Blitz, when people's houses were bombed. So far, the only negative to our household is the amount of pointless and irrelevant interruptions that the Matriarch insists on peppering my day with. Honestly, I couldn't give a bumhole's hair what's on her Instagram feed, but she's not taking my word for it.

However, I'll take a few months of that if it means you and I get to spend more time together.

Well done on reaching the four-month mark, son.

## Who The Hell Eats Rich Tea Biscuits?
Friday, 20 March 2020

122 days old

'You don't have to stop working, you don't even need to leave your chair, but can you keep an eye on Arlo for ten minutes while I do a few bits around the house? He's sleeping, so it will be easy for you.'

That's dialogue from your mother that contains reasoning and logic that's about as strong as a ninety-year-old anorexic woman's ankle.

I'll explain why.

In order for her statement to be accurate, she has to have some way of knowing that you won't wake up within the next ten minutes. This is intel that she doesn't possess, because you're already beginning to stir. And Mummy knows this. I know she knows because she's looking at you right this second, watching your limbs, head and torso move!

And I'm about to point this out when she enacts an exit plan that's bordering on teleportation.

Sixty seconds later, and I'm trying to listen attentively on a conference call for work, and you're rubbing your slobbery hands all over my face, while also proudly demonstrating the new words that you've added to your baby lexicon.

'Oooohh ahhhh errrr raaa ooooh.'

That's not the worst idea I've heard on a project call, but it's not the best either. Working-from-home rules are being enforced next week, Arlo.

And while we're on the subject of Mummy being a twat, she's filled up the biscuit jar with rich tea biscuits. Honestly, I didn't know rich tea biscuits were still a thing. Do people still go in for that? I would compare the experience of eating a rich tea biscuit to going on a date with an unperfumed piece of cardboard. I assume Mummy's taken these measures to stop me eating biscuits, which, admittedly, is a habit I've revisited since the new working-from-home conditions were put in place.

But I won't be beaten.

And I haven't been.

I temporarily empty the vile-tasting rich tea biscuits on to a plate, excavate the custard creams from the bottom of the jar and then put the rich tea ones back in.

I complete the exercise in under sixty seconds. This includes eating the newly liberated custard creams.

Next time, give me a formidable challenge!

## Whatever Doesn't Kill The World ...
Saturday, 21 March 2020

123 days old

Global pollution levels have dropped; the Venice canals have cleared because the absence of traffic on the water has allowed the sediment to settle; acts of kindness are becoming more and more common; people are taking to social media to offer their time, services and skills to anyone that could benefit from them. A friend of mine from university is a chef. Since he can't work at the moment, he's offering to teach people how to make bread online. Teachers are reaching out to support parents who are having to homeschool their children. My Thursday-evening Pilates class took place as normal, but from our living-room floor, using a videoconferencing app. For every life that Covid-19 takes, humanity finds creative and beautiful ways to strike back.

In some ways, I think you're missing out on witnessing what's happening. Covid-19 is terrible and crippling, yes, but humanity's response is powerful and unified. I hope that when the dust settles – and it will – the world will be a better place to live in.

# Mother's Day
Sunday, 22 March 2020

124 days old

Granny Smurf was pregnant with me when she was nineteen. My dad was never in the picture, choosing instead to bail out as soon as he learnt of my existence. When Granny Smurf told our family that she was pregnant, many responded with words to the effect of 'I'm so sorry to hear about that, what shall we do to fix it?' – implying she should consider having an abortion. This included, among others, my grandmother (your great-grandmother and Granny Smurf's mum).

But Granny Smurf ignored them all (clearly).

We spent my childhood living in one-bedroom bedsits. I still remember the sight and smell of the damp, and the condensation streaming down the walls. As a child, the time it took from me getting out the bath to getting warm, dry and dressed again felt like hours.

Despite the circumstances, for better or for worse, I'm the man I am today because Granny Smurf said no to having an abortion, and no to letting the many hardships get in the way of her being a mum.

My day job requires me to work thirty-seven hours a week between the hours of nine and five, Monday to Friday. I get an hour for lunch to do whatever I choose, and I can go to the toilet or make a coffee whenever I want during those hours undisturbed. I get twenty-seven days' annual leave a year, I get sick pay, and now I get five carer's days each year to look after you.

Mums supposedly get one day off a year. They are required to work the remaining 364 days. They are on call twenty-four hours a day; they don't get sick pay or holiday entitlement, nor do they get many chances to recharge their batteries.

Yet they keep going.

Shout out to all the mums, Arlo, especially your mummy, who shows up to work every day with a smile on her face and enthusiasm running through her veins.

Happy Mother's Day to all the mums of the world.

## The Struggle Is Real
Monday, 23 March 2020

125 days old

Do you know what I find to be a struggle in life, Arlo?

I'll tell you.

It's when I get you ready for bed, and you throw up down your pyjamas. Naturally, the contents of tonight's vomit are watery and therefore have soaked through to your vest. Parental protocol dictates that I'm required to change your whole fucking outfit.

Some struggles in life don't end quickly either, Arlo. Like when the above happens, and you're on your second outfit, and you go right ahead and defecate an unnaturally large deposit of faeces, large enough to ensure an up-the-back trajectory that travels far enough that I wonder if I need to wash your hair.

Those are the instances that make me sigh aggressively,

like I'm having a stroke, but I'm really annoyed about having the stroke, almost as if the stroke has happened at an inconvenient time of the day.

Do you understand where Daddy is coming from?

I should also admit that you went ahead and vomited again on your third outfit, but this vom was less watery, and so I didn't feel compelled to change your outfit. Instead, I gave it a quick wipe with the old muslin square so Mummy wouldn't notice, and then I put you to bed.

Nighty-night, son.

## Lockdown
### Tuesday, 24 March 2020

#### 126 days old

It's 8.30 p.m. and 27 million viewers, including us, have turned on their TVs to watch Prime Minister Boris Johnson address the nation. It doesn't take much to guess what he's about to say. My money is on tougher measures in order to slow the spread of the virus.

There was media footage over the weekend of large gatherings across many different public spaces. Too many people are not taking this seriously, which means the NHS will be put under even more pressure, the economic recovery will take the country longer and many more people will die.

As of yesterday, 335 people have died from the virus in the UK. The UK is tracking roughly two weeks behind Italy, and this tells us that things are going to get a lot worse before they get better.

The prime minister is going through details of the new measures right now.

As suspected, he announces that the UK is now effectively in a mandatory lockdown. Details are hazy, but I'll give you the summary points:

- All non-essential shops to close immediately. This also includes libraries, playgrounds, outdoor gyms and places of worship.
- Weddings and baptisms have been cancelled.
- Gatherings of more than two people are banned unless they all live together.
- People may not leave the house unless it's to exercise once a day, or to shop for essentials, such as food.

The police will be given emergency powers to enforce these new measures, disbanding illegal gatherings and issuing fines if need be.

These new measures don't impact us any more than yesterday. We've been self-isolating since last Wednesday. It does mean, however, that we won't spend any time with the wider family for a while. You will have to make do with Mummy and Daddy.

Sorry about that.

These measures are in place for three weeks, but things are changing all the time, so I guess we'll see.

# Working From Home: Ts & Cs
Wednesday, 25 March 2020

127 days old

I've sent the following email to Mummy, to lay out the new conditions for working from home. If Boris Johnson can do it for the country, then I'm fucked if I can't do the same in my household.

Hi,

As you know, the Covid-19 pandemic has forced people to adjust rapidly to new routines for the foreseeable future. This includes our family, especially now that I've been asked by my employer to work from home until further notice. To give our family every chance at succeeding through these tough and uncertain times, and to ensure we don't split up, I've taken the opportunity to set out the parameters that we as a family (but mainly you) will be following until this nasty business concludes.

The terms below are effective immediately and are not up for challenge, debate or review (unless my interests are being exclusively served).

Section 1a

You may not interrupt me:

- To show me something on Instagram –
  I promise you, I don't give a grizzly bear's
  shiny shit stain what it is; I don't care.
- To change Arlo's nappy, or to comfort him
  when he has a meltdown.
- Just for a chat because you're bored.
- To tell me that Arlo has gone to sleep –
  I don't need to know his daily statistics; you're
  his mother, and I'm more than confident that
  you've got this covered.
- To ask me to do any household chores. I'm
  afraid I'm busy providing the sole source of
  income for the family, so you will need to
  manage the housework along with being a full-
  time mum.
- To tell me something that's really important
  because it almost certainly falls into one of the
  following categories:
  - ♦ It's not important.
  - ♦ You've told me seven times already.

Section 1b

You may interrupt me if:

- You bring me a coffee or food (a task you can
  accomplish in complete silence).
- Arlo is in a happy, playful mood, in
  which case I will agree to several micro-

interruptions to allow me to cuddle and play with him.

- Arlo's life is at serious risk of ending.
- You bring me a new book (which you will first need to buy – please see my Amazon Wish List for inspiration).

Thank you for your patience and understanding, and thank you for committing to doing your little bit in helping to keep the family stable.

Now go and wash your hands – we've got a curve to flatten!

# Leave Charlie Alone!
## Saturday, 28 March 2020

### 130 days old

Mummy has completed her weekly house clear-out, and she's come across my cat, Charlie, my soft-toy BFF from when I was a baby. Anyhow, she thinks that Charlie stinks from years of being kept in storage, and she suspects that Covid-19 originated from him. I told her that she was fucking bang out of order for saying that about poor Charlie; that Charlie isn't stupid enough to travel to China, just in case he gets mistaken for a dog; and that if she ruins him by putting him in the washing machine, I will have no choice but to interpret her action as a declaration of war and respond accordingly!

Luckily, Charlie survived a light 30-degree wash.

# Tastes Great, Honestly
Sunday, 29 March 2020

131 days old

I return home from food shopping, only to be met at the door by the ardent security force that operates in our house: a one-woman unit called Mummy, who insists that if I would like to come any further into *my* house, I need to strip naked so she can wash my clothes.

*Look, if you want a piece of what I've got, woman, just ask politely. Or even impolitely.*

While I'm undressing, Mummy disappears, returning a moment later wielding two cans of Dettol and a demeanour that resembles a Pokémon Trainer who's about to compete in a high-ranking tournament event – she means business.

And it's business she delivers. She goes wild, gripping the triggers of both Dettol cans, much as a boa constrictor grips its afternoon tea. I can't see through the hazy cloud of bacteria-killing disinfectant.

*Cough, cough, gag.*

She *claims* that her target was the shopping bags, but I think she's missed the mark. My mouth tastes like a mad scientist's laboratory, and I now need to add an unplanned entry to my food journal.

CAN YOU THINK OF
ANYTHING BETTER
THAN BEING ON THE
RECEIVING END OF
A BABIES SMILE?

# April

## Glasses

Saturday, 4 April 2020

137 days old

Your new glasses have arrived.

Provided we follow strict protocols, we are allowed to collect them from the optician's, which, despite lockdown, is seen as a key-worker facility, meaning they've not had to close their doors.

It's been a long time since we ventured into town as a family.

It's quiet, but not eerily quiet. I was expecting eerily quiet – post-apocalyptic style. But aside from a few pigeons, my eyes can't locate any wildlife, the urban vegetation hasn't grown out of control, and we are yet to encounter anyone by the name of Max.

However, there are other members of the public, and we must be on our guard, ensuring that no one comes within two metres of us, including the small boy of about five who is currently screaming his way in our direction. Clearly, he lacks any understanding of what social distancing is.

As he approaches, I adjust my body weight, ready to roundhouse kick the little fucknut in the head. But fortunately for him, his mum suddenly appears and stops him in his tracks.

We arrive at the optician's. Mummy rings the doorbell (it's one of the protocols I mentioned earlier) while you and I stand back. A young woman in her twenties arrives and opens the door a couple of inches. She's wearing protective gloves and a face mask.

Mummy explains why we're here. The girl closes the door and disappears, returning moments later with your glasses.

*Well, that was surprisingly simple.*

We return home.

Once we're back, Mummy disinfects the paper bag that houses two sets of blue baby-sized Winnie the Pooh glasses.

And on they go.

On the cuteness scale, you've gone stratospheric. I know this because the scale is based on how high the frequency is when your mother lets out one of her squeals. This one hit such a high note that half the cast of *101 Dalmatians* arrive on the scene to see if everything is all right.

If I were in charge of the marketing department that was selling the idea of having children to prospective new parents, I'd slap the image of you wearing glasses on the artwork, and then wait for the population to triple in nine months.

A lot passes through my mind. I'm still gutted that you're in this position, but what's helping is that you've not thrown them on the floor (yet). Instead, you're staring at your parents wearing an oversized smile, one that tells me how you will leverage a tiny weakness into an incredible asset.

Now, let's send pictures to the grannies and see if we can't locate the other half of the *101 Dalmatians* cast, shall we?

## Relocating To Your Nursery
Tuesday, 7 April 2020

140 days old

You're twenty weeks old today. To mark the occasion, we've taken the difficult decision to put you to bed in your nursery tonight[6] for the first time.

Once again, it's another bittersweet development.

I love having you sleep in our room. But on the other hand, I'm getting fucked off with having the Netflix subtitles on because the volume needs to be low enough to avoid waking you.

I'm sure it will be fine. Your nursery has smiling-cloud stickers for you to look at as opposed to the underside of a shelf that houses books on stoicism, and if I were nearly five months old, I know what I'd prefer to fill my field of vision.

Do you agree? I guess we'll know by tomorrow.

---

6 NHS guidelines advise parents that their babies should be sleeping in the same room as them for the first six months due to the risk of sudden infant death syndrome (cot death). I didn't know this at the time.

# Sleep Report
Wednesday, 8 April 2020

141 days old

Last night can be recorded as a *partial* success. It started with you going down at 7 p.m. without complaint or any sort of shenanigans. You woke up for your first bottle at 6.45 a.m., which is when we get up anyway. So the bookends of the night played out as we had hoped.

It's the bit in between where we had a few hiccups.

You woke up crying four times.

This could be a product of your new environment, or it could be your teeth hurting, or it could even be the four-month sleep regression: where your sleep patterns shift, leading to more waking in the night. We have noticed more stirring on your part at night recently.

Before the relocation, when you stirred, Mummy would typically swing her legs over the side of the bed, lean into your crib and stick your dummy in your mouth, before reversing her leg-swinging movements and going back to sleep, hopefully achieving all of this without kicking me in the process.

I loved this arrangement because it didn't involve me in any capacity.

But now you're sleeping in your nursery, it's a different narrative. Your nursery is situated at the back of the house and our bedroom is at the front. It requires significantly more effort to enact the reunite-baby-with-dummy protocol, which, tragically, now includes me having to get out of bed for some dadding. I love dadding, but I'll admit to having grown accustomed to clocking off at 7 p.m. for the night.

I guess if the NHS and every other key worker can risk their lives every day by going to work to safeguard the well-being of the nation, then I suppose I can shuffle down the hall to stick a baby's dummy back in his mouth at night.

## Stocking Up
Thursday, 9 April 2020

142 days old

Mummy's shopping, and it's just us lads – *LADS!* You give me a look that says, 'Dad, it would really cheer me up if you put me in a box lined with cushions, and push me around the house as if I'm in a mine car, while humming the *Indiana Jones and the Temple of Doom* theme.'

Oh, go on then, if I must.

Honestly, the things we do for our children.

Mummy returns home armed with more food than there is in Granny Feeder's larder. That's obviously a joke. Tesco couldn't stock more food items than Granny Feeder does.

Anyway, the point is, we're all set to retreat indoors and shut ourselves away from the world while this nasty virus business plays out.

There is one small lesson I've learnt from all of this, Arlo. The lesson is that if you're going to stockpile tinned goods, make sure you have a tin opener!

It had escaped our attention that Granny Smurf had taken the only one we had when she moved out. Admittedly, it was hers, but we'd forgotten to replace it. Apparently, we didn't learn our lesson from the bottle-opener incident.

## Excellent, Smithers
Friday, 10 April 2020

143 days old

You, Mummy and I are in the living room. We've stripped you so you can have some naked time. The reusable nappies leave red marks on your legs, so a bit of fresh air helps reduce the redness.

You've been naked for almost fifteen minutes, and you haven't peed yet, which by my reckoning means one is imminent. I'm on the lookout for one of your baby-boners to appear – a sure sign of imminent urination.

Mummy is blowing raspberries on your belly, and I have my phone ready on video mode.

*Come on, buddy.*

'Why don't you do that thing where you kiss him on the neck and make him laugh?' I say.

Usually, Mummy's personality is coded to automatically reject any of my suggestions, but there's a rare vulnerability in the software. Whenever

I suggest she gives you affection, it glitches, and Mummy accepts my suggestion without question.

'OK,' she says.

I mentally imitate Mr Burns from *The Simpsons*, bringing my hands together. 'Excellent.'

Mummy begins blowing raspberries on your neck and, from my vantage point, I see everything.

*Come on, buddy.*

*Come on, buddy.*

*Come on—*

Your willy lifts up ... and you begin pissing all over Mummy.

*YES, YES, YES!*

It takes a few seconds for her to realise, but when she does – oh, boy!

'Oh my God, he's pissed all over me. Can you see it?'

'Yes. Yes, I can.'

'Wait, why have you got your phone out?'

## Gratitude
Sunday, 12 April 2020

145 days old

Today I'm feeling grateful: grateful for the doctors and nurses, the rest of the NHS and all the other key workers – delivery drivers, the police, the fire service, the shelf stackers and the cashiers. I'm grateful to Becky from Specsavers for posting your glasses strap through our letterbox the other day. I'm grateful for not being one of the many people who have been severely impacted by Covid-19. I'm grateful for living in a country whose leaders have worked hard to protect its citizens. I'm grateful to have a job and to get paid so I can pay the bills and afford food. I'm grateful to Disney+ and Netflix, which help keep us entertained. I'm grateful for having a healthy baby for a son who never stops smiling, and I'm grateful he pissed on Mummy the other day and that I caught it on camera. I'm grateful I have a nice home, that I have an unlimited supply of clean, filtered water, and I'm grateful for the cottage-cheese pancakes (don't you dare fucking judge) that Mummy made me yesterday, and for everything she does to look after us. I'm grateful not to be on my own during a time like this; I'm grateful for being in good health and high spirits. I've said this to you many times, Arlo: there is always someone out there who's been dealt a worse hand than you. There are no exceptions to this. It doesn't mean you're not allowed to feel shit sometimes, but when you do have a shit day, and believe me, you'll have plenty, gratitude can help you navigate from the dark to the light.

I'm grateful for being a dad.

Happy Easter, son.

## Baby Drive-By
Thursday, 16 April 2020

149 days old

Today has been our toughest day in lockdown so far. Mummy is struggling emotionally: she's had a Chernobyl-style meltdown because several of your reusable nappies leaked in a row. She misses her family and her friends, and she's had enough of spending most of her time indoors. It doesn't help that, last night, the government announced that the lockdown would continue for at least another three weeks.

To help lift her spirits, I've invented a new game: Baby Drive-By.

I'll explain the rules. Daddy puts you on his forearm and flips you over, so you're in a Superbaby position. I then fly you around the room in random-sized figure-of-eight patterns, each rotation taking us closer to Mummy. When we're close enough, we initiate the Baby Drive-By: you fly past Mummy as Daddy lifts your arm up—

And you slap Mummy across the face.

To escape retaliation, I do this while she's cooking.

Am I comfortable having Mummy's firstborn son slap his mother, while she's slaving away over a stove and suffering mentally from lockdown restrictions?

Ten-four.

## Shoulder Carry
Friday, 17 April 2020

150 days old

In the past, whenever I imagined having children, it was always the image of me carrying them on my shoulders that came to mind first. But I'd completely forgotten about that, until a few seconds ago, when

I lifted you up to take the seat that all sons should have the chance to take, sitting on the shoulders of their dad, holding on tightly to his cheeks while he awkwardly attempts not to drop them.

A massive milestone, boxed, packaged and on its way to the long-term happy-memory vault – a location that's become overcrowded of late.

# The Blame Game
Saturday, 18 April 2020

151 days old

In the last twenty-four hours, your mother has injured herself five times. She holds you responsible for every single one of them. I would jump to your defence, but that would probably mean taking the blame myself, or, heaven forbid, your mother taking some accountability.

First, she stubbed her toe while running up the stairs to respond to your demands. You were crying.

Next, she dropped a table knife on her foot; the same knife that sits on top of your formula tin. We use it to level off formula scoops.

Then she burnt the roof of her mouth gulping down hot chocolate too quickly, so she could turn you around to face Granny Smurf, who had video-called you.

The injury to her knee happened because she banged it on the landing skirting board – something she risks when carrying you downstairs because of the way she descends them (our stairs are steep and narrow and you have to sidestep down them – *God, that'll be fun when you start walking*).

Finally, she scratched her arm on your buggy.

Can you see how she's linked all of these to you?

Out of the five, my favourite is the toe-stubbing because, when you started crying, Mummy was sitting downstairs and I was upstairs in our bedroom. We both responded independently to your cries, sprinting quicker than a cheetah. But it was me who got to you first because of Mummy's little medical situation.

Having settled you, I left your room, only to find Mummy sitting at the top of the stairs blowing steam out of her nostrils because she could have stayed where she was and avoided the injury.

## Five Months Old
Sunday, 19 April 2020

152 days old

You're five months old today, and physically it's starting to show, particularly around your thighs. I don't mean to body-shame you, but if I lift you out of your Bumbo, the Bumbo comes with you. It's now a two-person affair to remove an animate baby from an inanimate object.

Instead of shipping you off to baby fat camp, we've enrolled you into a complex physical therapy programme. It's called a Jumperoo. It is a device that harvests high levels of excitement from you, and you love it. We throw you in it, and you jump up and down for fifteen minutes. After that, you're beat. It's great.

Despite constant dribbling all month, there's still no sign of any teeth. Mummy says we should expect teething for the next eighteen months. It's hard. I don't like seeing you in pain. We have this white powder stuff that provides fast-acting pain relief. Mummy refers to it as baby cocaine, but it's called Ashton & Parsons Infants' Powders.

You've settled into your nursery. You wake up more than you used to, but 99 per cent of the time we need only to stick your dummy back in your gob and switch Ewan the sheep on for a white-noise cycle.

Other developments include instinctively putting one foot in front of the other when held up, and standing with assistance for long periods.

You've rolled over from your back to your front once, but you haven't managed from your front to your back yet. We're days away from that happening, though, especially now you've found your feet.

The television has begun to capture your attention. I don't know if this is a good thing, a cause for concern or neither. Television always gets a bad rap as far as I'm concerned, but there's a difference between selling all the televisions in the house versus ensuring there's one in every room and that they're turned on 24/7. I'll read into it at some point.

Moving on to eyesight, you've adapted well to your new glasses. They piss you off, sure, but you tolerate them on your head. Apart from when you don't, and you eat them. The challenge often comes when you're lying on your back because you're such a nosy git now and you're always turning your head which invariably dislodges your glasses from your face and so you respond by throwing them.

Life during lockdown is getting harder, particularly with the weather's alluring temperatures and clear blue skies. I want to be outdoors exploring. But I try not to forget the benefits of being in lockdown: I can spend my lunch break playing with you, I can sneak in micro-breaks throughout the day for a quick cuddle, and my shortened five second commute downstairs to the basement means more time, morning and evening, for us to hang out.

Another benefit of having no life outside the house is that your routine is note-perfect. Mummy has an app where you input when you go to sleep and wake up, and it uses that data, along with your age, to predict nap times. It's the most accurate piece of technology I've found that's compatible with your personality. As soon as we catch you yawning, Mummy checks that app, and lo and behold, you're due a nap. Feeds and nappy changes are integrated with nap times as well. What the app doesn't do is teach Mummy how to raise her hand and wait patiently until I've paused the telly so that she can ask her question about the film we're watching. I've lost count of how many times she's said, 'Why is he doing that?' – only for the answers to be revealed in the next scene, or heck, even the next frame.

To round off the celebration of your five-month birthday, we've dressed you in a Superman Babygro, fashioned a cape from a muslin square, straightened up your glasses and stood you up with both hands on your hips for a photo – one you nailed with a smile of star-rivalling radiance.

Thanks for another happy month, son.

# Would Sir Like To Hear The Specials?
Monday, 20 April 2020

153 days old

Your interest is immediately piqued when Mummy and I eat. It's been like that for the last few weeks. It doesn't matter what it is you're doing, you stop it so that you can stare at our dinner plates with a curious glint in your eyes – longing, almost.

So, it is for that reason that Mummy and I have decided it's time for you to try solid food. I think the 'rules' tell us we should be waiting until you're six months, but fuck it.

For your first-ever meal, we present you with mashed avocado with a side of water.

Mummy does the honours of spooning your first mouthful, while Daddy holds the camera. Like we wouldn't capture this.

'Look, Arlo, what's this? Open wide.'

I can't tell if it's because you're teething and you shove anything and everything into your mouth, or that you've watched Mummy and Daddy eat enough times to know what to do. Regardless, you lunge forward with an open mouth, accepting what's on offer.

Your reaction is ... interesting. It's evident that you're registering new tastes and textures, and that you're not sure what to make of it, or what to do.

In the end, you spit it out.

Mummy tries again. Once more, an eager lunge forward followed by a confident chomp down on the spoon. But then you become clueless as to what to do next. It's fascinating to watch.

Again, out it comes.

Now it's my turn. The other day I wrote to you about how elated it made me when I placed you on my shoulders for the first time. I'm enjoying a similar experience now, as I make clichéd aeroplane impressions while trying to feed you.

It doesn't take long for my head to explode with a sudden lightning bolt of parental insight – so many things make sense to me: I now know why parents use so many wet wipes on babies' hands, something we'd never used until today; I understand why high chairs, ugly as they may be, are a vital household resident; I know why extra-large bibs are a 'need to have' and not a 'nice to have'; and I understand the phrase 'food all up the walls' in the literal sense.

What started out as a fresh snow-white bib (the colour, not the Disney princess), is now a snot-green rag that looks like it's been used by Slimer from *Ghostbusters* to blow his nose on when he has the flu.

You eventually swallow a couple of mouthfuls, and we call it a day. Mummy cleans you up while I look on Amazon and see how much an extra set of reusable wipes costs.

## Day Two Of Solids
Tuesday, 21 April 2020

154 days old

For your second solids meal, we serve up mashed carrot. It will be interesting to see if your table manners have improved since yesterday, but in case they haven't, we have wipes and spare bibs at the ready.

Mummy places the bowl down in front of you, and your attention is immediately drawn away from your starter dish – your fist. You lean over your Bumbo for a closer inspection. 'Oooohh?' you say with your face.

I load some carrot on to the spoon, start the imaginary aeroplane noises, and deliver the food into an open and eager mouth. Yesterday, we didn't have long to wait until you tried to return to sender by spitting your avocado out.

That's not the case today, because you've swallowed it immediately.

Good boy.

But was it a fluke?

Nope: you swallowed the second spoonful, and the third and fourth. How have you grasped this already?

*Cough!*

I don't remember ever having carrot in my eye before, so this could mark a first. Have you not been paying attention to the media? You should be covering your mouth when coughing, Arlo, there's a fucking pandemic going on!

Mummy takes over, and it doesn't take long for you to finish the bowl.

We're so proud of you. Mummy even sheds a tear, which she delicately wipes away, while I fish out chunks of carrot from underneath my eyelids.

## Broccoli And Banana Bread
Thursday, 23 April 2020

156 days old

Yesterday's meal was parsnips. You didn't eat a single mouthful.

Today, it's broccoli. Despite some screwed-up, sour-looking facial expressions, you devour the entire ice-cube-sized portion. This will be recorded as a success, along with the loaf of banana bread that I've just polished off.

Also, I've got the smallest of coughs, which means I need to 'officially' self-isolate for another seven days. You and Mummy have to self-isolate for fourteen days.

Thankfully, Granny Feeder is ready to take care of our shopping requirements. I've still got my gratitude hat on, Arlo. We're still all OK, but at the same time, I've opened up my wardrobe, and I can see my fuck-you-coronavirus hat inching closer to the front and begging to be worn.

# Fear
Monday, 27 April 2020

160 days old

You experienced a new emotion today: fear. All I did was push the start button on the food processor, but as soon as the engine revved up and the gears began grinding, your facial expression turned from a happy and passive one to one of abject terror.

The thing that surprised me was how much it shook me up. Seeing your face turn like that caused my insides to tear themselves apart. I had you out of your Bumbo and into my arms in a flash.

I remember ruminating on becoming a dad and about how important it would be that I got the right balance of being affectionate and comforting so you never felt abandoned, while at the same time letting you get knocked around a bit so you could toughen up. Both are vital to your development, and the balance is hard to judge correctly.

Seeing fear in your eyes for the first time has made me realise how difficult the task will be.

I now understand what the conflict must be like for parents when their children ask them to push them that bit higher on a swing or watch them jump off a taller wall or swim out that bit further in the sea.

I thought I'd be able to remain objective, but that was before I posted a sprint time of 0.2 seconds to reclaim you from your Bumbo seat and attempt to banish your fear of the stupid, loud, scary machine.

I think that's another 'Santa isn't real' moment for me today, Arlo.

## Daddy Day Care
### Tuesday, 28 April 2020

**162 days old**

6 a.m. I'm woken up by the sound of someone in pain. A lot of pain. It's Mummy. She's clutching her right side, and she can't move. She suffers from Crohn's disease, but she says it doesn't feel like a Crohn's flare-up, just that it 'fucking hurts'.

You're still asleep.

6.10 a.m. I ring NHS 111, and after a brief Q&A session with an adviser, they dispatch an ambulance to our house.

6.30 a.m. We've not had anyone here for almost two months, so it's strange to be hosting guests. The paramedics ask if they can go upstairs and see Mummy. They keep their shoes on. Mummy usually shits out her left lung when people even joke about walking on her carpet, but I surmise she'll make an exception this morning, especially as gas and air is on offer.

6.45 a.m. You've woken up. You find the two nice ladies dressed in green uniforms and wearing protective masks interesting. You even offer up a few smiles which I find reassuring, because you've not exactly had a hectic social life of late.

The paramedics diagnose Mummy with suspected appendicitis. She needs to go into hospital – possibly for surgery.

My first concern is Mummy's well-being.

A close second is how long I'll be looking after you by myself.

It's not that I object to looking after my son, but the last time I had you by myself, you were a completely different person and I could leave the house with you. I feel like any E-minus qualifications I achieved in parenting expired weeks ago.

7 a.m. The paramedics take Mummy away, and I update work to the effect that I won't be commuting down to the basement today. I'm having a Daddy-and-Arlo day.

*Eeek.*

8 a.m. You fall asleep for your first of four planned naps. I survey the house and take an inventory of what needs doing. If you have four naps a day, then household chores should be manageable, right?

9 a.m. I manage a cup of tea, one load of washing and not a lot else before you wake up.

Usually, I put jeans on to go to work but today I've selected joggers. How long do you think those joggers remain vomit-free? Twenty seconds.

I need the toilet, but it's a number two, and I don't want to leave you unattended, so it looks like you're coming along too.

I find the whole thing uncomfortable because you're looking at me in a strange and an almost accusatory way. It's not a crime to go to the toilet! Avert your eyes and give me some privacy.

9.15 a.m. I now know why you were looking at me funny on the toilet. It wasn't with accusatory eyes – it was with pity. Your eyes were saying, 'You call that a decent display of excrement? Buckle up, Dad, let me show you how the pros do it.'

And, by God, hasn't the pro demonstrated his ability in spades? I'm looking at a mountain of the brown stuff.

11.10 a.m. Nap number two. The house is a tip, but I prioritise a workout instead. This is because your mother is always complaining that she has no time for yoga, and my response is to tell her she should do it while you sleep. But now I totally understand where she's coming from. Still, I let the house suffer, and I sweat out a HIIT workout. Muslin squares are excellent for wiping a sweat-drenched forehead.

1 p.m. Mummy is OK, she's on the morphine, and she's due to have a CAT scan to determine if she has appendicitis.

1.10 p.m. Carrot for lunch which you demolish within sixty seconds. A new personal best.

2 p.m. Nap number three. I get my Tasmanian Devil speed on and fly through the following: hang out the wet (but clean) nappies, assemble the dry nappies so that they're ready to use, sterilise your bottle and, finally, polish downstairs.

I am physically and emotionally shattered. How did Granny Smurf do the single-parent gig full-time?

3 p.m. I strap on the baby sling, put you in it, and then, together, we hoover.

4 p.m. Mummy doesn't have appendicitis. Doctors don't know what it is, but they suspect a Crohn's flare-up. She will probably need to stay overnight.

*Overnight? Gulp.*

The house is now in reasonable shape. This means we can play. You're in a wonderful mood for your poor, old wet flannel of a father.

4.45 p.m. Final nap. I have just enough energy to make it to the fridge and pour myself a beer.

7.30 p.m. I dress you in your pyjamas, read you a *Star Wars* story, kiss you goodnight and put you to bed. You've behaved beautifully today. Thank you.

8 p.m. Mummy rings to say she is allowed to come home. They haven't been able to diagnose her, but the pain has subsided enough for her to be able to self-medicate with codeine at home.

I've learnt the following lessons about myself today, Arlo: Mummy has a much harder job to do than Daddy; I don't want Mummy ever to leave me; and if we're lucky enough to have more children, I would like them to have your temperament. Goodnight!

## Fuck You, Jumperoo
### Wednesday, 29 April 2020

### 162 days old

Arlo, your Jumperoo is a fucking cunt of a thing, and I want to destroy it. Why? Because try as I might, I can never get your fucking legs through the fucking holes, and, in case it's not clear, I'm finding it fucking infuriating right now.

STUPID FUCKING THING!

Obviously, your stupid mother has no issue operating it whatsoever, and thinks the thing has been engineered to perfection.

Oh, and yes, I did kick it, and yes, I felt guilty when that startled you, even though you weren't in it. You're welcome.

HOW DO YOU STOP YOUR BABY FROM GROWING UP?

# May

## Bottle Teats And Crocodiles
Saturday, 2 May 2020

165 days old

I used to believe that threading the bottle teats through the bottle rims was similar to disarming a bomb. Making skin contact with the teat was like the bomb going off. Every morning, my heart rate would shoot through the roof as I conducted the assembly of the newly sterilised bottle, desperate not to transfer to it from my hands any dangerous bacteria that could upset my little boy's undeveloped immune system.

I regret overreacting in that way. I've grown since then, Arlo. Nowadays I drag the teats through the rim like an unenthusiastic checkout operator pulls purchases through the scanner. Don't get me wrong, I don't purposely rub the teats under my armpits before screwing them on to your bottle (you're welcome), but neither do I treat the whole affair like walking a tightrope over a bask of crocodiles.

By the way, I had no idea a group of crocodiles was called a *bask* until I looked it up just now.

## Another Lesson Learnt
Sunday, 3 May 2020

166 days old

Mummy has stumbled on a video that dispels common baby myths. One of them was particularly alarming: that walkers and bouncers (basically your Jumperoo) aid in development. They don't – they damage it, forcing babies to use the wrong muscles in their legs.

Mummy quickly cross-references this new information (new to us at least) with several other websites, including the NHS, and confirms what the myth-busting video says.

To be honest, I'm not sure I buy it, but it's one of those things where once you hear it you can't unhear it, so while I don't think we'll be campaigning to have all Jumperoos banned, it does mean we've taken the personal decision to force early retirement upon yours.

'I tell you what myth they didn't dispel, which means it must be true,' I say.

'Oh yeah, what would that be then?'

'That in order to improve the mummy's well-being, the daddy should be allowed to buy a few *Star Wars* bo—'

'No, books and *Star Wars* do nothing for the "mummy's" well-being.'

*Such a fucking KILLJOY.*

# If You Can't Beat Them ...
Thursday, 7 May 2020

170 days old

You're getting grabby. I wonder if this is an early indication of kleptomania. You reach out and snatch at everything, including your mummy's underwear, which you aren't too happy about surrendering. I get it: you want something, I'm not letting you have it and you don't understand why because you're less than six months old. In the end, I cave. I give you back Mummy's knickers. I may or may not have taken a selfie with you wearing them on your head. Daddy may even have had a pair on *his* head as well ...

# One Of A Kind
Friday, 8 May 2020

171 days old

Because of Mummy's Crohn's disease, she's constantly low on iron. She tries to make up for this by eating as well as the Crohn's will allow her to, but being an almost full-time Mummy takes priority over structured mealtimes and micronutrient calculators. Those facts combined should tell you one thing – Mummy is always tired.

And yet, she can magic up enough energy, seemingly out of thin air, to be everything you need her to be and more. From the moment you wake up to the moment you fall asleep, she's there with a smile, a cuddle, and usually a fresh, clean bib and muslin square. It's one thing to make looking after a baby effortless (even though it's anything but), but it's another to do that while having less energy than everyone else.

The other day she sat down in the afternoon for her first break of the day. As she took her first sip from her cup of tea, the baby monitor went off, telling her that you had woken up early from your nap. She looked longingly at her cup of tea as if to say, 'I only wanted five minutes.'

I couldn't step in as I was due on a work call any minute.

Mummy put her cup of tea down to let it cool, as she often does, and made her way up to your nursery. If you had heard the way she spoke to you, you would have thought she'd just returned from a thirty-day yoga retreat. I could see and hear all of this on the monitor: she was smiley, playful and full of energy.

I told you once that you don't owe us anything for being born. Having a baby was our choice. You didn't have a say. I still mean that. But believe me when I say that you have a one-of-a-kind Mummy, who digs deep every waking moment to be everything and more for you.

# Reflux
Monday, 11 May 2020

174 days old

You have reflux. Looking back, you've been suffering with it for months. However, I didn't know what it was or what the signs and symptoms were. It turns out it happens because the muscles at the base of your food pipe aren't fully developed, causing milk to come back up after it's been swallowed. I find that difficult to believe since all you seem to do is exercise your food-pipe muscles.

I always assumed that babies vomit a lot, and it's just part and parcel of being a baby. But you've been sick a lot recently, and Mummy suspected something wasn't right.

A quick call to the nurse confirms the diagnosis, and she prescribes Gaviscon to help. You can record this as another fuck-up in the 'Ignorant New Parent' column.

# The Journey Ends
Wednesday, 13 May 2020

176 days old

When you were Dory, some of the standout moments for me were linked to sight, sound and touch. Every time I experienced one of them for the first time with you, my emotions rocketed, like the first time I saw you on the ultrasound machine or the first time I heard your heartbeat.

When you went from Dory to Arlo, I had two senses left to tick off: smell and taste. Smell is easy: the newborn-baby smell is something everyone recognises, not to mention the wonderful gift of nappy changes.

That left taste – something I didn't think I could have an emotion-rocketing experience from.

A few seconds ago, I was lying down with you on your play mat, eliciting some beautiful-sounding baby giggles by way of some armpit raspberry blowing.

My heart swelled to the size of a beach ball.

And now, you've turned your head to the side. You're facing me and you're smiling.

This is such a perfect—

You projectile-vomit in my face, with the majority of the offering entering my mouth.

Neurons light up in two separate regions of my brain and begin firing. One sends a signal telling me to spit the vomit out while the other sends a signal to ... I guess... the area that deals with eating ... instructing it to recognise that I have food in my mouth, that the food has been broken down and that it is time to swallow.

It was a race, Arlo, and the fact that I've just swallowed baby vomit confirms which region of my brain won.

In case you were wondering, baby's vomit tastes precisely as one would expect: like milky baby's vomit.

And that completes our father-and-son journey through the five senses.

# Look, But Don't Touch
Thursday, 14 May 2020

177 days old

There has been a *minor* relaxation of the lockdown measures, one of which means you can meet one other person outdoors. So you can start seeing your grandparents again.

Granny Smurf has come over to have garden coffee. We have moved the dining-room table away from the back door and positioned you on the floor in front of her. It is with mixed emotions that she watches you play. She loves that she can see you, but I can see in her eyes how desperate she is to pick you up for a cuddle. You're the grandchild she never thought she'd have, and she's gone from being able to hold and feed you every day to looking at you only from a distance.

It's similar with Granny Feeder and Grandad Tools later in the day when Mummy takes you up to their garden so they can have the same viewing experience.

Granny Feeder is struggling with social distancing. Her definition of two metres is at odds with that of a tape measure, and Mummy has to keep telling her to back off.

I get it, I do. It must be excruciating for grandparents. All they want to do is give their grandchildren a big, squidgy hug, and they can't, and you're at an age where you're changing every day. Granny Smurf says the same thing every time we send her a picture: 'How has he changed so much again? It's only been two days.'

But that's the way the cards have fallen, and it's pointless to yell at the dealer.

## Sun Cream
Saturday, 16 May 2020

179 days old

There are three things that I don't love when it comes to baby sun cream.

The first is the considerable amount of time it takes to apply, which is a surprising revelation given how small babies are. But the cream is on the thick side.

Next up is the paranoia that I've somehow missed a spot, which is stupid because I've put litres of the stuff on you and one could easily mistake you for a glass of milk.

The final thing I don't love is that when we take you outside for a walk, and even though it's 18 degrees and there isn't a cloud in sight, Mummy decrees that you're too cold and insists on you wearing a hoodie over your top half and a blanket for your bottom half.

Wonderful!

# Sitting
Monday, 18 May 2020

181 days old

You're officially a sitting-up baby.

It's one of those milestones where you don't simply do it one day, and it's done. It takes time to build up your core strength, at least enough to maintain a sitting position for more than a few seconds. You've been gradually improving your sitting-up record for weeks, making it difficult to know where to draw the line and officially claim that you can sit by yourself. Mummy thinks a baby needs to sit unaided for at least two minutes before it can be classed as 'sitting' which, as of today, is what you've done, hence us laying claim to you being officially a sitting-up baby.

I've been looking forward to this phase because it means we can just sit there and watch you playing. At the moment, that consists of putting anything you can get your hands on into your mouth.

# Six Months Old
Tuesday, 19 May 2020

182 days old

You are six months old. How the fuck is this happening so quickly?

As is becoming the norm, you've added a ton of new skills and lessons to your repertoire. You can now sit up. You grab at everything in sight which includes my hair and cheeks. You pass objects from one hand to the other and back again. Your communication is evolving, and you're getting better at telling us what you want. If you're hungry, you whine; if your teeth hurt, you dribble and whine, but at a different pitch. You reach out for objects, stretching your entire body as far as you can, which is great fun when what you want is on the floor, and I'm holding you up in my arms. You launch yourself towards the object without warning, and I have to react quickly so as not to drop you on your face.

We've finally turned a corner with the reusable nappies because they rarely leak. We use them all the time, apart from at night. Time in the evenings used to consist of your parents lying on the sofa, almost certainly with our phones, watching the TV. Now, we make up nappies for the next day and plan what you're having for dinner.

You're now on two meals a day, but I guarantee that will quickly be bumped up to three. This morning you ate porridge with peanut butter. Mummy read somewhere that it's good to introduce foods that are prone to cause allergies early. Peanuts is a big one with children, so it's a relief to say that it went down fine.

You have your probiotics every day. I still have no clue if they're working, but we will continue to give them to you. Food is the number-one priority for me in terms of your development right now. I want to get it right. One of the positives of lockdown means you're not left alone with Granny Feeder, who I'm convinced would dismantle my nutritional plans quicker than you can say chocolate.

To celebrate you being half a year old, Mummy has dressed you up in a lion-cub outfit that says 'Aroarable' on the back. And we've got you a present. It's a slice of lemon. I've been looking forward to giving lemon to you for months. Mummy starts the video, and I offer it up to you for inspection. It takes you less than a second to decide that it's going into your mouth, but it takes considerably longer than a second for you to react to the taste. Two seconds pass, three seconds pass. Anything? Nothing ... Seriously? It's a sour, citrusy taste – why are you not screwing your face up in disgust?

Cause you're a fucking lad, that's why!

'Lemon?' you say. 'So what, Dad? Try harder next time.'

Understood, son!

Still no teeth, and still no rolling over. I was sure you'd have logged both of those this month, but you haven't yet.

We've been in lockdown for almost two months now. A quick look at the government website confirms that over thirty-five thousand people have lost their lives in the UK. As far as we know, none of us, including the immediate family on both Mummy's and Daddy's sides, has been infected.

For the moment, we're all OK. Daddy can still work from home and pay the bills, and Mummy's invisible cape remains permanently affixed to her shoulders while she looks after you, me and the house – managing to do it all with a smile.

You laugh every day. You finish your food every meal. You keep still (just about) for us to stick your eyepatch on each day, and you keep *really* still for us to peel it off again. You go down for your naps without complaint, and you regularly sleep through the night.

Once again, thank you for everything, and congratulations on reaching the halfway point of year one.

# Off!
## Thursday, 21 May 2020

184 days old

Until now, you've tolerated your glasses. But that's no longer the case. You now see them as an adversary, one you have both the desire and capability to remove. It's become nigh on impossible to keep them on your face for longer than a handful of seconds.

If you're annoyed at having to wear glasses, spare a thought for your parents, who are struggling to conjure up enough willpower to keep continually affixing them.

After what feels like the hundredth time of me stopping the buggy and leaning in to reattach them, Mummy tags in, while I move to the side for a self-delivered counselling sesh.

She fares better. She uses toys that rattle to distract you, along with warm smiles and a high-pitched baby-talk squeal.

It's working, Arlo!

And now it's not working.

After a few seconds, you claw them off your head again.

The strap doesn't help either. All it means is that your glasses end up dangling around your neck, rather than you waving them around in your hand, which is a precursor to you dropping them on the floor.

*I told you this was fun.*

But how do I tell a six-month-old baby that he needs to wear his glasses to help strengthen one of his eyes because it doesn't work as well as the other? It doesn't help that your teething is particularly troublesome today, and you haven't done a doo-doo in your nappy in two days. *Can't wait for that one to reveal itself.*

Mummy and I have agreed to the following protocol: whenever one of us asks the other one why Arlo doesn't have his glasses on, this is not to be seen as an attack for being a shit parent. This is a reminder and a show of support, to help each other maintain the practice of ensuring you wear the damn things.

It would be easy to give in. No one would know, apart from us. But we don't. So, we'll stop the buggy a million times if we have to, and reapply your cute baby-blue Eeyore glasses to your head. Because love you and want to do the best for you, despite how fucking annoying it is – for all of us.

## Playnests
Saturday, 23 May 2020

186 days old

Not for the first time, Mummy's nursery experience has come in handy.

'He needs a Playnest,' she says.

'A what?' I say.

'It's basically a rubber ring that he can sit in and play in without worrying about falling over and hurting himself.'

'How much?'

'Fiver – second-hand. It would make our job as parents easier.'

*Easier.* 'I'll go and get the car.'

Mummy has found the Playnest from an ad on Facebook Marketplace. Despite being in lockdown, we're not breaking the law by going to collect it (at least I don't think we are), as long as we follow the guidelines and maintain social distancing.

We collect the Playnest, and then return home for Mummy to carry out a full-scale mandatory cleanse consisting of a 60-degree wash of the fabric that surrounds the ring and a thorough scrub of the inner plastic ring itself.

When it's ready, we place you in the middle for a test drive.

Mummy wasn't wrong, it's as simple as it is genius. You have enough freedom to move around while using your core strength to maintain a sitting position. And if you do topple over, the ring saves you from a face plant, and you're still at an angle where a bit of extra core work returns you to a sitting position. It's great.

Add in a few toys, and you're more than content.

I love a good parent hack, Arlo.

## Soft White Toys
Sunday, 24 May 2020

187 days old

The good thing about you having a white bunny-rabbit soft toy is that the vomit doesn't show up when you're sick over it. The not-so-good thing is that, when that happens, I invariably pick it up and pretend to cuddle it in front of you while we're playing ...

## Your First Tooth
Monday, 25 May 2020

188 days old

We finally have a tooth. It must have cut through in the night. These milestones are a tale of two emotions: of happiness and sadness. I'm happy that you're growing and developing, but I'm sad that this is all moving so quickly.

Congratulations, buddy – your first one!

This means teething will stop for a while, right?

## Where's Your Foot Gone?
Tuesday, 26 May 2020

189 days old

This morning I didn't know that I could fit your entire left foot in my mouth. This evening I do.

## Rolling Over
Wednesday, 27 May 2020

190 days old

We've spent an hour working on Operation Rollover. We got so close that at one point you did roll over, except you then rolled back over on to your back. The whole episode happened so quickly that Mummy and I doubt whether you rolled over in the first place. It's surreal. We're 99 per cent sure your torso touched your mat, but now you're facing upwards, and we don't know if we're making it up.

## Deflection
Friday, 29 May 2020

192 days old

You are lying on your play mat, enjoying your daily fix of naked time. Mummy sits precariously near the danger end. I don't, because I'm smarter than your mummy. I lie down next to you, but *away* from danger.

The inevitable happens: you start pissing. Mummy's reaction is to hold up her hand in front of her to prevent you from pissing in her face. It works. Her hand deflects the oncoming stream of urine away from her face and into my face – predominately into my right eye, where my pupil is pounded by a deluge of amber liquid like a blast from a fireman's hose.

The liquid smothers my cornea, iris and various other unfamiliar, scientifically-termed parts of my eye before encasing my eyeball fully and searing the optic nerve.

It stings, Arlo.

It really fucking stings.

# June

## Three Points!
### Thursday, 4 June 2020

198 days old

I've been awake for only five minutes, yet I've already won three shittest-dad-of-the-day points. First, I fell asleep *after* you had woken up. This meant that you also fell asleep again so that when I did eventually drag myself out of bed, I had to wake a sleeping baby.

One point!

Next, I changed your nappy and realised you had dropped a code brown, which meant I had let you drift back off to sleep with a dirty nappy.

Two points!

Finally, I placed you in your cot sitting up (because you're a pro at that now) so I could wash my hands. You fell back and hit your head on the cot bars, awarding me my third point, and thus allowing me to lay claim to a hat-trick.

As starts to the day go, I'm not killing it, am I? I might as well bag myself a fourth point and buy you that box of asbestos crayons on eBay.

## Lockdown Haircut
Sunday, 7 June 2020

201 days old

My hair looks like a cremated palm tree that's been on a heavy meth sesh.

It's coming off, Arlo – all of it!

Well, most of it is; grade two all over. Mummy is overseeing barber duties.

A DIY haircut – or YPDI: your partner does it – is something the UK has unofficially named a 'lockdown haircut'.

I'll admit, I'm a little anxious to see what's under all the mess. I told you last year, Daddy has been battling some thinning issues on top for the last decade, but life in lockdown has caused the hair growth to form a temporary safety blanket around the issue – one that's about to be sheared off!

The clippers are plugged in and switched on and you're placed in your Playnest to supervise. I want you to watch so that you don't freak out afterwards.

Mummy gets the show under way.

It's strangely transformative having a hairstyle overhaul, not that anyone has ever accused me of having any style, mind you – either in the hair department or outside it. Still, I no longer look like the under-the-weather palm tree. Mummy's first comment is that I look my age with short hair, but not a day older. *Such a poet, that woman.*

Now to examine the thinning on top. Mummy takes a picture and shows it to me ...

OK, so it's not that bad. I mean, it's not great, but it could be worse. There are definitely deforestation concerns, but no one is confusing me for Billy Zane just yet, which I proclaim to be a shame because a name that ends in Zane is a name I would exclaim to claim, if the Zane is game, and if the Zane is game and without disdain, I'll rename my surname and claim that of Zane, for the name Billy Zane is full of fame and acclaim and the flame I hold for that big name is most assuredly larger than a candle flame. BOOM – take that sleep deprivation!

## Meet Louie
Monday, 8 June 2020

202 days old

Your new favourite soft toy is a chimpanzee named Louie. Your decision to befriend Louie can be filed under 'Slightly Weird', because Louie happens to be a gift Daddy received from an ex-girlfriend from uni.

Strolling past the 'Slightly Weird' column, we arrive at the 'Definitely Ultra-Weird' column, which features an outstanding question as to why Daddy has kept Louie for, wait for it ... fifteen years.

I have a ... sort of ... answer. After uni, I packed away a bunch of old clothes that I knew I'd never wear again, but I maintained a social attachment to them, like my custom-made lacrosse drinking T-shirts. Somehow, Louie ended up in that same bag of clothes.

I'm sure I did this because I subconsciously saw into the future, knew I'd have a son, a son who would strike up a companionship with the primate ... *OK, even for me that excuse is lacking in quality.*

Regardless of how it happened – you're welcome.

## Increased Intelligence
Tuesday, 9 June 2020

203 days old

I am convinced that you know how the baby monitor works. That's why you stare directly into the lens of the camera after we've put you down for bed.

You stare at it, and then you spit your dummy out, and then emit sounds of displeasure that not even good old reliable Ewan can suppress.

You are entering a phase of your life where you routinely object to having to go to sleep. Furthermore, you've become adept at dismantling the structures that we've worked hard to erect.

Last night, after the fifth episode of spitting out your dummy and crying, Mummy picked you up for a cuddle because you weren't just sobbing, you were screaming in distress. Neither of us could figure out why.

We assumed it was teeth because that's what we always think, and until you're able to communicate effectively, a large part of our parenting will rely on assumptions and guesswork.

In terms of how distressed you were, last night was an exception, though. Usually, you begin your bedtime-disruption campaign with a whimper – one that gradually builds up in pitch and ferocity, until one of us yields and marches into your nursery to settle you back down. Sometimes, to increase the strength of this rod we're making for our own back, we give you a gentle rub on the side of the face to settle you off to sleep.

This is a fucking problem, Arlo.

Why aren't you going to sleep?

I'll tell you why: you're learning.

And don't try and tell me you're not in control of your actions, otherwise why else do you smile the biggest smile every time we walk into your nursery? I'm like, 'How are you smiling? You were inconsolable less than a second ago.'

The bigger the smile, the bigger the confirmation that you're learning how to outsmart your parents.

This is yet another stage of parenting that I didn't think we'd be facing yet. I thought this sort of display of cognitive manipulation was months, if not years, ahead of us.

Apparently not.

## Your First Head Injury
Wednesday, 10 June 2020

204 days old

I thought I would be the one to hit your head on the wall first (by accident, of course), but alas, it was Mummy. Your first head-to-wall collision came about from Mummy trying to pull up your dungarees too aggressively. You leaned back at the same time as she lifted the material up around your legs. Your shift in weight meant that Mummy didn't pull the dungarees upwards, but sidewards – into the wall.

We each reacted in different ways.

You cried. Understandable.

Mummy felt guilty. Also, understandable.

And I felt relief, because it wasn't me who did this to you, it was Mummy. Remember that, Arlo – Mummy. Spelt M-U-M-M-Y.

## Don't Get Suckered In
Thursday, 11 June 2020

205 days old

More of your bedtime bollocks today, son. Firstly, you resolutely opposed the idea of an afternoon nap, despite a valiant attempt by the Matriarch. You said – through your actions and your crying – fuck you to Ewan, fuck you to your dummy and fuck you to your light projector shining images of stars and planets on to your walls. Those three fuck yous combined to form one mega fuck you which was hurled at your parents.

Well played.

Mummy has just this second marched down into the basement and firmly thrust you into my arms, declaring, 'Your son has decided to be an arsehole for the day!'

I'm about to inform her that today is Dress Up As Daddy Day, but she looks ready-to-blow-a-gasket pissed and so I refrain, which I damn well want recorded as a rarity.

Instead, I tell her to get a cup of tea and sit down for five minutes.

I sit you on my lap so you can start bashing Daddy's spare keyboard, which is now Arlo's keyboard and it sounds like a portable washing-up bowl on a campsite, owing to the litre of dribble that's collected underneath the keys – I think I can hear frogs in there somewhere.

If you discount my slight discomfort at having to lean over both you and *your* keyboard – think Lurch from *The Addams Family* playing the organ at church – to type on *my actual* keyboard, we normally have a good thing going.

But your be-an-arsehole-for-a-day decision seemingly extends beyond nap time. You no longer want Arlo's keyboard, you want Daddy's keyboard, and you want to leaf through the pages of Daddy's journal, and Daddy's work notes.

*Sigh.*

It's now evening, and bedtime bollocks continues. I've put you down and you're crying. Except you're not crying, it's that half-arsed attempt at a cry, one that sounds like a crop-duster plane working a farm half a mile away. You're even pausing your *crying* to look towards the door for one of us to come and interact with you, you sneaky little bastard.

'Do not go in,' I say to Mummy.

'But he's crying.'

'No, he's not, he's acting. Don't let him get inside your head. I know he's not yet seven months old, but he's become a master parent-manipulator already. He's not upset.'

Sure enough, the periods of silence begin to overtake the periods of non-silence.

What's interesting about this conversation is that your mummy taught me this exact lesson. She knows child psychology better than me and if it were anyone else's child and the same scenario were being played out, Mummy wouldn't get suckered in.

How strange.

I suppose this could be one of those biological mother-child nuances. The number of times I've heard the line: 'Yeah, but it's different when it's your own.'

I wonder.

## Ice Cream
Sunday, 14 June 2020

208 days old

Today we went for a walk in the park with friends, and I learnt two valuable lessons about food and babies. Both while eating ice cream.

Lesson one: if you don't want your kids to eat junk food, don't eat junk food in front of your kids.

Lesson two: telling your adorable seven-month-old glasses-wearing baby that they can't have ice cream is an awful lot harder than I imagined it would be.

As far as nutrition's concerned, I figured we wouldn't give you any sugary processed crap for as long as possible. I can't see you queuing for a red-lentil dhal once you've got a liking for chocolate buttons. Same with sugary drinks: if you never experience them, you're more likely to form good water-drinking habits – something I want to encourage.

But the hardest thing about not letting you have any of our ice cream was that you weren't crying, grabbing or making any sort of fuss, you were just watching, with shiny, glistening, hope-filled eyes, like a dog at the dinner table on lamb-chop night.

I felt awful.

We eat very well at home, but I do give myself a couple of cheat meals at weekends. I now know that these can happen only when you're not around, otherwise it's not fair.

I don't mean to be a hypocrite, but you're too young to understand the concept of a cheat day, and I deem healthy nutrition to be paramount to your development, and to give in at the first test is to admit defeat from day one.

I'm not saying you can't have treats, because there are far too many social pressures for me to take a stance like that, but I want to hold you off for as long as possible, so you get a good run at consistently eating the best food.

In case you were wondering, my ice cream was lovely, Arlo – cookies and cream with the taste manufactured to perfection.

Please stop looking at me like that.

## Buggy Upgrade
Tuesday, 16 June 2020

210 days old

You're having a nap upstairs, and Mummy is standing in the middle of the living room, crying.

'What's up?'

She nods over to a new attachment for your buggy.

'Has that nasty thing hurt you?'

'No, it's Arlo's buggy. He's getting too big for his bassinet, and we need to put him in his grown-up buggy seat. But it faces outwards, so I won't be able to talk to him any more. He's growing up.'

*Ah.*

She's right. And it's not only your size that has bulged; it's your curiosity as well. Whenever we go outside, your eyes dart around with rapid precision. It's as if you're tracing star constellations.

It's yet another bittersweet parental realisation: I'm proud of the progress you've made, but saddened that you've taken another step away from being a baby.

There's no escaping them.

Learn to cherish them all, Arlo.

# A Delightful New Phase
Wednesday, 17 June 2020

211 days old

I think it's fair to say that you have entered a phase of your life that you won't depart until the day you die. It's called the tantrum phase.

I noticed it last week when you roared in protest at Mummy because she took away the bath sponge that you were sucking when it was time to get out of the bath.

You conducted similar protests towards me, when I reclaimed the television remote from your saliva-filled mouth. I wouldn't mind you playing with it – or eating it – but you keep biting down on the mute button when we have music playing, and having music playing without sound isn't exactly facilitative to the whole music-listening experience, is it?

Sticking on the subject of remotes: why is it babies are obsessed with them? I've seen this behaviour before, but I'm beginning to suspect it's more widespread. Is it because most remotes are black, and newborn babies perceive black more clearly than they do other colours? But you're not a newborn any more. You show the same fascination with my phone, which is also black.

Curious.

Anyway, back to tantrums: you throw down when we take your empty food bowl away;

you throw down when you're sitting, but you want to be standing; and you throw down while simultaneously contracting PTSD when I lay you down on your changing mat, your screaming and attempts to claw at my face serving as evidence for the diagnosis.

Welcome to the tantrum phase.

## One Big, Giant Anticlimax
Thursday, 18 June 2020

212 days old

The you-rolling-over saga has come to an end, and a great, whopping anticlimax of one at that. It happened like this: Mummy left you lying on your back and went out into the kitchen, and when she returned a few seconds later, you were lying on your front. Just like that, you've reached the milestone. I feel this is a massive piss-take on your part, given how much time we've invested personally overseeing your training, encouraging you with every shred of energy we possess. I reckon I've deleted over ten gigabytes of footage of you *almost* rolling over. For you to then go and do it alone is one giant ball of phlegm to the face. Don't you know there's absolutely no point in achieving anything in life, unless there's someone there to record it or, hell, at least witness it?

# Seven Months Old
Friday, 19 June 2020

213 days old

Seven months old today, and you're becoming mischievous.

It's as if the manufacturers that supplied the tiny little cogs in your mind have built newer and more capable versions, and they've begun installing them into your personality. The signs are faint, but they're there if you know where to look.

Like when you refuse to make eye contact, instead offering up a big, broad smile, when I ask you if you're up to badness. Or it's the fixed eye contact you give me as you slowly remove your glasses and throw them on the floor. This is where your personality development begins to ramp up.

You have favourite toys. Louie remains your number one. You have favourite foods and you have wants as well as needs now, like TV remotes or Daddy's computer keyboard. Your fake crying is woefully inadequate – it's pathetic, but it's a sign that you're developing the tricks and tools of your trade as a professional parent manipulator.

Up until now, everything has been subconsciously instinctive. You cried when you were hungry or in distress because two hundred thousand years of evolution had biologically coded those actions into your DNA. They're unconscious.

They're still unconscious, as they are in all of us, but now they're joined by other actions that are consciously performed.

You spit your dummy out when it's time for a bottle, you hold your arms out when you want one of us, and you've learnt to pull yourself up to a standing position without any parental assistance. The sofa is your go-to aid. Your increased core strength has meant your Playnest has been cast aside, abandoned. And it's early days, but you're showing initial signs of waving, clapping, and constructing melodies on your wooden xylophone.

You love your food. Mummy has introduced many new tastes and textures this month: lamb and apricots; salmon and sweet potato; cod, pea and potato; courgette, spinach and tomato; toast; Greek yoghurt. You give everything a go, but as I've said, you have developed favourites, like avocado and coconut yoghurt, which you gulp down like a parched desert wanderer who's found a well.

We've been in lockdown for almost one hundred days now. A light relaxation of the rules means you can see your family again, and you've spent time with our friends and their children. But those interactions have been restricted to the confines of the social-distancing rules.

Well, mostly they have. Your cousin Haylee, who is now eighteen months old, went and rescued your dummy from the floor the other day and stabbed it back in your mouth. And then there was my godson Eddie who's one: he walked into you, and then through you, while coming over to say hi last weekend. Still, you have responded well to new faces and people. Everybody gets a smile from you. There are no exceptions.

When you're in a seated position and there's something you want, but it's out of range, you stare at your legs as if they're the things stopping you from getting what you want. After a few attempts, you build up a *rocking* momentum, so that your torso carries your weight over from a seated position to one where you're lying on your tummy. Mummy tells me this represents your desire to move around on your own. This could be the start of your crawling journey, son.

I'll end, as always in our monthly recaps, with a thank you. Parenting you is beyond fulfilling.

PS: you've learnt to *give* kisses. They take the shape of wide-open-mouthed dribbles.

## Louie's Days Are Numbered
Saturday, 20 June 2020

214 days old

Your attachment to Louie the chimpanzee is a growing cause for concern. I think the two of you may be co-dependent. Mummy jokes that we need to get Louie microchipped so we don't lose him, but her comments have caused me to take stock of the Louie situation in a whole new light.

As I mentioned previously, Louie is a gift from an ex-girlfriend from *fifteen* years ago. I don't hold out much hope that Louie is still available for purchase at the local toyshop. He's an unstocked endangered species – possibly the last of his kind. I know this to be true because I've spent the last hour unsuccessfully looking for replacements online.

If we lose him, he's gone. Forever.

I've seen the attachment kids can form with their toys, particularly those that provide comfort, and the lengths parents go to to prevent any 'missing toy' reports having to be filed with police. My mate Martin, for instance, tells me that he's had to buy five versions of a small bear that his eldest loves to carry in his mouth, like a lioness carrying her cub. He says that his boy would be heartbroken if Bear suddenly went away for a permanent vacation.

I also recall seeing another friend's boy drop his teddy and react to the incident like he was having his intestines hole-punched.

So, what precautions can we take? Well, I might not be able to find another Louie, but I have found another cuddly chimpanzee toy that looks a lot like him, and is of a similar size. I'm hoping that a combination of you being only seven months old and your defective eyesight will mean we can execute a swap-and-replace strategy, consigning Louie back into storage for another fifteen years while seamlessly welcoming into our lives New Louie. The 'New' will be silent, so as to improve the odds of a successful subterfuge campaign. New Louie is made by Jellycat, a popular brand, meaning if any accident should befall New Louie, he can be replaced with a new New Louie, without alerting your attention.

Am I awful for doing this? Parents try this trick all the time with pets, don't they? Some kid's white bunny dies, but a quick trip to the pet shop resurrects the white bunny through another white bunny. Some even attempt this with grandparents. 'No, darlings, Grandma has always been a homeless crack addict. Now, do please be quiet, and eat your carrots,' says the wafer-thin mother from Kensington to her four children, each of whom was delivered by planned C-section.

We're mirroring that approach to spare you any pain. It's really an act of love.

Since I became a dad, I have been actively campaigning not to buy, and for others not to buy, any brand-new children's toys, because of the fleeting nature of them in a child's life, and the impacts to the planet that overconsumption is causing, particularly in respect to plastic. However, in the case of Louie, I'm prepared to bury my principles.

And I have done. New Louie is en route, all the way from the exotic region of the nearest Jellycat warehouse.

## Father's Day
Sunday, 21 June 2020

215 days old

Today is my first official Father's Day. Mummy put something together for me last year when you were Dory, but she's been marketing today as my 'first official Father's Day' all week. It begins wonderfully. I peer into your nursery from the doorway, and I'm welcomed with a big ear-to-ear smile from you, which hits all the right emotional cues with distinction.

Imagine the letter *u* in the alphabet. Now imagine it in bold, capitalised and with the font size increased from 11 to 300. That's about the size of an Arlo smile first thing in the morning.

We sit down to enjoy breakfast together: pancakes. As we eat, I meticulously study your facial expression, looking out for any signs of choking as you throw berries into your mouth quicker than balls are tossed at a fairground coconut shy.

Next, we drive to a quaint little village for a walk. It's busy, but not so busy that we can't maintain social distancing. Your appearance attracts the usual 'aww's from onlookers, who can't resist reacting to a cute baby in glasses. The sun is out, and the wind is absent. Perfect strolling weather.

The afternoon sees us sit down for a roast dinner that Mummy has cooked. Mummy has gone all out, to the point where I now have leftovers for the next three days.

The only wrinkle in the day was a nap-protest on your part, but that was OK as it meant a bit of extra play time.

'Have you enjoyed today?' Mummy asks me.

'It's been perfect,' I answer truthfully.

Last Father's Day, I spoke about the issues I had with Father's Day and any other occasion where a parent gets a card from their child that's signed off with 'You're the greatest Mummy / Daddy ever'. You'll recall I had some concerns about the underlying criteria that children use to define 'best ever'. I now have enough experience to admit that I was perhaps taking things a bit too seriously. This year in particular isn't so much about me being the greatest anything; it's about Mummy saying thank you. And receiving a thank you in the form of a card that's decked out with my favourite pictures of you is a nice way to be appreciated.

But I still stand by the belief that all the parents on the planet cannot *all* be the greatest ever!

## New Louie
**Wednesday, 24 June 2020**

218 days old

'It's here,' says Mummy, returning from the front door, having collected a parcel from the postman.

'What's here?' I ask.

'New Louie.'

I straighten my back, take a deep breath and divert all my attention to the next few moments. Crucial moments!

Old Louie has been sent to a secure holding area (the kitchen cupboard) to await the results of your introduction to New Louie. Old Louie is praying that you won't buy into this farce.

I sit you on my lap. Mummy appears, carrying a smile and New Louie.

'Look who I've got, Arlo!' Mummy says.

You look up, into the eyes of the smiling chimpanzee. You register recognition, and your face lights up.

*Oh, thank God for that.*

I'm sorry, Old Louie, but this is one insurance premium I need to take out. Imagine if we lost you. You know this is for the best.

Mummy skips forwards and hands over New Louie, whom you grab with two wide-open and loving arms.

We were worrying over nothing, Arlo. New Louie is a success, and poor Old Louie will now be escorted from the holding area, to live out the rest of his days in the loft.

But wait ... the smiling face that was full of recognition and delight slowly melts away, only to be replaced with curiosity ... and suspicion.

You're stroking New Louie's arm and it doesn't feel right. Mummy and I can read it in your face. And now you turn to me, and a give me a look that says, 'I don't know what's going on, but something's off here.'

It's fascinating to witness.

And now you're pushing New Louie away; you're not interested in him at all.

How? You're only seven months old. How can you tell the difference? Yes, New Louie has more fur than Old Louie, but that's it. You can love him the same, can't you?

Mummy takes New Louie away, steps back a few paces, and calls out to get your attention.

'Look who I've got,' she says again, before presenting New Louie to you for a second inspection.

But things play out the same: you react like you're seeing your best friend, and then you realise something isn't quite right as soon as you hold him.

You grow irritated after our fourth attempt, and you push New Louie away in disgust.

'Now what?' I say.
'No idea,' Mummy replies.

## Finger Food, My New Biggest Fear
Thursday, 25 June 2020

### 219 days old

Part of your introduction to the world of nutrition involves finger food – food you can pick up, play with, and explore in whatever format you wish.

I'm terrified of finger food.

It began a few weeks ago when you started coughing and spluttering. Mummy had to lift both your arms up in the air while I promptly shit my nappy.

'Why do you keep doing that?' I said.

'Because he's at risk of choking,' said Mummy, who hadn't picked up on the gravity of my concerns.

'Yes, I can see that, dear, but can we talk about why he's at risk of choking?'

'Because we're giving him solids,' she said, as if it were the most obvious thing in the world.

'Well, if he's at risk of choking, perhaps we should put the brakes on, and maybe stick with the pureed stuff?'

'No, it's fine, he needs to learn. You've just got to watch him, that's all.'

*That's all?*

And that was the end of that discussion.

The early excitement and fascination of me watching you eat pureed solids was replaced with something that contains as much excitement as ramming a high-powered jackhammer up my arse, and remains that way to this day.

I'm not fucking around here; this shit is serious. I lose half my body weight in sweat every time I have to supervise a course of finger food. The other day, you were eating berries. I was on import / export duty, monitoring everything that was going into your mouth or coming out of it. Every few seconds, I would open up your mouth to ensure you hadn't overstuffed it.

During one inspection, I opened your mouth and found it clear of berries, thus, leading me to conclude that there was no risk of windpipe blockage.

But then, all of a sudden, you coughed up a fully grown adult blackberry. You should have seen this thing, it just strolled out your mouth, like a mate does when he's returning to his friends at the bar, having been for a piss.

'It was probably stuck down his throat,' Mummy offered, by way of signalling that we could move the conversation on to another topic.

*Stuck down his throat?*

I was looking around for hidden cameras or some reassurance that I wasn't losing my marbles for being terrified of what was happening.

But no. This is one of the phases that, as parents who are responsible for you not dying, we are charged with overseeing.

Why am I bringing this up now? Because it's teatime and Mummy has prepared a little dish of pear chunks for you to sample. Once again, I'm on import / export duty, and I'm not enjoying my life right now. You've coughed a handful of times already. Admittedly, there hasn't been any choking, but I can't relax for a second.

Once you've finished your pear, we decide to give you Calpol for dessert because you're teething. I'm fine with this; at least you can't choke on Cal—

'Why-the-fuck-is-he-coughing?' I garble, fearing Berrygate all over again – but with a piece of pear.

'Quick, he's choking. Get him out,' Mummy says.

*FUCK!*

I yank you out of your highchair and practically shot-put you over your mother's arms, then I move into position to start giving your back a bloody good thump ...

'Stop, stop, stop. He's OK now. It's fine.'

There is nothing fine about this, Arlo, nothing at all.

And how the fuck are you choking on Calpol? *IT'S A FUCKING LIQUID!*

When you were Dory, the biggest fear I had going into parenthood was lack of sleep. If we're ever lucky enough to have another baby, my biggest fear will be finger food.

## Priorities Change
Friday, 26 June 2020

220 days old

When you were a newborn, your changing bag was almost the size of my 80-litre travelling rucksack. You had enough supplies to wait out a sixty-day siege in comfort. It was well organised; selecting a clean nappy was like retrieving a crisp white file from a filing cabinet. Everything had its home.

Nowadays, your bag resembles an empty family-sized crisp packet. It has just enough room to house a spare nappy, a vest and a pack of wipes. Items are launched into it the way you might dispose of garbage at the local tip.

We can chalk up this change to a combination of parenting experience and a shift in priorities. 'Pick him up and put him in the car so he stops crying, we can make do with what we have,' is not an uncommon sentence in our house, Arlo.

## Eggs And Ambulances
Sunday, 28 June 2020

222 days old

Today we're leaving you in the company of Granny Feeder for a few hours while Mummy and Daddy sit down and work through a list of things we need to do, which is a difficult task with you around. No offence. The latest government Covid-19 guidelines mean you're allowed to stay with Granny Feeder. However, since you've not been without both parents since before lockdown, we're unsure how you'll react.

But settle you do, which means we now have a large block of uninterrupted time to crack on with our tasks, without worrying about parenting.

We complete everything we want to accomplish within two hours.

Soon after, we receive an incoming video call from Granny Feeder. She reports that you've been as good as gold and that you've had scrambled eggs on toast for lunch. She also reports that you're behaving a bit sluggishly. She turns the camera around, and we can see that you are cuddling your Auntie Lisa; your head is nestled into her shoulder and you're in a torpid state.

Mummy and I both look at each other, each having the exact same thought: you're not a *nestler*. At least, not for longer than a few seconds.

We end the call to Granny Feeder.

'This is the first time he's been without either of us in forever, right?' I say.

'Yeah, since before lockdown,' Mummy says.

'Maybe he misses us.'

'Maybe he does. I think I should go and get him.'

'Yeah, I think you should.'

I can't put my finger on it, Arlo, but something wasn't right.

At least you held out long enough for us to finish what we needed to get done.

An hour later, I get my second video call of the day, this time from Mummy, who's driven to Granny Feeder's house to collect you. She looks scared shitless.

'I think he's had an allergic reaction to the eggs. Look at him.'

She turns the camera around on you. Mummy is right, you've come out in a nasty little rash. You've got red blotches all over your body. I think they're hives.

'I'm gonna call 111,' she says.

Ten minutes later, Mummy calls me again, crying. 'They're sending an ambulance.'

'I'm on my way.'

Except I can't be on my way, because Mummy has taken the car and I don't know if taxis are operating yet.

'Granny Feeder will come and get you now,' Mummy says.

Granny Feeder arrives, and you can tell she's been through emotional hell in the last hour.

'I don't understand ... I only gave him a tablespoon ... The first time you trust me to look after him, and this happens ...'

I feel for her; she only ever has her family's well-being at heart.

The ambulance is already there when I arrive. I march over and knock on the back. A young paramedic in his twenties opens up and invites me in, where I find you, Mummy and another paramedic (this one female).

'Look at him,' says Mummy.

*Fuck!*

The situation has intensified. Your poor little body is blanketed in hives and blotches. You look like you've spent the night in a sleeping bag made out of stinging nettles.

'Look at his poor ears,' Mummy continues.

Your ears have swollen up. It's like you've come off worse in a baby boxing bout in a play ring, your opponent having landed several right (and left) hooks to the side of your head.

But the paramedics are great. They quickly rule out meningitis and a host of other nasties before delivering their diagnosis. It's the same as ours: a suspected allergic reaction to eggs.

'Because he's so little, we'll need to take him in and let the doctor take a look,' says the female paramedic. 'I'm afraid only one of you can come because of Covid-19.'

Mummy looks stricken, but I know she won't agree to me going so I kiss you both, tell Mummy everything will be fine, and then exit the ambulance, leaving you – at seven months old – to experience your first official ambulance ride.

I drive our car home, walk through the front door, and sit on the sofa, staring into space. Try as I might, I cannot shed the image of your swollen little red ears and your hive-ridden body.

Mummy sends periodic updates. As usual, you're in high spirits. A nurse has given you a teddy to play with, and you've struck up quite the friendship. *Watch out, Louie.* He's a slightly freaky-looking bear, wearing the vilest shade of lime-green dungarees.

You need medicine, but first, the nurse needs to know your weight so the doctor can prescribe the right amount.

You now weigh 8.86 kg.

The medicine – whatever it is – does nothing. Next, the doctor tries steroids – the same steroids that Mummy takes when she has a severe Crohn's flare-up.

The steroids work. The inflammation reduces – as does the swelling.

At 7.35 p.m. a friendly-sounding nurse calls me up, telling me I can collect my family. *No need to tell me twice.*

Your face erupts into a broad smile as soon as you see me, and I return the affection.

I can't see any redness or hives, and your little ears have returned to their standard size and colour.

You're clutching the bear, the one with the dungarees in a vile shade of green. 'The nurses said he could keep it as he's been very brave,' Mummy says. I don't doubt that for an instant. Once again, your resilience was called upon, and once again, it arrived promptly and without complaint. You are a marvel.

After a long, character-building day, we all climb into the same bed. It feels like years since you last slept in with us.

You fall asleep with one hand holding Ewan and the other resting on my face. We name your new friend Eggsy – short for Eggbert. Granted, it's not the most original name given the circumstances, but it's been a long day, and we're all tired. Actually, come to think of it, we've named the bear after the very thing that landed you in hospital. That's like buying a get-well-soon candle for someone who's been in a fire.

Sleep well, my boy. Let's hope tomorrow brings less drama and fewer trips in an ambulance.

## Cruising
Monday, 29 June 2020

223 days old

I was expecting one thing to be different when I woke up this morning, and that was to find you next to me, which you were. But to my surprise, there were two additional variations to my routine. First, I was woken up at 5.45 a.m. instead of my preferred time of 7 a.m. That's despite you being in bed much later last night, so go figure. Second, how I was woken up was different. It wasn't by your cute, playful baby talk that carries from the nursery into our bedroom – my all-time favourite alarm clock. Instead, I had Arlo-sized claw marks, traipsing across my face in more directions than can be found on a compass.

*Ouch.*

You have a day ahead of you that involves lots of cuddles on the sofa with Mummy.

Granny Feeder has been on the phone to report that she's been to Tesco to buy a box of baby-food pouches. She is terrified of giving you anything that triggers another allergic reaction. I see this as an advantage for my war against grandmothers giving their grandchildren sugar-ridden treats. As of now, all sweets have egg in them, as do cookies, cakes, chocolate and ice cream. And if she checks the label and discovers I'm lying, I'll say that the foods are prepared in factories that *also* prepare egg products. 'It's not worth the risk,' I'll say. 'You wouldn't want your only grandson to die, would you? WOULD YOU?'

It's the end of the day, and it's bedtime. You're in a surprisingly buoyant mood so we sit and play for a bit on the floor of your nursery. You indicate that you wish to stand up. Mummy obliges, but she turns you to face your cot so you can hold on to the spindles without parental arm support. You're so proud of yourself when you do this.

Your confidence is growing.

But then, out of nowhere, you shuffle sideways and, using the cot to support your weight, you take two wobbly baby sidesteps.

Wow. Where did that come from?

I believe this is known as cruising, along with it also being one massive proud-dad moment.


## Don't Drink The Bathwater
Tuesday, 30 June 2020

224 days old

It's bath time, and Mummy and I are both overseeing the activity.

'Should we be allowing him to do that?' I say to Mummy.

'Do what?'

'Fill the sponge up with bathwater and then suck it out.'

'Oh yeah, that's fine. All kids do it.'

'I don't doubt that,' I say, 'but do those other kids' parents wash shitty reusable nappies in the bath sometimes?'

'Erm, well ... Poss not ... But I'm sure he'll be fine.'

I agree with Mummy because statistically speaking it's the smart thing to do, and if you die from dysentery, I can pile the blame on to her.

# July

## Goodbye, New Louie
Wednesday, 1 July 2020

225 days old

New Louie remains absent from your list of close friends. Truth be told, Mummy has boxed New Louie up, ready to return him to the store, ostracised, with his head held low and his tail dragging across the ground behind him.

You can imagine the other toys in the shop: 'New Louie, you're back! I don't understand. You were chosen by a child, to be loved, cared for and slobbered on,' says Leopold the lion.

New Louie can't look his fellow soft-toy animal residents in the eye. 'He didn't want me, so his mum sent me back.'

'Ohhhh nooooo,' say the other soft-toy animals in unison. They are distraught, not to mention worried for their own futures.

Echoing on repeat in the back of my mind is the advert that says, 'A dog is for life, not just for Christmas'. Then it hits me. *Dear Zoo* is not a children's book. It's a lesson about rejection, and how it can happen to us all for many seemingly unfair reasons, such as the shape and size of our bodies, or our personalities.

So, if New Louie is on his way out, and Old Louie is still in holding, still in the kitchen cupboard, who is your current BFF?

I'll tell you who: Eggbert.

Which is less than ideal because we're faced with the same problem again. Eggbert is of such a peculiar design that I think he was handmade, and so not replaceable.

Last weekend, we went to see some friends. Their little boy Harry owns Thunder the fox. I walked Harry's mum through my concerns about you forming attachments with irreplaceable soft toys.

'It's not worth it,' she said.

'Have you ever had to replace Thunder?' I asked.

'I haven't, but I've wasted about three tanks of petrol having to return to restaurants and other places because I've left him behind.'

That settled it, we need a plan. But what?

And how do we reduce the risk of losing an irreplaceable toy?

# Welcome Back, Old Louie
Thursday, 2 July 2020

226 days old

Despite all the risks I've called out about the loss of irreplaceable soft toys, your mother has decided to reunite you with Old Louie, and explore strategies for ensuring we don't lose him. I'm not on board with the reunion at all. Old Louie has been in holding for a while now, which means you've probably almost forgotten about him, and are slowly adapting to life without your monkey BFF. But trying to get your mother to see sense is like trying to blow up a bouncy castle by farting in it so, naturally, I'm overruled.

The other day, Mummy joked that we needed to get Old Louie microchipped, but I think she's inadvertently stumbled on a solution. Can you get microchips for toys? If not, I'd posit there's a market for it.

Despite my hesitancy, I'm curious to see your reaction given that you've not seen Old Louie for a while, and you've taken a shine to the newly inducted member of the family, Eggbert.

I start the video recording and give the nod to Mummy to commence the reunion.

One look at Old Louie is enough to transform your eyes into bright, shining stars. You smile the biggest smile and two outstretched, welcoming arms follow, accompanied by high-pitched, buoyant jabbering, aimed squarely at your best friend.

As parents, this is a joy to witness – it's magical. Though I still find it difficult to believe that a seven-and-a-half-month-old baby can form such an emotional attachment to a soft toy.

Even Mummy can't believe it.

'Oh my God, he really does love that monkey, doesn't he? We need to ensure we don't lose him.'

*YOU THINK?*

I won't pretend that my heart hasn't liquified watching your little reunion, but I want it on record, right here, right now, that I raised the potential loss of Old Louie as one giant ticking time bomb that's waiting to explode in about eighteen months' time.

If there isn't a product out there for microchipping toys, then I will call the vet and get Louie booked in. I don't care if it costs me a thousand pounds. The thought of you losing Old Louie after that display of affection isn't worth the emotional fallout.

And Eggbert: given how many soft toys we have under our roof, being the second favourite isn't to be sniffed at, old boy.

## Evil Daddy
Friday, 3 July 2020

227 days old

It's bath time, and I'm overseeing the operation. Despite what Mummy said the other night about it being perfectly natural and OK for babies to suck the bathwater from a sponge, I'm not OK with it.

So, evil Daddy has taken the sponge away, knowing a protest will follow. But it doesn't.

Instead, you take one look at me, and then you turn to face the water below, studying it.

What's going on in that wonderful little mind of yours?

It's fascinating. Through your facial expression, I can see neurons firing in a brand-new choreographed pattern, making new connections and rewriting the operation scripts for how you react to a change in circumstances.

After a few moments, your eyes lose that narrow focus, instead opening up wide, having settled on your next course of action ...

You lower your head down – *right down* – into the bath, whereupon you begin drinking from it. Fucking *drinking* from it.

You're lapping it up, like a basset hound returning to his water bowl after a long walk out in the sun.

I'm stunned, but also a little bit proud, of how quickly you problem-solved your way through this one, but enough is enough: bath time is over. I scoop you up in my arms and out of the bath.

And then the protest begins ...

## Pops Or Pumps?
Saturday, 4 July 2020

228 days old

A baby trump in your nappy triggers the following conversation: 'What are we gonna call farts when Arlo is older, pops or pumps?' Mummy says.

**279**

'I figured we'd go with air shits or shitless shits? Obviously, you get the deciding vote,' I say.

'For once, can't you be serious?'

'*Au contraire*, my sweet, I'm being very serious.'

'I'm not getting caught out in Tesco by "Mum, I've done a massive air shit".'

Arlo, tell Mummy from me that I'll start taking conversations with her seriously when she stops taking the fun out of everything life has to offer.

## Karma
Sunday, 5 July 2020

229 days old

You've learnt an amusing little trick today, Arlo – it's called continuous screaming.

I'm astonished that your voice box is still intact.

You have not let up all day.

It was funny, but then it became less funny, and now it's annoying.

You can relate to my experience because I've just recorded you screaming on camera and now I'm playing the video back to you. It's caused such a fright that you've stopped screaming. Mission accomplished. But now the bottom lip has arrived on the scene to do what it does best: quiver.

That there's a little thing called karma.

# Don't Be Stingy On The Spinach
Monday, 6 July 2020

230 days old

'I am loving Arlo's shits these days. They're harder and more contained since he started eating solids. We haven't had an up-the-back explosion in weeks. It's great. I honestly can't remember the last time I had to clear up a squidgy one that went up towards his neck. I think we should definitely keep feeding him spinach.'

I'll let you figure out the speaker attribution there, Arlo.

# It Was An Average Tuesday
Tuesday, 7 July 2020

231 days old

'Help!' Mummy screams.

Like Bruce Wayne responding to the Bat-Signal, I leap out of my chair, sprint up the stairs, and run into your nursery, while all the time making my first-responder siren impression: 'Nee-nore-nee-nore.'

I enter the crime scene and am instantly overcome with hysterics. Your dear mother, Arlo, is standing with a handful of the brown stuff in the palm of her hand.

'It just started coming out and I didn't have a wipe nearby, so I panicked and put my hand there.'

Perfect. This moment has turned what was, up to this point, an average Tuesday into a memorable one.

Don't forget to wash your hands, Mummy.

## Glow-In-The-Dark Dummies
Thursday, 9 July 2020

233 days old

It's all well and good manufacturing a glow-in-the-dark dummy, but if the dummy operator hides the damn thing under either Louie or Ewan, it makes it difficult for the parent who's assigned the job of reuniting dummy and baby to accomplish said assignment, not to mention making the glow-in-the-dark feature fucking redundant.

Wouldn't you agree?

Oh, we're dispensing with 'Old' from Old Louie. He's back to being just Louie.

## Learning To Crawl (Or Not)
Friday, 10 July 2020

234 days old

You are showing a burning desire to crawl along with a soul-crushing frustration because you don't know how. You've figured out that you need to do something with your legs, and also with your arms, and possibly at the same time. But you don't know what, or in what order. You've almost got the hang of commando crawling, but you end up going backwards instead of forward.

You find this frustrating.

Your frustration manifests itself with a contorted face and a baby growl that makes it difficult for me to distinguish between you filling up your nappy and venting annoyance.

Don't worry, son, what is a parent's job if not to teach?

I have devised a teach-a-baby-how-to-crawl programme that is designed to get you on the move without any assistance from a parent. A whole new world of exploration awaits you at the end of this programme.

First, we need to sort your legs out. You know they're needed, but you haven't figured out that you have to lift your hips up and bring your knees in so you can get into an all-fours position. Until now, every time I moved your legs into the correct position, you immediately lowered your hips, causing your legs to fold out to the side like a frog mid-jump.

To stop this from happening, I adopt the same all-fours position, but *over* the top of you. Imagine a Russian doll, or a coffee table sitting directly over a smaller version of the same table. From this position, I can use my knees like a vice-grip to wedge your legs together.

Now that we're both on all fours and your knees are secure, you're ready for the next step. I move your arms forward, so that you're in the early stages of a child's-pose yoga stretch.

Now it's your turn. All you have to do is lean forward and bring one of your knees with you ...

*Thud.*

That'll be your face on the floor, Arlo.

You knew to propel yourself forward, but you didn't think to bring a knee along with you, and the forward motion ended up being too much for your little arms to handle.

No matter. My training programme has an inbuilt pivot to be used if the dad-and-baby-on-all-fours set-up doesn't work, which it hasn't. I tie a scarf (hat-tip to Granny Smurf for this suggestion) around your midsection and hoist you up into a crawling position. This reminds me of the apparatus they use to liberate the eponymous whale in *Free Willy*, but smaller, a lot smaller.

You're loving this, you've got a big grin on your face, and all your limbs are shaking with excitement at being able to move freely, without face planting.

But with me taking your weight in the scarf, you're not grasping what you need to do. Instead, you're flailing your limbs in a randomised, excitable pattern. Think doggy-paddle swimming. And because you're not face planting, in Arlo world you assume you must be doing it correctly.

Wrong.

But this is Daddy's fault, so I correct the mistake by gently lowering the scarf so that the onus is on you to move competently ...

*Thud.*

Another face plant. This one brings real tears. Oopsie. It seems I miscalculated again, and your forward momentum carried you too far. You flipped over the taut fabric of the scarf and on to your face.

Luckily, you're too small to comprehend that I'm to blame and so you seek the comfort of my arms.

I think that's enough training for one day.

Sorry, buddy.

## Ball Games
Saturday, 11 July 2020

235 days old

Granny Smurf has stopped by to see you, and she's brought with her an extraordinary gift for you: your first ball. It's multicoloured. Intrigue washes over your face.

I sit you down in front of me, and I begin by rolling the ball to you. It doesn't take you long to work out how to roll it back. Your aim and action in rolling are a little bit off – OK, massively off – but you're forgiven because you're a baby and this is your first experience at interacting with a ball.

Next, Granny Smurf stands you up and takes you through the basics of ball kicking, something she never taught me as a child because my football skills are famously inadequate.

The high-pitched shrieks of delight tell me you enjoy ball games.

'Every boy needs to have a ball,' Granny Smurf says.

She's right, although I honestly don't know if that's a politically correct sentence. It's probably not as it's all too easy to offend these days.

It's nice to see you getting into toys. Good God, it won't be long until ...

'It-won't-be-long-until-we-can-get-him-a-lightsabre,' I say, both words and excitement exploding out of my mouth.

'Isn't that to do with shitty *Star Wars*?' Mummy says.

'No, it's to do with your face being shitty.'

'Good one.'

'You're a good one ... wait, that's not what I meant, er ... *Star Wars* isn't shitty!'

I digress, Arlo. You're now a little boy who is the proud owner of a ball, and you love it!

Also, fuck off, Mummy.

## Parental And Primate Awareness
Sunday, 12 July 2020

236 days old

We've not long been up, and we're all in bed together, having a lovely time.

'Arlo, where's Louie?' Mummy says.

Without pausing, you turn around and stare straight at your BFF. Mummy and I look at each other.

'He's not done that before, has he?' I ask.

Mummy shakes her head.

*I wonder.* 'Arlo, where's Mummy?' I say. You turn and face your mummy and throw her a smile.

This is massive, Arlo. FUCKING MASSIVE! This is the first time that you've demonstrated such awareness.

*But what about Daddy?*

'Arlo, where's Daddy?' Mummy says.

Not missing a beat, you turn back round to face me with yet another of your special smiles.

*Wow.*

What a bloody fabulous way to start the day.

# I Need More Detail
Monday, 13 July 2020

237 days old

'Try to describe it to me,' Mummy says.

'OK, well, it was brown, and it looked like shit, and it smelt like shit, and if there was a gun to my head and I had to hazard a guess as to what it was, I'd probably say it was shit,' I say.

'Yes, but I need more details for his app tracker. I need to know if it was small, medium or large, what shade of brown it was, and also the texture.'

'It was medium to large.'

'It has to be one or the other.'

'OK, let's go with large, but I've seen him knock 'em out bigger.'

'Shade of brown?'

'Darkish, like an oak tree that's been out in the sun too long, wearing only factor 30 when it should have gone for factor 50.'

'I'm gonna say dark.'

'You do that, my sweet.'

'Texture?'

'Hard-ish.'

'Like when he's had spinach?'

'God damn, no. Are you crazy, woman? Not that hard.'

'Fine. I'll say soft, but I'll add a note with more detail.'

'That's exactly how I would play it.'

'Fuck you!'

'I'm game if you are, baby?'

## A Prospective Modelling Career
Tuesday, 14 July 2020

238 days old

Mummy has taken you to see the eye specialist for a check-up. I'm working, so Mummy is keeping me updated.

The first update is to tell me that one of the nurses tried to get you to wear a face mask until her colleague reminded her that the compliance rate of an eight-month-old baby isn't likely to be high.

Next update is that Mummy has been approached by no less than seven staff members to tell her how cute you are, and that Mummy should try and get you signed up by a modelling agency.

Update number three is that Mummy has found several baby agencies, and she is going through fifty terabytes of baby photos to select some that will give you your best chance of getting paid to crawl down a kitten-walk.

Now an update about your eye. The doctor is impressed, and surprised, that you haven't developed a squint (*they always say that*), and in Mummy's words, says you're doing great.

The penultimate update is to tell me that she has registered you for several agencies, having supplied pictures of you with your glasses on and without them. Her words were: 'I wanted to appeal to a broader demographic.'

Finally, you've got new eyepatches, and one of the designs is a camouflage pattern, which is great as you're now a commando-crawling baby – albeit one who hasn't yet figured out how to go forward.

## You're Hired!

Thursday, 16 July 2020

240 days old

We've had a response from one of the modelling agencies – you've been hired! All they need now is a registration fee, and for us to book in a no-pressure, completely free photo shoot, where we don't have to buy anything. But if we did, your pictures would be on display on the A-list.

It looks like your modelling days are over before they've begun.

## Someone Got Out The Wrong Side Of Bed This Morning
Friday, 17 July 2020

241 days old

'QUICK, COME HERE!' I scream to Mummy.

She bolts up the stairs and into your nursery. 'What's happened? Is Arlo OK? Is he hurt? What's wrong with him?'

'Nothing. I wanted you to look at his baby boner. It's massive.'

'Are you fucking serious?' She's incredulous, Arlo.

'Dead serious, look at it, it's bigger than mine.'

'Hardly an achievement!'

Ouch. What's got her all in a pissy?

## The Look Of Disappointment
Saturday, 18 July 2020

242 days old

We're all set for a family day out to a place called Castle Ashby.

I say we're all set, but we're not; we're getting set now. Mummy has asked me to dress you and pack your bag, which is a potentially problematic instruction because – not for the first time – I've forgotten what I need to pack. I'm also suspicious of Mummy's decision to grant me charge of your outfit selection.

Still, I comply.

I select a dashing pair of red joggers and a blue stripy vest, before employing guesswork to pack your bag. As an insurance premium, I list to Mummy – *out loud* – everything I've packed, so she can remind me of anything I've forgotten. She tells me I've packed everything, so if I have fucked up, it's on her.

*Phew.*

We arrive at Castle Ashby and – how this has happened, I'll never know – Mummy notices your outfit for the first time. Call it shit mothering on her part.

'What have you put him in?'

'Clothes, like you asked. I think he looks like a cool little dude.'

'He looks a mess.'

'Outrageous. He's a beautiful, cute, smiling baby.'

'Why did I let you choose his outfit?'

'I was wondering the same thing myself, but then who am I to question the demands of the Matriarch?'

'I wanted to get some nice family photos, that's all.'

*Errr ...*

Twenty minutes later, and we find a picnic spot to change your nappy.

'Is this all the wipes we have?' Mummy says.

'Well—'

'This won't be enough,' continues Mummy, who's looking more and more dejected as the day goes on.

'Not with you gung-hoing them out of the bag like that. You've got to be economical.'

'I think you're being a bit optimistic.'

On the contrary, Arlo. Back in my uni days, I could make three sheets of toilet roll do for a couple of number twos, and several instances of personal relaxation.

'Did you pack the green bag for his dirty nappies?' Mummy says, having lost all faith in my competence as a father.

'Of course I did. Here it is, like you requested.'

'That's the green and pink one, not the green one.'

'How clumsy of me to make such an obvious error. We'll have to make do with what we've got, though.'

Mummy gives me a look, and then a sigh, telling me she's evaluating my last sentence, but for widely different reasons.

At least I know what to work on for next time ... or I could let Mummy do it.

# Eight Months Old
Sunday, 19 July 2020

243 days old

Eight months old.

Your separation anxiety when either of us leaves the room has grown, though I admit a tiny part of me likes it when you reach your arms out, wanting me to pick you up.

You get bored quickly if we lay your toys out in front of you. Mummy figured out that we should be placing the toy box in front of you and letting you rummage around yourself.

If I lie you on your back and hold your arms up, you immediately brace yourself for raspberries and kisses. You know it's bath time when you can hear the water running, and you know it's dinner time when you see Mummy get one of your bowls out of the cupboard.

But my favourite display of social recognition is when I hold out the baby sling to you. Honestly, it's like holding out a lead to a dog. Your face sparkles, and your legs begin vibrating. You love going out for walks in the sling and it's become one of my favourite things to do as well, because it's one of the rare instances where it's just you and me.

Your frustration at not being able to move the way you want remains in place. I mentioned crawling the other day, but it's not only your inability to get going on all fours. Cruising is also challenging because you don't have a lot of confidence in certain environments. This morning, for instance, I stood you up against the bannister railings in the hall, and you hated it.

You're always talking – you don't shut up. You squeal, you screech, you scream and you babble. If we're lucky, you still dazzle us with a bit of gentle mewling – something that softens even the worst day.

Mummy continues to knock it out of the park with your nutrition. You've still yet to sample sweets, chocolate, cakes or any sort of fruit juice, and lockdown has meant we've been able to maintain strict granny observations.

You do make a bloody mess with your food, though. A film I enjoyed as a kid was *Casper*. In it, Casper's brothers would eat, but because they're ghosts, the food would fall straight through their pale, ghostly bodies and on to the floor, building up into a large pile for Casper to sweep up afterwards. The scene you leave behind post-mealtime reminds me of Casper's brothers' eating habits.

The Covid-19 UK death toll has now reached over forty-five thousand. But because it continues to slow, and the number of new cases can be managed effectively by the NHS, the government has further relaxed the lockdown measures. Schools are set to reopen in September for all students. Swimming pools will reopen as well. We feel like we've missed out on a lot of pool time with you because of Covid-19, but we daren't be too eager to dive back in.

Now that you're eight months old, the image of you as a newborn baby has long gone. Mummy and I have been looking at old photos, and it's like they were taken from another life. I'm grateful for the photos and videos we have, and for the time I take each day to write to you.

As always, thanks for another month of happy memories, son.

## Your First Telling Off
Tuesday, 21 July 2020

245 days old

You've been told off by your mother today. It's the first time it's happened, and I found it highly amusing.

The reason for the Matriarch chastising you was because you wanted to flip your food tray upside down, and Mummy thought that you shouldn't. Your argument was that this seemed like a fun idea. Mummy's counterargument was that the tray was full of food, and you should be directing your efforts towards eating the food, not throwing it on the floor.

The best thing about the exchange was that you thought it was all a game – one you were enjoying immensely. Every time Mummy said, 'No, Arlo,' and put her hand on top of your food tray to stop you flipping it, you laughed and kept trying.

I didn't interfere or undermine Mummy, just like the parenthood manuals dictate, but I was giving you an invisible pat on the back the whole time.

You see, we're the same, you and I; whenever Mummy says 'no' to me, I feel a strong urge to do it anyway. I think the kids call this 'mad bantz'.

## 0.96 Seconds: Not Bad
Wednesday, 22 July 2020

### 246 days old

Don't make a big deal out of it, but you stood on your own without any help from a parent or from any other stationary object. I'm joking, Arlo. Of course, we're going to make a big deal out of it – a big fucking deal – because it's awesome. And so are you. You enter the leader board clocking a respectable time of 0.96 seconds for your first free-standing attempt.

## Meet The Brown Team
Thursday, 23 July 2020

247 days old

Before you began eating solids, Mummy and I always knew what to expect with a dirty nappy. We knew the smell, the colour and the consistency. The only surprise would be the volume.

Today, thanks in large part to the exotic nutritional plan Mummy has concocted for you, it's an entirely different narrative. Every nappy change is like a workplace Secret Santa: you never know what you're going to get, only that it will be shit.

But over time, and through careful analysis, I've noticed various patterns emerging – characters, if you will. Allow me to take you through my findings of who we might meet when changing your nappy.

The Silent Assassin. Despite parents regularly peeking in from the side of your nappy, there is no sign of any poo, and aroma levels remain the same as when you're wearing a clean nappy. But you were straining so hard only moments ago, a balloon-sized tear fell from one of your eyes; an action that usually presages a heap of the brown stuff. But we can't see or smell anything, so what gives? It's not until we lie you down and fully undo the nappy that we find the little chap: a small offering that's taking refuge in your baby bum crack – invisible and un-smellable to all: The Silent Assassin.

The Smelly Assassin. Like the first, but you can smell it a mile off. The thing that strikes me as odd about The Smelly Assassin is that, once again, it's such a small offering hiding in the trenches. However, it has enough destructive aromatic capabilities to eviscerate all surrounding life. There's a lot of testing of the gag reflex when The Smelly Assassin strikes.

The Jumanji. There is an abundance of undigested food and foliage in a Jumanji nappy that you'd be forgiven for thinking you were standing in the heart of a jungle. There are bits of green bean, broccoli ... whole pieces of carrot ... possibly even something moving? There's clearly a short supply of stomach acid when The Jumanji's in town.

The Mary Poppins. It looks like it was made and packaged by a premium chocolate maker. It's tightly packed and presented – it rolls off the nappy and into the toilet, without leaving a single skid mark. This is my favourite type of nappy change. You could even say it's practically perfect in every way ...

The Illusionist. Mummy met this guy recently; she thought you were all finished up when you released a second helping – and then a third. Mummy was caught so completely off guard that she ended up having to collect it in the palm of her hand. This guy rarely shows up to the party, so you're never prepared for it when it does, which is exactly what The Illusionist wants.

The Saddam Hussein. All aromatic evidence points to a nappy of mass destruction. But, no matter how many times you carry out a ground-floor inspection, you can never find any evidence because there is nothing to find. That's despite no one believing that to be the case. You're like, 'There has to be something here, right? Farts don't smell that repulsive, do they?' But then I remember when your mother was pregnant ...

Finally, allow me to introduce you to the ALL IN ONE: unclassifiable on the Bristol Stool Chart, it is to the nappy-changing world what Voldemort is to Harry Potter. Staring down at it is worse than watching your parents have sex. The ALL IN ONE possesses a lethality that makes Hiroshima seem like a whisper in the wind, and it has a volume so vast that even Marcus Aurelius himself would be unable to plot his next move. The smell is death. Expect to go through an entire pack of wipes. In fact, why even bother? Run the bath, throw the outfit away, and triple bag the nappy, for THE ALL IN ONE is The Smelly Assassin, The Jumanji, and The Illusionist packed together and off their faces on anabolic steroids – offered up as one giant, gag-inducing, fingernail-possessing, eye-stinging mess.

And there's no need to feel an ounce of parental guilt for having a beer afterwards. You've earnt every drop and more if you've been first on the scene to an ALL IN ONE.

Cower in fear, you weak and wretched excuse for a mortal, for I am the harbinger of death and destruction to your nose and your spirit!

I found that quote in the 'About me' section on the ALL IN ONE's Facebook profile.

# Back-Seat Driver
Saturday, 25 July 2020

249 days old

It's evening. Mummy and I are watching the telly when, all of a sudden, we hear you cry. I race upstairs to put Ewan and your dummy back to work, but that fails. *Strange.*

I don't pick you up. Instead, I bend over into your crib and comfort you by way of a belly rub to get you back off to sleep. You're almost there ... but then you start crying again. And now I've got the Matriarch whispering through the monitor, advising me what my next move should be.

'Pic ... m ... p ...' The signal is terrible, so it's mostly static I can hear.

'I can't understand you,' I whisper back.

She repeats herself three more times, but I still can't hear, so I ignore her.

You're still not happy. I carry out a quick sniff test, but unless it's The Silent Assassin, it's not a dirty nappy that's the issue.

I lean in even closer, so our faces are touching, and I rub your head. This is working, Arlo. You've stopped thrashing around. You stop crying.

There, there. You just needed your daddy, didn't you?

I'm about to back away when I see your mother out of the corner of my eye slowly creeping into view, moving ever so delicately on all fours so you don't see her. Having abandoned whispering garbled orders to me through the monitor, she's arrived on the field to take charge of the operation. And now she's got her hands on the bars of your cot; she's lifted her face into view and she looks like fucking Gollum. I'm trying to hold it together and not laugh.

'I said, pick him up,' she hisses.

'No. He's almost asleep,' I hiss back.

'Has he done a poo?'

'No, I don't think so.' At this point, Arlo, I should remind you that Mummy doesn't know about the names I've given to your nappy episodes.

'Are you sure? Sometimes he does a sneaky one that hides, and it doesn't even smell that much.'

And that does it for me, I start giggling, which causes Mummy to start giggling, and now you've started giggling ... nope, sorry, you've started crying – really crying – and now screaming.

Mummy gives me the 'well I did try to tell you' look, and then says, 'Do you think now's the time to pick him up?'

'Well, obviously I'm gonna pick him up now!'

## Two Columns
Tuesday, 28 July 2020

252 days old

Since you were born, I've been keeping a chart of sorts in my head. This chart has two columns: 'Things I Love About Arlo' and 'Things I Don't Love

About Arlo'. In fact, let's reclassify the second column so that it reads 'Things I Find Slightly Annoying', or even better, 'Things Arlo Does When Acting Like A Bellend'.

Only items or behaviours that are consistently performed can be categorised in either column. So, for instance, you being a great sleeper goes into the 'Things I Love' column, and the odd times that you do wake in the night are ignored because they're one-off examples.

To date, everything about you has gone into column one. Column two has remained empty, gathering dust. Until now.

The first entry comes courtesy of a charming little vocalisation that you've newly developed. The best way to describe it is that you sound like a constipated Wookie having a stroke. It's by far the most prevalent vocal pattern coming out of your mouth these days, which isn't fun at the moment because I'm in the jeweller's buying, or trying to buy, Mummy's birthday present. I'm trying to explain (through a face mask) what I want, and all I can hear is: 'Huurh aaaaahnr awwggggghhh HUURH.'

No matter how I respond, whether I ignore you without making eye contact, ignore you with eye contact, tell you to be quiet, try and distract you with something else, or any other 'fill in the blank', the response from you is always something like: 'Uughghhhgh wuuh huurh raaaaaahhgh.' Which is annoying because this is probably the only time in my life that I get to storm into a jeweller's wearing a mask without being arrested. Admittedly, holding up a jeweller's shop isn't my top fantasy – that one involves Jessica Rabbit and a Marmite sandwich, but you don't know that, so I'll ask you to please vacate column two!

And for anyone who feels sorry for you because I have a column dedicated to my beautiful eight-month-old baby boy that's entitled 'Things Arlo Does When Acting Like A Bellend', they should know that when you make this sound, you do it while smiling. Not the cute, playful smile that we all know and love. No. These smiles are different. They're impish. They say, 'I'm not a toddler yet, but here's a little taste of what you and Mummy can expect next year.'

'Aaahnruh huurh aarrragghuuhw,' is what I say to that.

# August

## The End Of Something Beautiful
Saturday, 1 August 2020

**256 days old**

I come bearing the worst news. News that has made my day more depressing than attending a funeral with Eeyore. It started out with you getting upset over something, and no matter what I did, I couldn't settle you. This isn't what's made my day shit. What's made my day shit is that I thought for old times' sake I'd whip out my trusty NFF card, and play you 'The Yogi Bear Sex Song':

> Yogi couldn't hold it in, prem-jack, prem-jack.
> Yogi couldn't hold it in, he's a prem-jack bear.
> He's a prem-jack bear! He's a prem-jack bear!
> Yogi couldn't hold it in, he's a prem-jack bear.

If anything, it made you worse. And this is what has broken my heart. Why don't you like the song any more? It worked wonders when you were a newborn.

So then I switched to a more age-appropriate choice and put on a nursery rhyme playlist, and you settled immediately.

I'm not angry, I'm disappointed.

## Your First Fall
Friday, 7 August 2020

262 days old

Another first for you today, son: you fell over from a standing position without a set of arms to catch you. It shook you up, and you did cry, but Mummy soon calmed you down with a cuddle.

Toppling over for the first time heralds a new chapter in your life, as you must now begin to assess your choices and calculate – as best you can at your age – the risk versus the reward. Sometimes you'll get it right, and other times you won't. I'm afraid that's the price you pay for learning and developing your physical limits.

## Live Piss-Free Or Piss Hard
Sunday, 9 August 2020

264 days old

It's fallen on me to put you down for your second nap, but before I can do that, I need to change your nappy. I go about my business but refrain from removing the dirty one because I notice you have a baby bone-on which, as we know, is a sure sign that you're about to dispense more urine.

Right on cue, you release a stream of pale amber liquid.

But I capture every millilitre in the dirty nappy because I've been at the parenting gig for almost a year now and I know precisely what to expect. My actions are automated.

Once you're done, I remove the dirty nappy.

And I lean over my shoulder to grab the new one when ...

I hear it before I see it – the sound of a rainbow-shaped arc of piss launching out of your willy, sailing through the air, and *thudding* on to your changing mat.

I'm caught entirely off guard, to the point where I just turn around and stand there watching it like a dickhead – a man frozen in time, in shock and in despair.

*How?*

I don't even bother trying to contain it. What's the point?

And now the sound is less of a *thudding* and more of a *splashing* – your changing mat beginning to look like a cluster of miniature gold-coloured hot-spring pools, huddled closely together and giving off steam.

And who the fuck separates a piss into two separate sessions anyway? If you need a piss, you go for a piss, you don't clench up halfway for orange slices!

The vast quantity of urine has meant that it's travelled *down* to the top of your changing mat, and now your hair is sopping wet.

Piss on the skin is easy to dab away, but a wet head of pissy hair is different. I should really dunk you in the shower, but I'm not going to, because honestly I cannot be fucked. So I dab the back of your head using a muslin square, change your nappy and your clothes, and then I put you down for your nap.

I have no regrets, apart from the entire episode happening.

## Tread Carefully
Friday, 14 August 2020

269 days old

It's morning, and I'm thinking to myself how best to approach the next conversation.

You see, for the last four nights in a row, you've woken up multiple times. However, Mummy and I can't quite agree on the exact number: I think it's never more than twice a night, but Mummy states that's because I hardly ever wake up. She says this as if it's an action I can control, which I'm silently thanking God I can't.

I know you woke up at least once last night, but judging by Mummy's frequent yawning, I suspect it was more.

'Did you hear him last night?' Mummy says curiously, but not resentfully. Not yet at least.

'Which time?' I say, as if I'm as tired and weary as she is.

'I know, right? He's never done this before. I wish those front two teeth would come through.'

'The heat doesn't help. But at least he soothed himself back off to sleep.'

The look Mummy returns suggest I've royally fucked up on my word selection.

'Are you kidding? I was up three times.'

'Well, yeah, but you only put his dummy back in and put Ewan on, didn't you?' By saying that, I've gone all-in at a high-stakes poker game without looking at my cards. I hope I've bluffed correctly.

'Well, yeah, but I'm still tired.'

I reach both arms over the table and collect all the chips – which I fucking deserve! 'Yeah, me too, I heard you get up every time ...' I say, lying to the mother of my child who endured a hospital stay of six nights to bring you back home, and who still has to massage her C-section scar because it hurts. I didn't hear shit.

'How did you sleep? What does your Fitbit score say?' Mummy says.

*FUUUUCCCCKKKKKKK!*

'Erm, not sure. Let me take a quick look.'

As I pick my phone up, I slide my finger up across the glass and turn off Bluetooth. I then load up my Fitbit app and watch the sync bar start up. Mummy shuffles over so she can see. She acts curious, but we both know this isn't a case of satisfying curiosity. No, this is an inquiry to establish how much of a piece-of-shit dad I am for not waking up in the middle of the night.

Fortunately, my quick thinking has worked. The sync bar stops, and an error message pops up saying 'Sync not complete'.

'It keeps doing that recently, doesn't it?'

## Pandora's Box
Sunday, 16 August 2020

271 days old

Mummy showed Rebecca a photo of you, and at first Rebecca thought your legs were slightly bowed. She quickly followed up with, 'Actually, I think it's the angle of the photo.'

Too late – the lid to Pandora's box now lies open.

First, we take it in turns to walk down the hallway with you while the other parent lies down at the other end, staring intently at your legs, looking for evidence of any curvature. This exercise is tough because you can't walk unaided yet and you're hopelessly inconsistent at how you plant your feet: sometimes you cross one foot over the other, as if you're a supermodel strutting in heels. Other times you lazily stagger forward because you know we're holding on to you and we won't let go. You look like a baby kung-fu master demonstrating his drunken-boxing technique.

We can't get visual confirmation, so we play the self-blame card instead. 'It's our fault if his legs are bowed – he's not even nine months old and we've been letting him walk with us for ages.' 'He's been standing up since he was three months old, should we not have allowed this to happen?' And on it goes.

This is another reminder of how unqualified and unprepared every new parent is – something I must have forgotten. There's no guide to peruse, no manual to read and no television referee to confer with upstairs. But then I think to myself that's an excuse and I should have researched the dos and don'ts of babies learning to walk.

The problem with researching is that babies are always either in a phase, transitioning from one phase to another, or in some other scenario that has the word 'phase' attached to it. I can't keep up. It's overwhelming, and I guess I've gone, 'Ah fuck it, we kept you alive for the first six months, we'll be all right winging it from here.' Plus, I have taken the admittedly lazy view that if Mummy thinks it's OK then it must be OK: Mummy is a natural with children. But now she's worried, and that sets the sirens off.

A cup of tea and ten minutes on Google drains us of our anxiety and makes us both feel quite silly. We've learnt that children often have bowed legs owing to a condition called 'physiological bow legs'. It's where some of the bones in the legs had to rotate in order for the baby to grow in the womb, and it's expected to self-correct by age three or four.

Did I mention we're also pretty sure your legs aren't even bowed?

The parent odyssey is a strange odyssey, Arlo, but it's never once boring.


## Nine Months Old
Wednesday, 19 August 2020

274 days old

Nine months old today and our toughest month since the newborn stage. This month can be summed up as a period in which you are continually frustrated at not being able to walk unaided. One of us has to accompany you with a hand for you to hold on to – something we do bent over with a rounded, boomerang-shaped spine.

Both Mummy and Daddy's backs are in pieces.

We'd love for you to crawl, but you flat-out refuse. My days of being a crawling instructor are over before they began.

Speaking of frustrations, there are more of those in general, these days. You want to do more stuff, but you can't tell us exactly what the more stuff is, and so you ball up your fists and scream, often going red in the face. You are becoming an angry little man at times.

Sometimes I find it amusing. Other times I'm more sympathetic. I know what it's like to want to be able to do something but not have the knowledge or skill set to execute it, like getting your mother to explain with logic and reasoning why she needs to reorganise the kitchen three times a day.

Mummy is remarkably intuitive at reading your body language, though. The other day you were with me, I was sitting down and you were standing up holding on to my leg, shouting. Mummy studied you for a few seconds and then said, 'He wants you to move your leg out of the way, walk with him over to the coffee table and let him bang the tea coasters.' I don't know how she picked up on all of that, but that was exactly what you wanted to do.

Other times, we don't have a clue.

Your cruising is getting better, but you still lack confidence – the exception being our bed first thing in the morning, which is something you can do well, but only in a leftwards direction because of your eyepatch.

Sticking with mornings, it used to be that we'd have a lovely half hour with you between us in bed, playing with toys after you finished your morning bottle.

Not any more.

You push your empty bottle away and then make for the edge of the bed, where you slide off, feet first and on your tummy. You stick the landing every time.

You wave unprompted if we say 'bye-bye', and you still lose your shit if you see the carry-sling. You give Mummy big wet kisses, but you're hesitant to give me kisses because of my chin stubble.

You're still besotted with your mate, Louie. Mummy was sorting out your toys the other day, and she came across Eggbert, who you've not seen for a while. You took one look at him and pushed him away. I don't know what's going on between you guys, but you're currently not on speaking terms. Louie is still number one, even though he is in desperate need of a bath, owing to his crusty hands and feet, all of which spend an unhealthy amount of time partying in your mouth.

Still no new teeth, though the top front two are eager to burst forth. It's like looking at two bloated pieces of rice, pressed up against a piece of pink cling film – *ouch!*

While this month has been the hardest physically, it's offset by your new personality developments – still such a joy to drink in and watch. You might have started getting angry and frustrated, but you're still a smiley, happy, sociable little guy, who's growing more confident each day.

Covid-19 can cunt off now. Everyone has had enough. The good news is that the death rate has slowed, so you can't deny the effectiveness of lockdown, not to mention the carefully controlled relaxation of certain measures.

With it being the nine-month mark, I guess that it means we're 75 per cent through our first year of parenthood.

I can't believe that.

Mummy has already begun planning your first birthday.

Thanks for another month, son. Now, will you please start crawling?

## My WhatsApp Conversation
Friday, 21 August 2020

### 276 days old

It's the end of a long and challenging workday. Luckily, I need only climb one flight of stairs to get a dose of my all-time favourite mood improver – an Arlo smile.

You don't disappoint, you're pleased to see Daddy. You start squealing, like a winner in a raffle where for once the prize isn't a shitty second-hand bar of soap.

Come here, son, let's have a cuddle.

I lift you up, give you a kiss and absorb the power of your warm, loving smile.

But now you're not smiling.

The excitement is over, and you've got serious business to attend to that takes place on the floor.

Which is why you're throwing your weight over my arm to get down.

I place you down so that you're sitting on your play mat, but I suspect that my action will be met unfavourably.

And it is.

As soon as I back away, you begin to whimper. Your whimpering communicates three things: that you don't want to sit down, that you want to hold on to my hands and go walking, and that it's likely to be a while before I can sit down and have a cuppa.

Nonetheless, I live to serve, so we're off on our adventures, hands in hands.

First, you walk from the living room to the dining room, and then into the kitchen. Then you want to retrace your steps back through the kitchen, through the dining room and into the lounge.

And then you want to do it all over again.

And again.

And again.

After the fifth circuit, I receive a WhatsApp message from my back, reminding me that unless I want every single one of my discs to crumble, I should position myself sensibly.

You disagree with my back's concerns. You feel that a crumbling disc will regrow overnight, so long as I drink a large glass of milk.

We continue: from the lounge to the kitchen, from the kitchen to the lounge.

I'm now in quite a bit of pain.

It's time to offload you – somehow.

Granny Feeder has given you Haylee's electronic baby walker. You love it. You can't get enough of the lights and the sounds and how much you can bash the shit out of it. As soon as I steer you towards it, your eyes light up and your pace increases.

My back is about to get a reprieve.

We arrive at the walker. I carefully plant your hands on it, while at the same time slowly backing away.

Success: the walker has your undivided attention.

Failure: the walker no longer commands even a scintilla of your attention.

It's been redirected to your selfish prick of a dad, who hasn't seen you all day and who, instead of valuing the short amount of time he gets to spend with you before bed, fucks off to the sofa to sit down. 'I don't think so, Dad,' you say to me with your eyes.

I ignore you.

'Whhaaaa,' you say with your lungs.

God damn it! I get up from the sofa and approach you. You stop crying and beam.

I bend over and receive another WhatsApp message from my back. This one says:

Is this really how you want to play things?

## The Happy Song
Sunday, 23 August 2020

278 days old

We've spent the day in Dartford with GG and GG Hazel. Granny Smurf tagged along too. You slept for the entire journey while travelling down and, after a lovely family day out, it's time to drive back home.

Ten minutes into our journey, you announce your displeasure at being buckled in.

'Whhaaaa.'

Granny Smurf is in the back, and she's trying to distract you with peekaboo games and toys that rattle.

No dice.

'Whhaaaa.'

And now you're thrashing your body, trying to escape from your car seat.

I would try 'The Yogi Bear Sex Song', but I know from having my heart crushed last week that it doesn't work any more.

But then ...

I remember something. When we were on holiday last year with our friends who are all parents, they told us about 'The Happy Song' by Imogen Heap, a song that's been scientifically crafted to soothe babies, who respond better to plosive vocal sounds like 'ba' than to sonorants like 'la'. Hence, the former features in the song a lot.

I load up Miss Heap's song and press play.

'Whhaaaa—'

You stop crying. Immediately. It doesn't even taper off gradually; it's like someone cut the power to the Arlo speaker. Absolute silence.

Once the song finishes, we move to 'Hop Little Bunnies'. It doesn't take long for you to start getting upset again.

Once again, I call on Miss Heap to aid us, and oh boy, does she deliver.

'Whhaaaa—'

Again, the reaction is instantaneous. Incredible.

I put the song on repeat and take a vote in the car on the following question: 'Would you rather listen to this song on repeat for the next hour, or listen to Arlo crying?'

The results, which are subject to zero Russian tampering, come in. It's a landslide victory for Miss Heap.

## Don't Fuck With My System
Tuesday, 25 August 2020

280 days old

It's morning, and you've woken up in a cantankerous mood, made worse from Mummy having the audacity to lay you down on your changing mat. But before she can change your nappy, she needs to tack your eyepatch on. This is always the first job we do.

'Pass me out an eyepatch.'

Your eyepatches are stacked on a shelf nearby. I select a patch and hand it to Mummy.

She eyes both me and the patch suspiciously.

'Where did you get that from?'

'From the pile of eyepatches. You know, the one that's three feet from where we're standing – the one you've just watched me take it from. Perhaps you suspect some sleight of hand? I told you on our first date, I failed magic at school ...'

'I know that! Where in the pile did you take it from?'

'I took the one that was sticking out the most, I guess.'

'So not from the top?'

'I don't think so, no.'

At this point, I should note that you're not crying per se, but you are whining, and the volume is steadily increasing.

Mummy ignores you. Instead, she takes the pile of eyepatches and lays them out individually on your cot mattress.

'I had them organised so he gets a different colour each day, and you've messed with my system.'

'You have to be joking.'

'No, I'm not. It took me ages to organ—'

'That's not what I meant.'

'You picked this red pirate one.'

'Arrrghh, me hearties.'

'But you should have picked a green camo one.'

'Where, I can't see any camo ones anywhere.'

'They're right in front—' She gives me a look that says she is not amused by my awesomely funny, and in no way clichéd, dad pun.

I almost had her, Arlo.

Mummy re-stacks the eyepatches, and I mentally add one more item on my to-do list this afternoon.

A few hours later, and Mummy has taken you to Granny Feeder's. I make my way to your nursery and re-engineer Mummy's eyepatch-stacking system, organising them by theme – all the camo patches are together, as are the red pirate ones.

Would you say that was a worthy investment of my time? That's rhetorical. Of course it was, you silly boy.

## What Keeps Me Going
Wednesday, 26 August 2020

281 days old

The hardest part of being your dad these days is the look you give me when I leave you to walk downstairs and go to work. It cripples me. It's a look of complete despair and disappointment, and then, in a stunning finish to the routine, you drop the bottom lip in a way that leaves me feeling like I'm a piddling, substandard excuse for a parent. Honestly, you'd rival Nana the dog when she gets booted out of the house in the Disney classic *Peter Pan*.

This has become a problem because of where you are developmentally. You love to play now, and you love to have a playmate. I don't know if you're becoming a Daddy's boy, or if it's more the novelty factor because we don't get to spend a ton of time together, but we have become excellent mates.

Admittedly, I don't help matters. If I have a meeting that finishes early and I have a few minutes before the next one starts, you can be sure I'll sprint up the stairs to have a few minutes with you. But if I'm honest with myself, this is selfish of me, because I fill your face up with the hope that Daddy is here to play games and split his spine open by hiking up and down the house with you. But then I have to go back downstairs, and you go from joy and excitement to despair.

This crushes me.

Your cousin Haylee has recently started nursery and your Auntie Lisa found it difficult leaving her. I understand a little bit of what that must be like now.

The thing is, I live for those moments in the day when I get to play with you. They keep me motivated, and they give me something to look forward to. I remind myself again that I'm lucky to be working from home full-time, and that I've had more time with you in your first year alive than most dads ever get. It's all a gift.

Still – that bottom lip ...

## Finally

Thursday, 27 August 2020

282 days old

YEAH, BABY! YOU'RE CRAWLING!

I'm so, so fucking proud. Look at you being all mobile without needing any help.

My back sends me a WhatsApp:

Let's make up. I hate it when we argue.

Included in the message are some emojis that lend it an air of credibility and sincerity.

You have now unlocked a whole new level of human experience and a new sense of freedom awaits. I can't wait to see how you take to it.

A few moments later and you're back to your standing position, bashing a tube of nappy-rash cream on the table. But then you drop the tube and it lands on the other side of the table. Your default response is to look for my hand so I can walk you round to get it. You can cruise, but you're not great at tackling corners yet.

But this time, I withhold my support.

Instead, I tell you to sit on your bum and crawl around. I use hand gestures to help get the message through to you. Amazingly, it works! You drop to your butt, turn on to all fours and crawl around the other side of the table to retrieve the tube of nappy cream. Your face is beaming, and so is mine.

Considering you cracked crawling only five minutes ago ...

You clever little creature.

We both deserve to swell with pride over your actions.

Well done, son, I've already submitted your Mensa application.

This is hands down my biggest proud-dad moment yet.

## Camping
Friday, 28 August 2020

283 days old

It's 5.30 p.m. and the car is packed, ready for a road trip to South Wales for our first family camping trip. We're going with Sean and Rebecca, and their kids, Olivia and Carson. We're meeting them there.

All that stands in our way is the four-and-a-half-hour car journey.

Obstacle number one strikes while I'm trying to fasten your seat belt – which also happens to be the obstacle. We've got you a fancy new car seat that spins around, making it easier to throw you in and extract you again. But it's taken me nine months to figure out how the old one worked, and now I've got this new bit of kit with a lever-and-pulley system that's more complex than Robin Hood's tree house. I've tried my go-to problem-solving technique of swearing at the thing, but it's no use and I've now had to hand the reins over to Mummy, who solves it with a flick of the wrist.

*How does she always know how to do these things?*

At least that means we can hit the road.

It doesn't take long for you to start crying. It was expected: it's the end of the day, and it's almost time for bed. I'm trying to connect my phone to the car's Bluetooth (we've borrowed Granny Feeder's car for the weekend as it has more room), but that too has mounted an opposition against me. I try swearing again, but it fails. In the end, I play a 'Hop Little Bunnies' playlist on my phone and place my phone near you in the back of the car. This works.

6.30 p.m. Our first planned stop. We've pulled into a service station to change your nappy. Hopefully, you'll sleep for the remainder of the journey.

Neither Mummy nor I can be bothered to faff around with face masks, and I dread to think what the state of the changing-room facilities in a motorway service station are like, so it falls to me to change you in the car. I lie you down in the passenger seat, which is slightly slanted and made of leatherette – brilliant if you want your baby to slide down and have the back of the seat contort his neck, but not brilliant if you want the baby to lie still so you can change his nappy.

Why didn't I change you on the driver's side? Because I'm an idiot. I'm now having to use my left hand to do the wiping, which is problematic, because I've strictly always been a right-hand wiper for both our arses. At least I'll know for next time.

I get shit on my hands, which I wouldn't usually mind because it comes with the territory of being a non-dextrous parent, but I've used the last wipe, and naturally, the new pack sits under a mini-mountain of luggage.

Luckily, a patch of grass and a squirt from the tube of hand sanitiser come to my rescue.

We're off, again. Mummy has fixed the Bluetooth issue, and now Miss Heap is sending you off to sleep.

We should be looking at an uneventful few hours from here on out.

9 p.m. You've woken up but you're as still and silent as a rock. It's strange – and by strange I mean disturbing: it's like you're on the precipice of a heroin overdose. You don't seem to be in any distress, and I can see your chest moving up and down, so I know you're alive – but all you do is silently stare.

Mummy is thirsty, but we've run out of water – well *we* have, *you* haven't. And so I watch your mother suck from your midnight-blue rocket sippy cup to relieve her parched throat. You can't fault the woman's in-the-moment problem solving.

10 p.m. We arrive at the campsite. We're having to share a tent with Sean and Rebecca because there was only one space available. Somehow, this is allowed under Wales's current Covid-19 guidelines. But the virus is not my main concern right now. My concern is that we have a tent that is housing a six-month-old, a nine-month-old and a two-and-a-half-year-old. The six-month-old is a breastfed baby. I don't think my Fitbit sleep score will be breaking any records tonight.

Can I just say something? I didn't actually realise we would be sharing a tent until this week, *after* we had booked up and committed to going. Mummy insists that she told me weeks ago and that I agreed. This is something I don't doubt for a second, but I'll confess to you, Arlo, that it's pretty obvious that I wasn't listening, so I guess I deserve everything that's coming my way – which I can guarantee is not a good night's sleep.

Granny Feeder has bought you a travel cot which sits snugly beside our blow-up mattress. It takes a while, but eventually we get you off to sleep.

??.?? a.m. I'm not sure what time it is, but Olivia has woken up protesting that she doesn't want to stay in her sleeping bag. That's despite the temperature being on the low side. For context, I'm in joggers, ski socks, a vest, a long-sleeved top and a jumper, and I'm under a duvet ... and I'm still cold.

'Olivia, get back in your sleeping bag,' whispers Sean.

'No, I don't want to,' she replies – and then begins to cry.

'Shhh, shhh, shhh, OK, OK, if you don't want to that's fine, but you have to be quiet as Arlo is sleep—'

'Whhaaaa.'

You are fuming at being woken up. Mummy and I try everything we can to settle you back down, but it doesn't work, so we bring you into bed with us and continue repeating all our tricks: cuddling, shushing, face stroking, rocking, etc.

After what feels like forever, you begin to quieten down and settle ...

'Whhaaaa,' roars Carson.

'Whhaaaa,' you roar back.

Welcome to our first camping holiday.

## Sand, Water And Fitbit Scores
Saturday, 29 August 2020

284 days old

Yesterday I said that my Fitbit sleep score wouldn't be breaking any records. I lied. I woke up to it telling me that if you record less than three hours' sleep, it won't present you with a sleep score. Though I sometimes doubt its accuracy, I believe it when it tells me I've not been asleep long enough to generate any statistics.

It wasn't this dismal when you were a newborn.

I mean, what did we expect? Two babies and a toddler in the same tent.

Still, two and a half hours ...

Last night was like playing dominoes: the dynamite edition. Once one dropped – or detonated – the rest came toppling down, exploding as they fell. I can't believe I'm saying this, but I'm glad you're a bottle-fed baby who sleeps. I can barely talk. Blinking is painful. We will *need* to do better tonight.

I muster enough energy to eat breakfast, and then we set off for the day.

We walk around a place called Tenby, a quaint little harbour town that's home to an impressive collection of golden-sand beaches and 13th-century medieval town walls. Pastel-coloured buildings huddle together, many of them standing shoulder to shoulder, looking out to the open sea on sentry duty. We stop for breakfast in a modest, but warm and welcoming café, and then after we explore one of Tenby's sandy coastlines. The weather is 17 degrees and cloudy, which means it's warm, but not so warm that we have to faff around applying sun cream. Tourists smile at you as soon as they see your glasses. You smile back.

In the afternoon, we take you to the campsite pool. You've only been swimming once before. You love it. I throw you in the air, teach you to throw yourself off the side, and Mummy performs a test to see if you still remember how to hold your breath underwater. She does this by pushing your head beneath the surface which, admittedly, is a solid way to test the hypothesis. I can confirm that the knowledge has been retained, although remind me never to let Mummy test you to see if you can dodge incoming traffic.

Despite the challenging start, it's been an awesome day.

But now the sun is dropping, and it's time to think about bedtime. I cannot handle another night like the last, Arlo – I can't!

Our strategy is first to get you to sleep before putting you down in your travel cot. Mummy feeds you your bottle and gets you ready for bed, and then I load you into the buggy and walk around the campsite until sleep takes you.

It doesn't take long.

Now for phase two: transporting a sleeping baby in the buggy, to the travel cot, preferably without waking said sleeping baby.

I push the buggy right up to the tent entrance. Then I hand over Ewan and Louie to Mummy so that she can rehome them in your travel cot. Next, I carry you in delicately, like the oversized wad of C4 that you are, shushing rapidly and begging for the bomb not to go off, before gently laying you down in your cot. I then throw the relay baton to Mummy, who takes over with the shushing, presses Ewan's belly and strokes your face. You don't wake.

Success.

??.?? a.m. 'Whhaaaa.'

## Is This The Afterlife?
Sunday, 30 August 2020

285 days old

I think I'm dead.

This feels like death anyway.

I'll never know how, but you didn't wake up last night. Our other tent residents ... eight times.

There are two positives to come out of this. Firstly, spending more time awake means more opportunities to use the toilet. It was a cloudless night in an area that doesn't have much light pollution, and that meant stars, Arlo. It's been a while since I've gazed at stars. Even in my sleep-deprived state, I find a sky full of stars a wonderful sight to absorb. Second, I've learnt that, when camping, sliders are a much more practical footwear solution than flip-flops, especially if it's cold and you've got two pairs of thick ski socks on. Hat tip to the Matriarch for that handy camping hack.

I repeat the same resurrection routine as the previous morning: coffee, a slap around the face, some dribbling and a quiet word with myself that's interspersed with a few tears. Afterwards, our group makes ready to go, and we head to the seaside.

Much like its colleagues, the beach we're visiting is a thing of beauty. It's guarded by a headland, a rocky promontory that acts as a giant dais supporting the ruins of Tenby Castle – ruins that have been battered by the sea and bruised by the wind. Time has ravaged its features.

The warm weather has drawn large crowds: families, dog owners, retirees. The image, if seen from above, would look like a giant dot-to-dot kids' puzzle on a golden-yellow backdrop. I can hear laughter, gleeful shrieking, dogs barking, and parents bestowing warnings of 'don't go out too far' to their children. Today is a great day to be in the ice cream business.

Say what you will about dummies, but if babies face plant the sand, having a dummy in their mouth is what we in the parent business like to call a 'good thing'. Unlike poor Carson, who, despite Rebecca's repeated attempts to the contrary, was born with a revulsion towards dummies, and now finds himself with a mouthful of powdered glass.

I'm looking at him, and I have no clue what our next move should be. Honestly, he's imported a huge helping of sand into his mouth.

'Well, what am I supposed to do with this?' says Rebecca. She looks around and grabs a bottle of water from nearby. 'Fuck it. I'm gonna waterboard him and see if that helps.'

A combination of water, tweezer fingers and gravity relieve Carson's mouth of *most* of the sand.

Arlo, if it were only me looking after you, we wouldn't be going to the beach, at least not a sandy one. It's rife with stressful scenarios that I wouldn't be keen to take on. But I'm with Mummy, who, as we all know, knows more than she should about this type of stuff, so we're here. Incidentally, Mummy has introduced me to another clever little baby hack: talcum powder. A quick rub of the white powder removes almost every grain of sand. Incredible.

This is the kind of shit that new parents need to know. Up until an hour ago, I was fearful of taking babies to a sandy beach, but now I know you need only a dummy and some talcum powder and the execution of a successful day at the beach becomes achievable, though I still probably wouldn't brave it alone.

It's our last evening and I cannot wait to get into my bed tomorrow. I'm walking you around the campsite again to get you off to sleep. I'm approached by a rather rotund man who possesses fewer teeth than an anteater and has more ink on his skin than a consortium of giant octopuses in their ink sacs. He smiles at me and says, 'I remember those days.'

IS THERE A MORE
PERFECT MOMENT
THAN BEING
CALLED 'DADDY'
FOR THE
FIRST TIME?

# September

## Rather You Than Me
Tuesday, 1 September 2020

**287 days old**

I'm delighted to wake up in my own bed this morning.

You, on the other hand, not so much. You've woken up in a foul mood, and it's Mummy who's having to deal with you because I have to go to work. I don't feel guilty that I can't help. I feel guilty because I'm glad that I can't help. Is this a thing? Or am I a worthless, good-for-nothing arsehole?

## Er, Come In, Houston
Wednesday, 2 September 2020

**288 days old**

I'm about to put you down for the night when I notice we're a bedtime-routine participant down. Louie is AWOL.

'Where's Louie?' I say.

'Shit. I've left him at Mum's,' Mummy says, while fear, panic and dread terraform the muscles in her face.

'When was the last time he went to sleep without him?' I say, my face mirroring hers.

'Not since Arlo named him his BFF.'

This should be interesting, then. We go through the rest of the routine: clean your teeth, change your nappy, read you a story (tonight it is *Where's Mrs Hen?*), place you in your baby sleeping bag, turn Ewan the sheep on and finally say goodnight.

Mummy and I go downstairs, turn the monitor on, and we wait ...

For thirty seconds.

That's when the screaming starts. You are not happy.

But it could be a coincidence. You often decide that you won't go to sleep without making a fuss.

Except it's not, because both Mummy and I have tried to settle you multiple times, and nothing is working. Mummy calls Granny Feeder.

'Mum, I've left Louie at yours, and Arlo won't settle.'

'I'm on my way,' says Granny Feeder, who knows this is life and death.

She arrives at the door ten minutes later, carrying your pal Louie. You stop crying mere seconds after your BFF has joined you in your cot. You guys are now having a cuddle. Another thirty seconds and you're fast asleep.

Houston, we have a problem, a big fucking problem. Why couldn't your favourite toy be an empty can of Strongbow?

'I'm going online right now to see if we can get a replacement,' Mummy says. 'What if we lose it?'

*What if we*—? My brain downloads a ten-gigabyte file that contains a list of possible responses I can use. All of them contain some variation of the phrase 'I fucking told you this', but that won't help matters, so I refrain. OK, I might have said it once … OK, twice. Shut up – you can't even count yet.

In Mummy's defence, when I raised this initially, it was all theoretical thinking: *what if* Arlo forms an attachment to Louie, and then loses him? I also recall thinking that we wouldn't be faced with this scenario for months.

Evidently, that's not the case. You should have seen your poor little face. You were devastated.

Mummy spends an hour online, but to no avail.

I send a message to my ex-girlfriend from fifteen years ago asking if she can remember where she got it from – that's how fucking desperate the situation is.

She can't. But she has a son, and knows this is important. She suggests getting one similar to see if that will work, but you and I both know that it won't.

I'm fucked if I know what our next move is. In the meantime, I've hired a security detail to watch Louie at all times.

## Please, Daddy
Thursday, 3 September 2020

289 days old

'Whhaaaa.'

'Come on now, buddy, you don't need me to come over and get you. If you sit on your bottom, you can crawl over,' I say encouragingly.

'Whhaaaa.'

'Try and sit down, Arlo – there's a good boy,' I say, while repeatedly pointing to the floor.

You understand what I'm asking you to do, but you're hesitant to act. I know you're capable of dropping from a standing position to a sitting one, but I've only ever seen you do this on a soft surface, like on your squashy play mat, and right now, you're standing on a hard surface. I believe this is the reason for your hesitation, and why you're shouting at me to come and get you.

But your shouting isn't working, nor will it work. I am unperturbed by your demands. I am an unshakeable mass of rock; one devoid of empathy.

You change tactics. You gently hold out your hand to me, proffering an opportunity for me to help a little boy who is sad and wants his dad. As the icing on the cake, the bottom lip arrives on the scene and begins trembling. My Achilles heel.

I refrain but it's excruciating.

'You can do it, buddy, Daddy believes in you.'

Nothing. Just that face, that lip and now a pair of watery eyes. I CAN'T TAKE THIS ANY MORE!

'OK, OK, you win ... Daddy is coming ...'
*Stubborn little bastard.*

As soon as I give you what you want, your bottom lip leaves the scene, to be replaced by a victor's grin. You're looking at me as if to say, 'Look, Daddy, I was always going to get my own way. I don't know why you bothered with that "I am an unshakeable mass of rock" bollocks. Next time, do what I say. Got it?'

## Daddy Is Not Invisible
Friday, 4 September 2020

290 days old

I've had a horrendous day at work, but it's over now, and it's time for us to play together before you go to bed. I walk up the stairs and locate your gaze. You smile. Usually, the end-of-day smile lingers in my direction, and there's often some enthusiastic arm flapping and shrieking.

Tonight is different: after a *brief* smile, you get right back to your business of bashing the cushions of the sofa – all without my input.

*That's odd. Usually, you want my attention immediately.*

I walk over and crouch down behind you and begin blowing air on the back of your head. You turn and give me a non-enthused, perfunctory smirk. And now that's done, you've gone back to bashing the cushions.

Eventually, you turn around, smile, and hold out your hand.

*About bloody time!*

But alas, you were using me to get from the sofa to the middle of your play mat, so that you can play with your new abacus that Granny Smurf bought you. As soon as you're near enough, you let go of my hand, sit down and begin spinning the coloured beads, without giving me a second glance.

*Is this how it feels to be a stepping stone?*

I try absolutely everything: I run circles round you, blow raspberries in your face, I even go and fetch your ball and place it down in front of you, like a dog trying to distract its busy owners.

Nothing.

*WHY WON'T YOU GIVE ME SOME ATTENTION?*

Oh, and just so you know, I think abacuses are pathetic.

## The Arlo Demolition Squad
Saturday, 5 September 2020

291 days old

Your crawling development is moving forward at pace. You're quicker, more stable and more confident.

This has led to a new game where either Mummy or I use your plastic stacking cups to build a tower, and you then race over and knock it down with one almighty baby-sized swipe.

This is fun, but then it becomes less fun.

Like right now.

You're not giving me enough time to fully erect the tower. I can barely stack my third cup before the Arlo Demolition Squad (ADS) arrives, shattering all my hard work. This is pathetically stupid, but I'm getting a little annoyed and competitive, to the extent where I've taken to cheating.

As you approach, I slide the cup-tower away from you, and then I turn and position myself so my back is between you and the cups; my action thus delaying the ADS's efforts long enough for me to complete construction.

I wonder how many other dads cheat against their almost-ten-month-olds?

## Those Were The Best Of Times
Monday, 7 September 2020

293 days old

Do you remember the walks we took in your sling? I do. They were the best. I'd get close enough to the windows of parked cars so that you could see our reflection, and I'd pull silly faces to make you laugh. Your arms and legs would shake with giddy excitement as you squirmed with delight, and then I'd make another face, and we'd laugh again. And then an attractive female would pass us by, making some sort of 'Aww, it's a cute baby in glasses!' comment, and Daddy's mind would wander to a place that it perhaps shouldn't, but then we'd carry on our merry way with not a care in the world, because all that mattered was a father spending time with his only son ...

Those were happier times, Arlo ... long forgotten and, I fear, never to be recaptured.

That's because you've grown, and now when you get excited and kick your legs, you back-heel your old man straight in the fucking bollocks. Actually, let's dispense with the plural as you seem to favour the right one, which is possibly the one you originated from. I've taken four successive heel kicks with each shot finding its mark.

Now, anyone reading this might think, 'Hang on a minute, the baby is strapped to a sling. Just cup your balls, stop moaning and go and find a window.'

What an excellent idea.

There's just one issue: my bollocks are exposed because I have to hold on to your hands to prevent you from tearing off your glasses and launching them further than an angry Angry Bird, which I'll admit is more preferrable to a week's worth of night feeds, but only marginally.

Looks like it's the buggy for you from here on out, son.


## Free Rein, You Say?
Tuesday, 8 September 2020

294 days old

'Can you get Arlo ready this morning? You have free rein on his outfit,' says Mummy, who I presume was struck by lightning in the middle of the night.

'Free rein?'

'Yep, just put him in his star-shaped leggings and use this vest.' She chucks it my way.

'Right. Just so that I'm up to speed on this morning's developments, I have free rein to dress Arlo in anything I want, so long as I put him in his star-shaped leggings and this vest that you've thrown at me?'

'Yes,' Mummy says.

You know, Arlo, I honestly don't think she believes she's said anything even remotely close to being considered contradictory.

## Chase
### Wednesday, 9 September 2020

### 295 days old

You've learnt to play chase, and the results are, as you would imagine, delightful.

Chase version 1.0 sees you standing up and holding on to the sofa. You take it in turns to coast down the right side and then the left side, while I chase you making loud noises and banging. You respond by shrieking, like a golden eagle uttering its battle cry while high on laughing gas.

You get so excited that your whole body vibrates, and you trip and topple over on more than one occasion, though that never stops you from wanting to play again.

'Look out, son, Daddy's coming to get you!'

# New Dangers
Thursday, 10 September 2020

296 days old

In the two weeks since you learnt to crawl, you've gone from a jittery, unbalanced, wary amateur to a confident, strong sprinting professional who covers floor space quicker than a Jackie Chan slap to the face. Once again, I'm amazed at how quickly you're developing these new skills.

But as your eyes are opened up to new freedoms and landscapes, mine and Mummy's have been opened to new hazards, red flags and dangers that threaten to reduce the number of days that we remain your legal guardians.

Had you asked me before I became a parent if I thought the underside of a dining-room chair would become an adversary, I would have baulked. Not now. The underside of any chair is now a threat, as is the dining-room bench, open doors, hot drinks on the table and Grandad Tools's power drill, which is here temporarily while he works on a few DIY jobs around the house for us. One of those jobs includes new bookshelves for you.

It's not only the crawling, it's the combination of crawling with cruising, along with your surge in strength and ability to pull yourself up, that has upped the risk rate: the three skills complementing each other in a way that means, with the exception of climbing stairs, you can get anywhere you want.

At least our backs get a break.

But as one obstacle is cleared, another rises higher and stronger to replace it. It's a good job we've ordered the stair gates.

## Zero Confidence
### Saturday, 12 September 2020

### 298 days old

'Right, I'm off to Mum's. He needs a vest and a Babygro, and some Snufflebabe on his feet and chest 'cause he's a bit snotty.'

'I know.'

'Are you sure?'

'So sure.'

'Do you want me to leave his clothes out?'

'You don't need to do that.'

'Or shall I get him ready for bed?'

'You definitely don't need to do that.'

'I'm going to get him changed.'

'Fine.'

Arlo, if someone asked Mummy to rate my competence levels, on a scale of one to ten, do you reckon it's optimistic for me to say I'm at least a two?

## The Big Three
Sunday, 13 September 2020

**299 days old**

One of the many phenomenal places that Mummy and I have been lucky enough to visit is the Serengeti in Tanzania. We were out on safari one morning, and we hit the jackpot. In the space of twenty minutes we saw a leopard, watched a herd of elephants cross our path, and found a cheetah lying down near the roadside under an acacia tree that was within two metres of us. It was incredible. We couldn't believe how many high notes we hit in such a small amount of time.

When I woke up today, I didn't realise that Mummy and I would have the same experience with parenting.

It began a few seconds ago when I decided to see what happens if, instead of holding your hands so you can walk, I hold you under your arms, around your upper torso. I begin my experiment: while walking and holding on to both of your hands, I change my position. You don't protest. Mummy is sitting a few feet in front of you holding out her arms. Still with my assistance, you begin walking towards her. But then my arms fall away without you noticing, and just like that, you take your first few steps unaided.

Wow.

WOW!

Was it a fluke? Let's repeat the experiment and find out, after we've set the camera up, of course. Now it's Mummy's turn to hold you, which she does in the same way as I did before. I smile and encourage you towards me by way of some fancy arm-flapping.

The same result.

You're wobbly and unstable, and I don't think I can take you hiking yet, but at a little under ten months old, you have taken your first steps.

Joy.

Delight.

Esteem.

My parental pride levels are hovering above the Earth's upper atmosphere, showing no signs of making a re-entry. That's a problem, as I'm somehow expected to return back to work.

Severely lacking in concentration, I sit at my desk staring at the screen while not reading anything.

I can't believe you took your first steps.

'Quick, quick! Come here!' screams Mummy from upstairs in your nursery.

*Fuck – what's wrong?*

I explode out of my chair and sprint up two flights of stairs, down the hallway, and into your nursery to find you on your changing mat. You don't seem to be in distress, you seem ... content.

'Look at this,' Mummy says to me, even more excited than before. She leans her face in close to yours and says, 'Arlo, say mum, mum, mum, mum, mum.'

You're silent ...

But then ... 'Mum, mum, mum, mum, mum.'

And now Mummy is hopping higher than a kangaroo that's been cross-bred with a pogo stick. She's screeching so loudly that my eardrums have begun exploring painless ways to commit suicide.

It's yet another wonderful moment, though, so I'll let her off.

Once again, I ask, is it a fluke?

No, son, it most certainly is not. After repeating the experiment, I can officially confirm that your first word is 'mum'. Now our parental pride levels have escaped Earth's gravity field and have found refuge in the deep reaches of space among the millions of brilliant, shining stars that reside in our galaxy.

What a great day to be your parents.

Five minutes later and we're debating how best to position your new stair gate, when you shout down from below, indicating that our attention is required. Our staircase is open on one side, so we can see you clearly from the top of the stairs and watch out for threats.

But you're not content to be left alone; you want to be involved in the stair-gate discussions because you feel like you have valuable insights to offer, and so you crawl to the stairs, lift yourself up, and then, for the first time in your short little life, you climb up on the first stair – unaided by anyone or anything, other than your strength and your courage.

I can't take much more of this. That's three massive milestones in under twenty minutes.

The Serengeti's got nothing on you.

## Say 'Dadda'
Monday, 14 September 2020

300 days old

I've spent all of my free time trying to get you to say 'dadda.' My speech training rivals my crawling training both in effort and success ... because you've not come close to saying it.

## My Little Marine
Tuesday, 15 September 2020

301 days old

It's morning, and you're in our room. You're reaching to get from my side of the bed to the radiator which sits underneath our bedroom window, about two feet away. Usually, you manage this task with relative ease. But this morning, you're finding it difficult.

Why?

Well, for starters, you're standing further back than you need to be to reach it. As I said, the distance from our bed to the radiator is about two feet, yet for some reason, you're standing double that.

A quick carpet inspection reveals that there isn't any lava, quicksand or shark-infested water in your way.

What gives?

You're stretching out your arm and you're puzzled as to why you're not close enough to stumble forward and grab hold of the radiator.

And now you're getting frustrated, so you start growling and shouting. Mummy and I can't understand it, it's like you've regressed. Why has your perception of distance changed so much?

Hang on a sec ... now I understand.

The answer is heartbreaking.

For the last few days, you've not been wearing an eyepatch because, until we restocked yesterday afternoon, we'd run out.

What we're seeing is the result of you not wearing an eyepatch for a few days.

Your confidence has evaporated like steam from a kettle. Your perception of distance needs recalibrating. It's not only affecting you transitioning from the side of the bed to the radiator either, your cruising speed has slowed. Usually, you storm out of the gate stomping through any toys that are unfortunate enough to be in your path, screaming in delight as you enjoy the new freedoms you've trained so desperately hard to acquire.

But now, every step you take is done so with a nervous shuffle, like it's your first day at nursery. You're tiptoeing reluctantly, and it doesn't take long for you to abandon the practice altogether and resort to crawling, all the while continuing to voice your frustrations.

This is shit for all of us. I hate that you don't understand why you could do these things yesterday but not today, I hate that we can't explain the truth to you, and I hate that one of your eyes doesn't function as optimally as the other.

But then I remember that this issue with your eye makes you unique, and with a challenge like this you're all but guaranteed to come out the other side stronger.

When athletes train, they train to perform as well as they can at the peak of physical fitness, when they're feeling at their best. Their conditions, and often their environment, are designed to maximise performance. But, if you're a soldier, like a Navy Seal or a Royal Marine, you're trained to perform at your best under terrible conditions, and when you're feeling at your worst.

I'm choosing to think of this as your soldier training; that's why one of your eyepatches has a camouflage pattern.

Train hard, my little marine; the results will be worth it. I promise.

## Code Red. I Repeat, Code Red.
Thursday, 17 September 2020

303 days old

Granny Smurf has been looking after you today – something she will now be doing once a week.

Let's all take a second to appreciate this awe-inspiring thing called childcare.

It's the end of the day, and you guys have returned. Granny Smurf confirms that you have had a wonderful day and that you have behaved beautifully.

This is welcome news, Arlo. And it's reassuring to hear that you're having fun with people who aren't Mummy or me. Remember, Covid-19 has meant you've spent hardly any time away from us.

Granny Smurf is debriefing us on the day's adventuring when Mummy assassinates her excitable mood with a question.

'Do you know where Louie is?'

'Erm ...'

*Oh fucking hell, no!*

Mummy and Granny Smurf begin rifling through your nappy bag and searching under the buggy, but it soon becomes apparent that he's not here.

'I definitely left the house with him, because Arlo was holding him. But he must have ... dropped him.'

RED ALERT! I REPEAT, ARLO, WE HAVE A RED ALERT!

Granny Smurf immediately leaves the house and retraces her steps, canvassing the pavement, hoping and praying that she can locate your fallen comrade.

I look at my bank balance and mentally start designing catchy missing-monkey posters. *It should include bananas and trees ... and a reward.*

Mummy begins pacing up and down, entering a full-on panic meltdown. I catch a few snippets of her witterings: 'He will be inconsolable ... why haven't we bought a replacement?' Then she looks at me and says, 'Why did Arlo have to make friends with a toy that we can't replace?'

*For fuck's sake, how many times?*

Once again, I know replying with 'I told you so' won't help, except I did fucking tell her, Arlo. I even began your transition from life with Louie to life without him when Mummy decided we were too cruel, and that we had to reunite you both.

But then, before I can respond, my attention is caught by some movement by the hallway door. I look up and can see the smiling face of a chimpanzee who's waving at us. Louie has been located, and Granny has brought him home.

We've had another narrow escape. Maybe I should design those reward posters for the next scare. And believe me, there will be a next one!

## Oopsie
### Friday, 18 September 2020

304 days old

It's 6.10 p.m. and you're ten minutes late for your bedtime bottle. Mummy is getting ready to go out with one of the NCT mums. I tell her to leave all of the parenting duties to me.

'You got formula, didn't you?'

'Yes, I got the formula, don't worry. I'm going to prep his bottle now. You take your time getting ready and have a night off.'

I walk into the kitchen to get my hands on the shiny new tin of formula that you and I went out and procured all of twenty minutes ago. But I can't find it. *Strange.*

Suddenly, my face contorts, like that of Arnold Schwarzenegger in *Jingle All The Way* when he's asked if he picked up a Turbo Man doll, because I didn't buy the formula.

If we back up a sec, I'll explain why twenty minutes ago I didn't buy something that I was certain I had bought.

We were in the shop, and I had marched straight to the formula aisle, but the formula boxes were empty. I then went to the checkout to ask for one because I imagined they might keep them under the counter. But instead, I scanned all the other items ... and completely forgot to ask for formula.

*Fuck!*

Back to the present, and I'm panicking. I check the drawer where we store all your baby equipment, and I can see there is already a tub there. I open it, and I'm presented with mere dregs, like what remains of a dust pile after you've already swept it up.

Although ...

Perhaps that's a slight exaggeration, and there's more than I realise. These days, you're a 7-oz-formula-sized baby, which means we need seven scoops.

*This is going to be close ...*

I manage the first three easily enough. The fourth is a struggle, but it's there. And there's still more formula left!

Arlo buddy, I think we're OK—

*Thud.*

Fuck, fuck, and FUCK!

I've knocked the formula tin over, and it's landed ... top side down.

No more formula.

Wait, what if I just scoop it up? No one would know, Arlo.

I'm about to begin a daring salvage attempt when the Matriarch arrives on the scene and sees the mess.

'What happened?'

'Erm, well ...' If only you were close enough so that I could blame you.

'You knocked it over?'

*So much for Mummy's night off.*

'I did, I'm sorry. I need to go out and get another one. Can you watch Arlo?'

## Ten Months Old
### Saturday, 19 September 2020

**305 days old**

Ten months old and you've decided to go it alone. You crawl with confidence.

You can pull yourself up from challenging positions. And when you do want a hand to hold on to so you can walk, it's now one hand only, which means we don't have to bend over as much. Everyone told us that we would rue the day you made it out into the world on your own, but we don't, we welcome it.

Sure, we've had to buy a stair gate and drill it into our newly plastered wall, and we've had to think about the positioning of certain items around the house that you like to trash the shit out of. Come to mention it, two sets of the blinds are fucked, our dining-room table has more dents and scratches than it did last month, and you get more bumps and bruises from falling over these days. But bumps mean cuddles, and cuddles are great, especially as you're not a cuddler. Also, my back is happy for inanimate objects to be trashed instead of my lower spine.

You've taken a few more unaided steps, but they all required encouragement and manipulation from Mummy and me – manipulation in the form of letting you think we're holding on to you by your upper torso when we're not.

One thing I dislike about your new-found freedom is your inability to lie still for nappy changes: fuck my life, you're now a squirmer. Remember, I'm nowhere near as capable as Mummy is at anything in the 'Fiddly Baby Stuff' column. Such items include putting your eyepatch on, cutting your nails (the only thing I flat out refuse to do) and, as of now, nappy changes with a baby who spins round quicker than a corkscrew section on a rollercoaster.

Circling back to things you like to trash, you have upped the frequency of how often your glasses are taken off your head and hurled away, and it takes a great degree of patience from Mummy and me to keep continually affixing them, though I'd be lying if I said you hadn't beaten us a few times this month.

Staying on eyesight, the dip in confidence you displayed the other day after having a three-day break from your patching has levelled out, and you're back to your usual self. Mummy took you to the hospital yesterday, and the doctor was most impressed at your progress. The main takeaway is that your 'weaker' eye isn't as 'weak' as it was but it's important that we carry on with the eyepatching, which I'm sorry to say means enduring Daddy's pirate impressions every morning.

You've begun a promising career in acting.

That's a lie.

You've started acting, but you're terrible.

You fake laughter – which is woefully obvious, as is the case with your fake coughing and fake crying. It is amusing to watch, though.

You can now stack and unstack all of the rings in your ring stacker, and you have begun to show off and do things for attention, especially at mealtimes. You amp it up when Granny Smurf is visiting. This behaviour is overwhelming evidence that you are my son.

You have also begun to demonstrate imaginative play. We play this game where we smell your sock, pull a face and tell you it's stinky. This is a game that you initiate by shoving the sock in our faces. You anticipate our reaction.

Playing chase has now developed into a two-sided affair where we take turns to chase each other. I'm sure you can imagine how delightful this is.

You've said your second word. It's not 'dad', or 'dog', or 'ball', or 'fuck'. It's 'yeah'. It didn't quite hit the same emotional high note as saying 'mum', but then some words in the English language aren't as exciting as others. Hopefully, it won't be long before you learn Daddy's favourite word, 'defenestrate'.

As always, thanks for another month of the parenthood gig. No two months are the same.

## The Power Of Calpol
Tuesday, 22 September 2020

308 days old

Yesterday, you started to come down with a cold. We were hoping it would pass during the night.

But it didn't pass at all. I think it was about 4 a.m. when Mummy collected you from your cot and you came into bed with us, along with Louie and Ewan.

It's now mid-morning and, wearing a stormtrooper Babygro, you resemble a young cadet, training to be indoctrinated in the ways of the Empire. But you've not turned up to Death Star school (where today's lesson is about droid interrogation). Instead, you're lying on the sofa cuddling Mummy and feeling sorry for yourself.

But then the Calpol kicks in. You depart both Mummy's arms and the sofa, before crawling over to the stairs. And then – *and then* – you only go ahead and climb right to the top without any help, though I was obviously close by.

I don't get it. When I'm sick, I want to rest in bed all day watching Marvel films.

Yet you've chosen to climb the stairs.

And let's not gloss over how much of a big deal this is. A flight of stairs might not be much to an adult, but to a ten-month-old baby who's sick and who's never climbed stairs before ... I guess it's the equivalent of an adult climbing a tree; something I love to do, but never when I'm ill, Arlo. That's too silly, even for me, who's often documented as being very silly.

And let's spare a thought for poor Louie, your BFF, who's naturally been by your side all night while you've been showering him in snot. He is drenched in the stuff, Arlo – like a baby kangaroo, bathing in the mucus of his mother's pouch.

It's now 3 p.m. and guess who feels like shit? I'll tell you: Mummy and Daddy. Yup, looks like we're all going to be ill at the same time.

Lack of sleep was my biggest fear before you were born, but runners-up on that list were periods when all of us were ill.

*Can't wait!*

## How To Pivot: Parenting Style
### Wednesday, 23 September 2020

309 days old

God, I feel like shit. So does Mummy, and so do you still. We need to seriously adapt our parenting standards. How can we make today easier? Let's take a look.

- Television – it's going on all day.
- Glasses – fuck 'em. If you want to wear them, great, and if you don't, well, I'm not arguing with you.
- Calpol – you can have it as often as the guidelines permit. Our temperatures are fine, but we all have snotty noses. Granny

Smurf reminds us that this is *not* a Covid-19 symptom. Not that it matters, because we're not going anywhere.

# Yeah But No But
## Thursday, 24 September 2020

310 days old

According to Mummy's NCT chat group, you saying 'mum' doesn't count as you recognising who Mummy is. Mummy doesn't buy this, and I think I can understand why. If 'mum' isn't your first word and is just noise, then that means your actual first word was 'yeah'.

I can't describe how utterly underwhelming that is. Actually, I can. It's about as underwhelming as the *Game of Thrones* finale.

# A New Word
## Friday, 25 September 2020

311 days old

It's bath time, and you've decided to side with your parents regarding the whole 'is-saying-mum-really-saying-mum-or-are-you-just-saying-mmm' debate. Not only are you definitely saying 'mum', but you're also saying 'mama', 'mummy', 'mamacita'. It seems like you can say every variation of the word 'mum' in English,

French, Spanish, Latin, Ancient Greek and the local dialect of wherever E.T. lives. Yet you cannot manage 'dada'. Heck, I'd even take 'da'.

I'm not jealous, and I'm not taking it personally.

OK, I am.

'Arlo, say dadadadada. Say dadadadada.'

You're not interested. You're bashing the shit out of the glass shower panel. You would not believe the amount of time I've invested recently trying to get you to say 'dada'.

Now I'm sulking. I know I shouldn't, but I am.

But then—

'Daddy.'

*Oh my God, you said it. You said 'daddy'!* Hearing it is like taking a Zeus-made lightning bolt to the chest: electricity pulses through me, invading every atom of my existence.

Mummy and I look at each other in shock. It was clear. Too clear. How have you skipped the easier ones and gone straight for 'daddy'? Probably because I've been drumming it into you since you started saying 'mum'.

What a moment this is for me.

But is it a fluke?

It's not.

You repeat 'daddy' a few more times, dispelling any and all doubt.

Entering your vocabulary at word number three is 'daddy'.

It's surreal to hear that. I've been referring to myself as Daddy since 16 March 2019, when I discovered I'd been accepted for a new job application. Usually, if someone referred to me by my job title instead of my name, I'd be insulted.

But not this job, son. Not ever.

*Yikes, you said 'daddy'!*

## What Did We Used To Do?
Saturday, 26 September 2020

312 days old

We were supposed to be away this weekend. We had booked Granny Smurf in for babysitting. But the latest Covid-19 restrictions (they change all the time) have fucked that up.

However, Granny Smurf still wanted to babysit, so she stayed over last night, and now she's downstairs with you, feeding you breakfast.

Mummy and I are lying in bed, and we don't know what to do with ourselves. We can't go back to sleep because we're parents and our body clocks have adapted to our routine. Granny Smurf is only downstairs, so making you a brother or sister is off the cards.

We try that weird thing that people used to do, and talk to each other, but our conversation is mostly about how we don't know what to do with ourselves because we don't have to worry about you. I suggest toast in bed, which becomes the most adventurous and exciting thing we achieve with our morning off as parents.

# The Fickleness Of Humans
Wednesday, 30 September 2020

316 days old

Mummy has returned from a walk to the shops with you. She enters the living room looking most aggrieved.

'Are you OK?' I ask.

'I forgot his glasses.'

'That's OK. I'm sure you won't go to hell.'

'It's not that. No one stopped me to say how cute Arlo was.'

Bastards. Those fickle bastards, Arlo. How fucking dare they? Whack a pair of glasses on a baby, and none of them minds forgoing the social-distancing guidelines to come up, cough and stare at you. But take them away, and apparently you're just a normal baby. Which is not fucking true, you are the cutest.

Those cunts!

# October

## An Hour Of My Life Gone
### Thursday, 1 October 2020

317 days old

Mummy is visiting Granny Feeder, and it falls to me to lead the bedtime operation.

*Alone.*

It's 6.10 p.m. and I've sat down with you to feed you your bottle. We're having a lovely cud—

You decide it is imperative that you stop feeding, and slide off the sofa. I check the bottle; you've not even drunk an ounce.

You cruise to the small table nearby and begin smashing two drink coasters together like you're a percussion instrumentalist recording the remake of *Fantasia*.

A quick snatch-and-grab move on my part has you nestled back in my arms to continue the bottle feed.

That's better, this is h—

Now you're screaming at me while also pushing me away. This is both annoying and upsetting. Pushing me away isn't something you've done before so, firstly, thanks for that. Secondly, I'm taken aback by your strength. Have you been working out?

I repeat the previous sequence: I release the baby, check how many remaining ounces there are in the bottle, recapture the baby and continue feeding the baby.

I do this no fewer than ten times. For anyone that's counting, we're on double fucking digits, Arlo!

Eventually, your bottle is drained down to two ounces. *Fuck it, that'll do.* Let's get you to bed.

My next job is to clean your teeth. Let's see if you behave.

*Side note: although I'm writing in the present tense, I think we all know where this is going.*

Back to teeth-brushing. You don't behave. You shake your head in every geographically possible direction. Getting the end of the toothbrush in your mouth is like trying to get Donald Trump to treat a woman with respect.

Next, we move on to the nappy change, and I'm going to dispense with the build-up – your cooperation is non-existent, and you counter every move I make by standing up. *Standing up?* Why the fuck are you standing up?

Changing nappies is hard enough with a wriggler, let alone a baby who's standing up. Will you please work with me?

Somehow, I get the nappy fastened, and I dress you for bed.

I'm ready to throw in the towel.

I sprint through story time, completing *Where's Mrs Hen?* in under ten seconds. Then I say good night and put you to bed, and press play on Ewan before heading to the kitchen to make myself a coffee – a strong coffee, one that's strong enough to beat Dwayne Johnson in a bench-press competition.

But before I can take my first sip, I'm alerted to some activity on the baby monitor. You've lost both your dummy and your pal Louie, and now you're crying.

Ten seconds later, and your dummy is back in your mouth and Louie is back in your arms. Ewan is serenading you off to sleep.

Now, back to that cof—

Right, mister! You didn't lose your dummy, or Louie. You purposely threw them out of your cot. I know this because I'm watching you do the same thing again – don't pretend you don't know exactly what you're doing.

I don't bite. I let you do without your dummy and Louie. I will not be drawn into the mind games of a ten-month-old.

But my non-compliance doesn't bother you because you've now begun crawling around your cot, rounding up the rest of the cot's inhabitants – no doubt hashing out some sort of machination to drag poor Daddy away from his coffee again. In no particular order, you've lined up: Stripes, a stripy bit of cloth attached to a star; Roary, a dinosaur with your initials embroidered into his right foot; and a white penguin-type character who I swear wasn't there this morning.

You're babbling away at them. I think Roary is capturing meeting minutes and evolving an action plan for the next steps.

I give it ten minutes before I break up the union meeting, push play on Ewan (again) and give you back your dummy and Louie, who you begin punching. After ten minutes, you drift off to sleep.

I check the time: it's 7.10 p.m. This whole charade has used up an hour of my life.

*An hour!*

At least I can drink my coffee now, and by coffee, I mean iced coffee because it sure as hell isn't warm!

## A Live Demonstration
Friday, 2 October 2020

### 318 days old

'So you pinch lightly, give both thumb and index finger the smallest of wiggles, and then, as you pull back, you give it another little pinch to get underneath, and then you can release the tissue. Never wipe! That can lead to sores,' Mummy says.

Oh, in case you're wondering what the heck is going on here, Arlo, Mummy is using me to perform a live demonstration of how to wipe a baby's nose. Apparently, I've been a bit heavy-handed in the wiping department when I should have been in the business of light pinches and wriggles.

Who knew?

# Run For Your Lives
## Saturday, 3 October 2020

### 319 days old

We've gone out for lunch. You're sitting quietly. Too quietly! A quick look at your expression reveals why – you're exporting waste.

'Who's taking him?' Mummy says.

'I'll go,' I say. It's been a while since I've had the privilege of an out-in-public nappy change. Refresher training will do me good.

We enter the changing room, and it takes me all of four seconds to regret my decision.

Peeling back the front of your nappy reveals that we have a major clean-up operation ahead. It's one of those nappies where you look like you're wearing one of Mummy's thongs, except your thong is made entirely of shit. It's covered your willy, balls and the bit above, and it's seeped into the lines above your legs.

It also smells like a cesspit. It's basically a cross between a Jumanji and a Smelly Assassin. There is undigested food all over this mess.

But before I begin the clean-up, I bend your legs back so that I can take stock of what's going on behind—

OH MY FUCKING GOD!

We have an ALL IN ONE. I repeat, we have an ALL IN ONE.

How can a baby produce this much waste?

This stuff is thicker than a folded-up bath towel – it's travelled halfway up your back and, unfortunately for me, you're wearing a disposable nappy, which means the feeble defences of the top of the nappy liner have been effortlessly breached – like Poseidon demonstrating his power in full and destroying a child's sandcastle on the beach.

If you look like you're wearing a thong of shit on your front, from behind you look like you're wearing a pair of literal shit-shorts.

Before I can even think about how I'm going to approach this mound of mess, you start not just crying but wailing. The intensity is ferocious; you sound like a witch whose fire-making spell has malfunctioned and shot a ball of flame into her face.

'WHAAAA! WHAAAA!'

I pick up my wet-wipe-shaped machete and enter the jungle, knowing I won't come out the other side as the same man.

I hack, slash and lacerate my way forward – trying to clear a path and rid us of the fiendish faecal foe – but it's like trying to empty the Atlantic Ocean with a yoghurt pot.

My 'machete' is quickly blunted, leaving me no choice but to discard it and reach for another.

I have spares. Whether they're enough is impossible to say.

I take another wet wipe, then another, and another – using up six in total.

The entire ordeal is torture, but I somehow make it to the middle of this brown foliage mess – my fingernails resembling that of a potato gardener who forgot his gloves.

I go through another six wipes.

I've now cleared the worst of it away, but my hardship and misery can't end until I somehow remove your vest without getting shit on your limbs.

After more lifetimes than a cat, I remove your dirty clothes and eventually fasten the new nappy, knowing that I haven't done a perfect job of cleaning you up. That's despite working through twelve wet wipes.

I bag up your dirty clothes and re-dress you, before finally stumbling out of the facilities – broken, beaten, changed forever, and all but assured of contracting PTSD.

When we return to our table, Mummy throws me a look of concern. 'Everything OK?' she asks.

*Where would I even begin?*

I can't bring myself to report what happened. The memory is still too raw, and Mummy will only laugh.

'Fine. Everything is fine. By the way, I think Arlo needs a bath tonight.'

## Antibiotics
Sunday, 4 October 2020

320 days old

I've woken up feeling the most refreshed I've felt all year because Mummy put me in the loft last night to catch up on some shut-eye. You've woken up multiple times over the last two weeks, and, because I'm about as effective as a waterproof jacket made of paper when I'm tired, Mummy decided it was better for all of us if I went and had a decent night's sleep. I didn't even set my alarm.

But I'm awake now, and you'll no doubt be wanting your bottle soon. Let's see what time it is.

*Fuck!* It's 9 a.m. I've slept for ten hours!

I march downstairs to find the most unusual of circumstances. Firstly, Mummy is feeding you your bottle, even though you should have had it two hours ago. What's more, Mummy looks fucking wrecked, which is a big deal because unlike your wet paper bag of a dad, Mummy copes well without a lot of sleep.

'Oh dear. Talk me through it,' I say.

'He started waking up at midnight and wouldn't go back to sleep. He was crying and burning up, so I took his temperature, and it was 39.7.'

*FFFFUUUCCCCKKKKK! Now I feel like a piece of shit for sleeping through all of that.*

'39.7! Why didn't you wake me? I've been asleep for ten hours.'

'I was about to, but then I tried not to panic. I gave him some Calpol to bring it down. That did work, but now it's gone back up again.'

I place my hand on your forehead, and it feels like a nuclear meltdown waiting to happen.

'I think I'm gonna call 111,' Mummy says.

Thirty minutes later, and you're all wrapped up to go to the hospital. The doctors are not taking any chances; they want you in for a check-up. Because of Covid-19, only one parent can take you still, and Mummy insists it be her.

Three hours later, I get a call from Mummy who tells me two things: first, you bit her while the doctor and consultant were present; and second, that your results are in.

'He's got a viral infection that's spread to his ear, and they want to give him antibiotics,' Mummy says.

I've been waiting for this day to come since you were born, Arlo. In short, I am against anyone on the planet taking antibiotics unless they absolutely need it. As effective as antibiotics are as a drug, they are not without risks. Antibiotics might kill the nasty bugs, but they wipe out many of the good guys in the process. This process alters the balance of your microbiome and can sometimes have unfortunate consequences, like increasing the odds of a particularly nasty bug called C. diff (clostridium difficile) appearing, which inflicts a lot of unpleasantness on your digestive system, and it's a fucker of a thing to get rid of.

Autoimmune and digestive system problems are hereditary on Mummy's side of the family. Mummy spends a lot of her life in pain because of her Crohn's. It's not fun to watch. That's why I insisted we include a probiotic with your formula and why it was important to me for you to eat the best possible diet.

But now you've got an ear infection, and the doctor wants to give you antibiotics, a course of action that could undo a lot of our hard work. Or, it could do nothing apart from fixing your ear and removing the pain.

Mummy knows this, and she's already asked the doctor the questions I would have asked. 'If we don't give them to him, the risk of a perforated eardrum increases,' she says, relaying the doctor's answer.

I conduct a five-minute research campaign on Google into the antibiotic they want you to have – amoxicillin. I read one study on mice that proved that they would most likely alter your microbiome, but it's hard to say in what way. Plus, it's a study on mice not humans, so it might not count for shit.

There's another variable in all of this: while Mummy has hereditary digestive issues, I have hereditary ear issues. Hearing was a real problem for me as a child. It still is. Granny Smurf once had a perforated eardrum as well, and she still shudders when she thinks back to it.

In the end, we agree to not roll the dice on your ears and give you the antibiotics. I should add that this has almost certainly been a problem for you for over a week, and what we thought was a cold followed by teething was this infection. Basically, pain that could have been avoided.

A few hours after you take the first course of antibiotics, you begin to perk up, and I'm wondering when the hell Elon Musk is going to get round to inventing a translation machine for babies.

## No Antibiotics
Tuesday, 6 October 2020

322 days old

You've woken up with a rash that is covering your entire body. It seems we can add penicillin to the list of things you're allergic to. At least, that's the opinion of the doctor, whom we obviously called right away.

It's another day of doing very little for you and Mummy.

## The Calpol Administration Dilemma
Wednesday, 7 October 2020

323 days old

I'll tell you a baby task that seems simple on paper, but in reality is the opposite: giving a baby Calpol in the middle of the night.

The first decision is where to draw it up. Do I leave the bottle in your nursery and try and draw it up in the dark where I can't see how much is in the syringe? I would hate to overcompensate. My aim in giving you Calpol is *always* to relieve you of pain – not to send you into a coma.

Perhaps I should draw it up in the kitchen with the light on. But then I have the joys of traipsing back through the house in the dark, stubbing my toes on the stair gates.

It doesn't end there. Next, I have to give you the Calpol.

But how?

Do I turn your light on or leave it off? If I leave it off, then I can't see anything, because my eyes are still readjusting from having the light on in the kitchen. If I turn it on then your head perks up, and, despite being ill, you're like: 'Fuck, Dad, are we playing? Let me grab Louie.'

Then I need to decide if I'm picking you up out of the cot, or giving it to you while you're lying down, where the risk of choking and spluttering increases.

Do you understand my pain? There are just too many decisions.

I can't take it!

## Pink Elephants and Stair Gates
Thursday, 8 October 2020

324 days old

You have adversaries, Arlo, two of them – each causing you anguish and frustration, though they differ in how they antagonise you.

The first is a pink elephant that blows plastic balls into the air. It's loud, ugly and annoying. And it scares the absolute crap out of you. It's been in our house for a while but you've never taken much interest in it until recently. I'm not sure why you're scared of it, but it has large eyes and a sadistic smile, just like an evil clown. Don't worry, I will rid you of this enemy. After all, if you can't count on me who can you count on?

The second adversary is harder to remove. Well, it's not, but I refuse. It's this thing called a stair gate, and it's stopping you from climbing the stairs.

You don't like it.

You scream at it and you hit it.

But the stair gate is indifferent towards your emotions.

Unfortunately, this is just another shit fact of life because you will always come up against adversaries and obstacles. Right now, it's a scary pink elephant and a stair gate, but at some point you'll come up against bullies, rejection, things you don't want to do and things you don't think you can do. And every obstacle or adversary that you remove or overcome from your path will be replaced by another. This is inevitable.

But that is also where you will find periods of growth and development. If the pink elephant is scary, then stay away from it. If the stair gate is in your way, then learn to climb over it or go round it.

You will learn this. I promise. It just takes time. So for now, carry on hitting the stair gate. It still won't move, but maybe you'll realise that you don't need it to.

## Vest Versus T-Shirt
Monday, 12 October 2020

328 days old

Mummy has asked me to dress you in a vest, T-shirt and dungarees. I begin with the vest.

'No, that's not a vest. That's a T-shirt,' Mummy says.

I counter with: 'Erm, it is a vest, it has poppers at the bottom.'

'That's still a T-shirt.'

'It's not. A T-shirt is what I'm wearing right now.'

'No, you can still get T-shirts with poppers on the bottom.'

Mummy hands me the vest.

*Now I'm really confused.* 'These are identical.'

'No, they're not, the T-shirt has poppers on the shoulder as well as underneath, and the vest only has poppers underneath.'

'Surely it doesn't matter – both items of clothing will go with his dungarees.'

'I know, but you have to change him because I know that it's all wrong.'

*[Insert image of a man deepthroating a pin-pulled live grenade.]*

## I Take It All Back

Tuesday, 13 October 2020

**329 days old**

It seems my grade-A parental advice has worked. You know what I'm on about, don't you? I mean the bit where I used poignant and deep metaphors to describe overcoming the stair gate.

Not only have you listened to me, but you've now found a way to get *around* the stair gate. I take everything back. Stair gates should be immovable and never challenged, trifled with, or even stared at.

Alas, you've learnt to pull the thing away. I shouldn't be too surprised as it's a free-standing one that we're forced to use because we have an open staircase – something both of your grandmothers love to hone in on when they visit. 'The baby will fall to his doom' is a line I've heard uttered many times.

Anyhow, Mummy shot upstairs to quickly put some washing away, leaving you in what she through was a self-contained, baby-proof environment. When she returned to the top of the stairs, she found you halfway up, en route to lend a hand with the washing. You were wearing a wide grin and a look of pride that said, 'Look what I can do, Mummy.'

Maybe the grandmothers have a point.

The downstairs stair gate has received a new classification. It's no longer an unpassable gate, it's a minor delay; one your parents can no longer leave up to chance.

## Eleven Months Old
**Monday, 19 October 2020**

335 days old

Eleven months today.

You've developed an obsession for both lights and books. Naturally, I approve of the obsession over books. The light one, however, is a little strange. Whenever I lift you out of your cot, the first thing you do is put your arm up in the air to touch the lampshade. Come to think of it, that's the first thing you do when I pick you up in any room.

Granny Feeder is to blame. She has a crystal chandelier in her front hallway that hangs low enough for you to touch, which you do at every opportunity. It has already sustained heavy damage since this routine has been in place, but that's on Granny Feeder.

Your resistance to our wishes has grown stronger, and we are on track for some exciting toddler adventures. You push our faces away if you don't want to be held, and the look of revulsion you pull when you don't want any more food is comical. You screw up your face so much that it looks like it's about to implode, almost as if we were trying to feed you battery acid.

You open drawers and bang them shut. You pull out chairs and bang them against each other. You assume that Mummy puts clothes on the radiator for a game – one where you *have* to pull them all off.

But with new challenges come new rewards. I cannot explain how much joy I get out of watching you take steps on your own. You totter along forward, wobbling from side to side like a pair of windscreen wipers – it's delightfully funny. You need to be in the right mood for it, and you still require encouragement from Mummy or me, but you're progressing. When you took your first steps, you leant forward and fell into our arms as you approached, using us as a safety net of sorts. But now, you steady yourself and take pauses – you regroup, and then set off again.

I love how you combine climbing, cruising and walking to get to where you want. Like I said, it's a joy!

Another joy is going out for our afternoon walks. You like to hold one of our hands (more a finger): one parent pushes the buggy, while the other walks next to you with an outstretched index finger for you to clasp.

Our run of good fortune has finally come to an end: you're no longer sleeping through the night. I think you've slept through only once or twice this month. I guess we always had this coming.

If you wake any time from 3.30 a.m. onwards, you stand a strong chance of coming into bed with us, which, when you're not clawing at our faces, is nice.

Covid-19 remains ever-present. I recently heard from my employer that we would be working from home at least until the end of March 2021. Again, I try and focus on the positives in the face of tragedy, and one positive is that I still get to spend more time with you than I would have in a pre-Covid-19 era. That said, the virus will almost certainly ruin your first birthday, but that's a minor point, given that people are dying. And I say ruin, I'm secretly happy about this. I think a large crowd would overwhelm you, especially as you've never had to face that sort of situation before.

Arlo, I cannot believe we're almost at the end of the first year.

## Rook To Bishop 5
**Wednesday, 21 October 2020**

337 days old

I'm about to commence the most challenging game of chess ever. Why challenging? Well, for starters it's not even like normal chess, it's speed chess but with prison rules. And then there's my opponent. He is as ruthless as he is skilled – his chessboard agility makes Bobby Fischer look like an oversized tub of butter.

Fortunately, I've selected the white chess piece, a pawn shaped remarkably like a nappy. I have the starting advantage, but can I make it count?

I begin. I grab my opponent, flip him on to his back and pull him towards me. I move in to take my first piece by wrapping up his nether regions in the nappy-shaped pawn.

He resists. His body convulses while he's performing a corkscrew manoeuvre. I'm momentarily taken aback by his speed and dexterity. This is my first mistake. My opponent seizes the moment, capitalising on my hesitation, and he escapes.

I need to focus and do better. *Come on!*

I try again, but this time I bend my head *over* and park it on my opponent's chest, immobilising him to forestall a second escape. With my world upside down and the weight of my head pinning him in place, I now have time to deploy my nappy-wrapping attack.

It's a struggle, I feel dizzy, but after sending my rook to bishop 5, I leave the battlefield as the victor – even if the nappy application is at best substandard.

My opponent isn't happy. He gives me a look that says, 'Daddy, I didn't like you doing that to me.'

'Tough shit, it's bedtime,' I say.

But the look was misdirection, and I've taken the bait – again! My mini opponent has Usain Bolted it to the other end of the bed on all fours. He tries to make it over the edge, but I counter with an Olympic move of my own, this time from the world of diving. I Tom Daley it over the bed with two outstretched hands that find their mark: two cute, adorably pudgy ankles.

I drag him towards me.

He tries to resist, like a victim in a horror movie scraping his nails on the wooden floorboards, but instead of screaming in terror, he giggles and shrieks in delight.

I don't shriek, or giggle. Instead, I pick up the Babygro that's on my right before bursting into tears.

*How does Mummy make this appear so easy all the time?*

I flip my opponent on his back and try to get his left foot in to checkmate the bastard.

He resists, successfully evading every attempt I make. In the end, I have to roll my body *into* him and lock his leg up and under my arm, so I can use one hand to loop the trouser-leg end of the Babygro before repeating the same trick on the other side.

My opponent scratches and punches, but I weather the assault like a tough-skinned punch bag.

The arms are a fucking joke – he parries every attempt with ease.

I'm about to give up when my opponent makes a rare error, allowing the Sky remote to distract him.

*Perfect.*

I flip him on his back, shove the Sky remote into one of his hands and thread the other through the Babygro sleeve. Then I snatch the controller out of his hand and shove it into the other, and repeat the threading action.

Success.

Let's hope my opponent stays still for checkmate—
*Thud.*

The Sky remote is on the floor, and my opponent has yet again vanished to the other side of the bed.

I'm a thoroughly drained and depleted chess player who is being outmanoeuvred by an eleven-month-old.

Eventually, I hold him in place long enough to pop the final popper.

I let out a sigh and roll over on to my back.

*Checkmate.*

I'm supposed to feel like the victor. I feel like anything but.

The total time for this chess contest was two minutes thirty-four seconds.

I never want to play chess again.

## Good-News-Bad-News Story
Thursday, 22 October 2020

338 days old

Good news: you fell over, but my dad-reflexes kicked in and I swooped in to save you before you could hurt yourself.

Bad news: I was holding a hot cup of tea at the time, and when I launched myself to save you from injury, the tea departed the cup and arced perfectly, before swan diving right down my dick hole – burning the top third of my urethra, and causing me to scream out in pain, like an injured Wile E. Coyote after he's yet again been bested by the Road Runner.

# A Good Day To Piss Hard
Saturday, 24 October 2020

340 days old

It's been a while since you've pissed on me. Evidently, you felt the same way, as you pissed on me not once, not twice, but three times today! We'll split the accountability: 50 per cent you for pissing on me and 50 per cent me for allowing it to happen.

By the way, did this particular description of you pissing feel less enthusiastic than the rest? Like I'm phoning it in, and that I don't give three cunting shits about my fans? Why did I bother writing about this when it's barely a half-arsed attempt at creating something I can be proud of?

# Ouch!
Tuesday, 27 October 2020

343 days old

'Your son has had an accident,' Mummy says. I can hear her crying over the phone.

*This doesn't sound good.*

'What happened?'

'I parked up outside Lidl, put him in the trolley ... then I turned around for a split second to get his glasses ... and the trolley rolled away.'

Shit.

'It hit the curb, and he came tumbling out and landed on his head.'

I mentally try to perform some basic calculations, estimating from what height you fell from and what the likely impact to your head would have been. At the same time, I'm baulking at how nuts that is for a first reaction because how on earth can I possibly work that out? I got a D in GCSE physics, and I only managed that by cheating.

'The bump on the side of his head is huge,' Mummy continues.

'Where are you now?'

'I've taken him to Mum's as it was the nearest place. He's having a cuddle with her now.'

'Call 111 and see what they say.'

I've lost count of how many times we've dialled that number this year, Arlo.

Mummy reports back fifteen minutes later. The doctor wants to see you. He warns Mummy not to let you sleep for any longer than one hour, in case you've injured your brain.

One hour passes without a visit from the doctor.

Mummy sends me a video of you inhaling a banana like a starving dog who's been fortunate enough to stumble upon discarded leftovers but needs to eat it quickly before anyone else shows up.

Another hour. Still no visit from the doctor, but there is another video that comes my way. This time, you're standing next to a chair, shaking the shit out of it while smiling. The act suggests to me that you're unlikely to slip into a coma today.

The doctor arrives and gives you the once-over. No blood in your ears and the swelling on your head means that the damage is on the *outer* side of your skull and not on the inside, which is good news.

At 5 p.m. Mummy walks through the door. She looks spent of all energy. You don't fare much better. You have enough strength to hold out your arms to me, which are duly met. I hold you for as long as you will permit (four seconds).

And now you've crawled over to your large wicker toy basket. You're looking at me as if to say, 'Dad, be a good lad and open the lid, I want to play with my toys.'

I'll open the lid, son, on one condition – don't drop it on your head!

I think poor Mummy needs a cup of tea.

## A Cruel Mistress Is Fate
Wednesday, 28 October 2020

344 days old

It's first thing in the morning, and you want to walk from your toy basket over to the French doors. No doubt to bang on the glass.

Total distance is two metres.

To prevent Mummy having a mental breakdown, I'm staying ever so close to you so that I can shield you from any more bumps and bruises.

You're a foot away from the French doors when you trip.

I react instantly with my dad-reflexes, but alas, the glass door beats me to the metaphorical – and non-metaphorical – punch.

I wait while your brain registers pain, plots the pain on the pain scale, and then sends a message to your vocal cords with the results, telling you how loud to scream.

Judging from the noise, it's a sizable welt.

'Arlo, Arlo, Arlo ... it's OK, buddy. Shh shh shh, otherwise Mummy will—'

'What's up with him?' screams Mummy from upstairs.

'Nothing, he had a tiny tumble, but I think he's—'

*THUD THUD THUD* – the Matriarch has arrived on the scene to personally perform triage. She looks like an antique collector, meticulously examining a priceless Egyptian amulet for signs of forgery.

'A tiny tumble. Have you seen his head?'

A quick look reveals another shiny bump to the collection, and now it's my turn to feel shit.

You're not having the best week, are you, son?

# November (Again)

## Fuck My Life
Wednesday, 4 November 2020

351 days old

3.45 a.m. 'Whaaaaaa.'

Mummy retrieves you from your cot and brings you into bed with us, which we wouldn't normally do this time of morning, but we think you're coming down with a cough so we've cut you a break. You're welcome. Hopefully you will repay our good deed by going straight back to sleep.

4 a.m. It's Cuban band practice, and my forehead is the stand-in prop for a set of bongo drums. Understandably, I want band practice to end immediately, so I confiscate the drums by rolling over so you can't get at 'em.

4.01 a.m. It's now animal impression time and you're pretending to be a female gorilla grooming her young. This time, the back of my head is the prop stand-in. I should add more context: not only are you a female gorilla, but you're also one who is brand new to grooming, and as such, you've not quite developed the finesse needed for delicate fingerwork – all of which equates to you harrying the back of my head while tearing out tufts of hair, which is annoying and painful in equal proportions.

Once again, I seek to end the activity. This time, I pull the cover up and over my head in the hope that I can get back to sleep.

4.02 a.m. Arlo, we're not playing hide and seek.

'Dadda?'

No mate, it's too early for all of this. Lie down and close your eyes. Mummy pulls you in closer to her, and we all try and get back to sleep.

4.05 a.m. I'm not kidding, would you get off my fucking face? Otherwise, I'm going to crack an egg over your good eye. Mummy is tired, I'm tired – and you should be tired!

??.?? a.m. Mummy is now pushing me towards the side of the bed. I throw her a disgruntled 'What the fuck now?' look, to which she responds by telling me that I'm lying on your head.

I look down. She's not wrong. I am indeed lying on your head. Why? What a great fucking question. I'll tell you why: you have decided to position yourself—

Hang on, let me back up a sec. We have a king-sized bed, and none of the bed's inhabitants are overweight. Sure, one of them might be a bit chunky, but he's not turned one yet!

Anyway, you have positioned yourself *across* the bed and nestled your head under my arse, and Mummy is worried about a broken neck and permanent paralysis on your part, so once again, I'm awake.

Why can't you lie in formation along with the rest of the bed's residents?

5.30 a.m. It's Cuban band practice *again*.

Fuck this, I'm making myself a coffee.


## You Can Clap ... Sort Of
Friday, 6 November 2020

353 days old

You've finally learnt to clap today. It's long overdue.

Admittedly, you're not *fully* clapping, but you're almost there. You hold one hand up like a statue and slap the other against it, like an actor who soft-claps when it's announced he's lost out to a colleague for that best supporting actor Oscar. He wants to appear sincere in defeat even though he's gutted he lost out and he loathes the chap who won it.

Well done on the clapping.


## Arlo The Electrician
Saturday, 7 November 2020

354 days old

I need to apologise for misjudging you, Arlo. Up until now, I assumed that your ongoing campaign to bash the crap out of everything you came into contact with was purely to irritate your parents.

I was wrong.

I now recognise that you were installing a new alarm system in the house. One of Mummy's cousins is an electrician – perhaps you've picked up a few tips.

Now, I'm making an assumption here, and that is that the alarm you've installed is a silent one, and only you know when it's triggered, because neither Mummy nor I ever hear it. However, we're convinced it's in place.

You might ask how we can know that.

Well, no matter where you are in the house and no matter what you are doing, as soon as one of us leaves open the door, the stair gate, the washing machine, the dishwasher or the fridge, you immediately stop what you're doing and sprint-crawl to where the alarm is being triggered for a thorough inspection – something that usually entails more banging. *Christ, we're back to the banging.*

The dishwasher is the most sought-out location. Like the lost city of Atlantis, or Shangri-La, it entices you as a shiny object entices a magpie. However, despite considerable speed on your part, the door closes just as you come within touching distance, and the contents remain a mystery for another day.

But it's OK, because as soon as we shut the door, you can begin to vent your outrage and protest at the injustice of it all by – you guessed it – banging the absolute fucking crap out of it.

# Building Birthday Presents
Sunday, 8 November 2020

## 355 days old

How are you nearly one?

Mummy and I have been busy: we have spent the evening building your birthday present. I say 'we' – Mummy was in charge of selecting what to watch on TV, and I was in charge of construction. Your present is ... well, I'm not sure what it is. It's made of wood, and Mummy boasts that it has a range of capabilities. Ready for the list? It's a see-saw, a climbing arch, a slide, and a hammock (cushions and blankets each sold separately).

I guess we can call it a climbing gym.

We both think you'll love it. You certainly love ignoring us when we tell you not to climb the stairs – or climb anything, come to think of it.

Assembling the gym has left my hands with more blisters than you have soft toys – both palms look like the face of a spotty adolescent.

This present is extra special because it's been shipped all the way from the USA.

Why the USA?

Again, that's something else I'm not 100 per cent sure on either.

I recall the conversation. 'Can't we can get a wooden climbing toy for him from the UK?' I said.

'No, silly, we need this one because it's a four-in-one and it converts into a slide,' Mummy said, speaking to me in the same tone she speaks to you.

'We have slides in the UK, though ... right? I mean, I'm pretty sure we definitely do.'

'Yes, but this one has multicoloured rainbow rungs, and you can use it for many different things. You're just going to have to trust me.'

At best, her argument is as strong as the rationale for erecting an ice bridge inside a furnace.

But it is your first birthday and it's one we have had to cancel all our plans for, so I let Mummy win this one and tell her that it's fantastic and that you will love it. I have no doubt you will.

But why is it coming from America?

# Dear Arlo
Monday, 9 November 2020

### 356 days old

One year ago to the day, I was eagerly awaiting Mummy's confirmation that you were on your way to meet us. To distract myself from the anticipation, I wrote you a letter.

I'm not eagerly awaiting anything right now apart from the release of *Black Widow* on Disney+. But I figured I'd do the same again, for a couple of reasons. First, I can once again share some more of the lessons that I have learnt, particularly this year, in a formal way. Italics makes it formal because I said so. They're lessons that I believe will be of value to you as you grow up. Second, I've called the book *Dear Arlo,* so I need to get the phrase in somewhere.

Here goes:

*Dear Arlo,*

*What a strange and surreal time it is for us both: for me, embarking on my new journey as a father, and for you, embarking on your journey as a human. Both of our journeys are moving in parallel, while at the same time, a virus continues to visit devastation and tragedy on the inhabitants of the planet. Covid-19 has brought home the point that your circumstances are always capable of changing – sometimes in an instant – by forces that you don't and can't control.*

*Consider the following equation:*

## *MEANINGFULNESS + CONTENTMENT = HAPPINESS*

*I've spent much of this year thinking about three areas, or lessons, that I see as being crucial to understanding this equation, so that you may obtain that which everyone seeks: happiness. In fact, let's call the equation the happiness equation. Even though I vehemently dislike the word 'happiness', I do have my own interpretation of what it means to me, and what you can do to achieve it for yourself, even in difficult times.*

*To understand the happiness equation, and to install its framework into your personal life operating system (OS), you must practise and master these three lessons. I'd like to take some time now to go through them with you.*

391

*Lesson number one: fall in love with showing up each day and giving it something – even if it's only one small thing.*

*Instead of fantasising about becoming a bestselling author who gets seven-figure advances, I focus on writing something down each day, even if it's only a few sentences. I do this because writing is meaningful to me, so I ensure it's part of my life. What's more, I take satisfaction in having the opportunity to write a few sentences each day. This is critical because that's where I find contentment, and you need both meaningfulness and contentment to balance the happiness equation.*

*If you're standing in the middle of an empty Olympic-sized swimming pool, and you dream of nothing more than it becoming full, it will never happen. But if you can commit to adding one drop of water a day – and feel satisfaction that you have the opportunity to add one drop a day (again, contentment) – the pool will eventually fill up, and you will feel highly motivated along the way. Drip, drip, drip is the path to achievement, and possibly some sort of enlightenment.*

*Don't train to run a hundred miles; train to run. Don't aim to read a book a week; aim to read regularly. And don't try to drop five pounds in weight; try to eat one healthy meal every day. Install routines and good habits and learn to love repetition. Do this, and you will never be beaten by disappointment, because each day will be the same as the last. This takes practice, but I assure you it is a worthy pursuit.*

*Lesson number two: seek out those you can cultivate deep, expressive relationships with, and then share your life with them. And for those where that isn't possible – throw them out.*

*I've been lucky enough to have some truly wonderful experiences in my life – resulting in great memories. But they all have something in common. Whether trekking in the Sahara Desert, or spending an evening indoors playing board games, it's the people surrounding me that have served as the true architects of those great memories.*

*Make no mistake, tomorrow is never obliged to show up and present itself to you – we never know how long we've got to spend time with the people that matter most. So commit to choosing today over tomorrow, because tomorrow is unreliable, but today will never leave your side.*

*I think we've all been reminded of the importance of relationships this year.*

*My third and final lesson: learn to tell the difference between lessons that you learn, and lessons that you practise. And then select your practices based on your priorities, and practise every day. This is the most important lesson, and it underpins the first two.*

*You can learn to count to ten, ride a bike, cook a beef Wellington, or speak Mandarin. Those are all lessons you learn. But not all lessons can be learnt. Some can only be practised – for example, gratitude, kindness or adding one drop of water to the pool each day. You don't take a seminar* and suddenly find you know how to be the perfect partner or the perfect parent. Stoic philosophy has taught me that.

Let me share some examples of how I do this. I commit time each morning and evening to be fully present with you, enjoying your company and observing how you have grown and developed over the last twenty-four hours. I do this without checking my phone or worrying about my to-do list. I keep a gratitude journal, and I write at least three things in it each day, no matter how small or unimportant they may seem to other people. Yesterday, I wrote that Mummy made me a hot chocolate. Can I say that I'm always present whenever I'm with you? And can I say I've never taken Mummy for granted? No. That's why I practise – to minimise the chances of this happening and to maximise the chances of it not happening.

All three of these lessons form my interpretation of meaningfulness and contentment. And remember:

### MEANINGFULNESS + CONTENTMENT = HAPPINESS

Happiness isn't a euphoric feeling; it's not achieved by acquiring things like money, status, power or even recognition. You have to structure your life and fill it with meaningful pursuits and, just as importantly, be content that you've learnt to embed meaningfulness in your life.

I've found liberation since adopting that framework for myself because I'm never wishing my life away waiting for one thing to happen –

*one event that will change my life for the better, whether that be more money, fame, a dream job, respect or a large social media following.*

*Instead, I have learnt to appreciate what's in front of me today, and to cherish the process of working towards a goal, with the goal itself becoming secondary: instead, the process becomes the space which I draw motivation and satisfaction from – or, meaningfulness and contentment. Because of that, I can say without hesitation that I am deeply happy.*

*And you can be too.*

*I hope this advice is of value to you at some point in your life.*

*Last year, Mummy traversed pregnancy brilliantly, and the labour even more so. But then she handed over the baton to you so that you could begin your life. The baton exchange was a smooth transition, and you matched the same brilliant pace and fortitude that Mummy showed. You have demonstrated resilience every day, and you conclude the first year of your life with distinction. For that you have my pride, my gratitude and my love. Top marks, buddy.*

*Next year will be more of a challenge, but I'm confident you will succeed magnificently – like your mummy did when she brought you into the world.*

*Thank you for an exceptional year, son.*
*Love, Dad*

*PS: today you learnt to say 'car'.*

# Appreciation
Tuesday, 10 November 2020

357 days old

Thanks to Covid-19, you still haven't met all of my closest friends. Two of them are a married couple living in the US, Abdi and Steph. They have a little boy who's two, named Gabriel. While scrolling through Facebook, I notice a post from Steph that says, 'You should be here today, but you're not. Instead, you will always be in my heart.'

Steph had a miscarriage earlier in the year. Gabriel's brother or sister was due today.

I can't stop drawing parallels.

Their baby was due almost exactly a year after you arrived. Steph and Abdi went through a complicated road to pregnancy with Gabriel, like we did with you. Their experience helped Mummy and me when we voiced our frustrations at not becoming soon-to-be parents. They understood.

While I can't relate to any parent who has lost a child, I vividly remember the night we thought you were dead, ten weeks into Mummy's pregnancy. That night has left a scar. Not one of pain, but one of relief and gratitude.

We've gone from being told we probably wouldn't have children naturally, to Mummy falling pregnant, to then thinking we'd lost you, to learning that we hadn't lost you, and then to your arrival, and our first year as parents, with its various medical ups and downs. It's been one hell of a narrative, and it's one that could have gone in a different direction at many points.

But it didn't.

Steph, Abdi and Gabriel weren't so fortunate.

When I put you down in bed tonight, I will do my best not to suffocate you as I squeeze you tight, and remind myself how blessed Mummy and I are to have you.

Your life is a story of 'what is', not one of 'what could have been'.

Not everyone gets that.

## Sky TV Versus Sentimentality
Wednesday, 11 November 2020

358 days old

It's 6.10 p.m. We're all sitting on the sofa when Mummy gets up and shuffles to the kitchen. I scoop you up and follow. Mummy takes a bottle from the rack and empties a 7-oz pot of formula into it.

This will be your last bottle of formula. Tomorrow, you move on to cow's milk. How many of these bittersweet milestones have we had this year, Arlo? Too many to count.

Mummy's eyes are watery. She walks over to us, both arms outstretched so that we can have a family cuddle – at which point you pistol-whip her in the face with the Sky remote.

You must have purloined it when we were sitting on the sofa.

And now Mummy is crying, but for widely different reasons than I imagined.

## Stick To What You Know
Thursday, 12 November 2020

359 days old

For reasons unknown to me, I go for a stand-up wee. This is something that never happens. As I finish up, I re-familiarise myself with the shake-yourself-dry-while-standing protocol: 'Remember to still aim down when shaking. Otherwise, urine droplets will land on the floor... and possibly your hands – and we don't want that now, do we? No, we do not.'

But then, all of a sudden, an almost-year-old hand – followed by an almost-year-old arm – appears from under my ball sack. Fortunately, I'm almost empty, otherwise I would have pissed on the arm.

You reach over and *into* the toilet bowl, and I deploy dad-reflexes to stop you from—Too late.

You've hand-printed the inside of the toilet.

*I should probably look into washing that hand.*

I grab you by the wrist, walk you out of the toilet and into the kitchen. Everything is still hanging out, and I'm certain the neighbours next door can see through the window. What I'm not sure of is the following:

A: if they saw a few droplets of urine splash down on your head because you didn't give me enough time to shake.

B: what their first reaction was to a grown man walking an almost-year-old baby out of a toilet with his willy hanging out dripping piss on his head.

C: why we have blinds for every single window in the house bar the kitchen.

If I've learnt anything in the last few minutes, it is that I need to stick to what I know, and that's sit-down weeing.

## This Amazing Woman
Friday, 13 November 2020

### 360 days old

I know of this woman, Arlo. She's very special. She cooks all your meals from scratch, using fresh ingredients, and she washes all of your clothes. If she wakes up in the morning before you, she panics and quickly loads up the baby-monitor app to check that you're still breathing. She's the only one that cuts your fingernails and she's somehow able to do this even when you're thrashing your limbs about. She brings you into our bedroom after every bath and delicately massages your body all over with coconut oil. She holds your hand while you're doing your business in your nappy. Every night, without fail, she whispers this phrase in your ear: 'Night night, sweet sleeps, love you lots, see you in the morning, night night.' Sometimes, not by choice, she spends the whole day at A & E with you, waiting for a doctor to tell her that you're all right and relieve her of the panic and the feelings of nausea that all mothers endure when their children's well-being is in danger. This woman takes photos and videos of you every day. She never stops talking to you or about you. She describes to you everything she does, and she does this to help you develop your knowledge and understanding of the world. She dances with you. She puts her soul into your well-being, and she would do anything to ensure your safety and contentment. She never loses patience. When this woman smiles, she gives off a radiance that illuminates the space around her, and if you're lucky enough to be in her company, then the brightness will engulf you too. It will elevate you to a place of comfort; one where you're reminded – even if only for a second – of the beauty of our species. You're incredibly lucky, Arlo, because this woman saves her biggest, warmest and most loving smiles for you.

I know of this woman, Arlo, and she has this job that she works 24/7 – never taking a single second off.

This woman is your mummy.

## My Boy
Monday, 16 November 2020

363 days old

You wear an eyepatch for a few hours in the morning. You wear glasses … most of the time. You can walk. You're wobbly, often holding both arms up in the air to help you balance, but you can do it. And you can talk. You can say 'dadda', 'mumma', 'yeah', 'Lisa', 'car', 'what is it', and 'who's that'. You can turn the pages of a picture book, uncovering the animals that are hiding behind the flaps. You can play hide-and-seek. You hold up your dirty socks to our noses so that we screw up a face and make silly sounds to make you laugh. You sneak up on Mummy every morning while she pretends to be asleep. You can fit some shapes through some of their designated slots in your shape sorter, but you have trouble with triangles – you always give up on them. You can climb the stairs, and you can slide all the way down them again. You can open and shut the kitchen doors, and you can shake the blinds. You bash on the basement door when Mummy asks you to 'go and get Daddy'. You can crawl at astonishing speeds, and you can kick a ball (sort of). You can drink water out of a sippy cup without a parent needing to hold it up, and you can suck from a straw. You like the swings and you like nature – trees fascinate you, particularly on a windy day when the branches are swaying in the air. You hold out your hand every time we go for a walk because you like to hold on to one of our fingers for comfort. You have a best friend – a chimpanzee named Louie, who comforts you every night when you go to bed. You call out for Mummy whenever you're upset, and you call out for Daddy whenever you want to play. You love it when I throw you up in the air. You smile all the time. You are a tottering, babbling biological encyclopedia who teaches others as much as you learn. You inspire me to become better, and you have given me a purpose that has the weight, height and strength of a mountain. You are the most beautiful small human being, and you have a Mummy and a Daddy who are utterly and hopelessly besotted by you.

You are my boy.

## An Ode To Dadding
Tuesday, 17 November 2020

364 days old

I thought this book would be full of entries about sleep deprivation, feelings of worthlessness and arguments with Mummy, all because we're exhausted, and we don't have a clue what we're doing. I'm not saying there's been none of that. There has – tons. And I'm certainly not suggesting we know what we're doing. I don't know any parent that does. But I like to think we're at least stumbling indirectly and broadly in the right direction. We get things wrong and we make mistakes, sure. But we try and learn from them.

Every day I fall in love with my job of being a dad. I've had other jobs that I've enjoyed, but they've all reached a saturation point where I get bored, and they don't satisfy or challenge me any more. And so I've left them to pursue something else.

Not this job.

Not my dadding job.

It keeps me on my toes by throwing up new challenges every day. I'm constantly upskilling and training.

I love hearing you talk – especially when you say 'dada' – and I love hearing the pitter-patter sounds that you make, crawling around in the room above me. I love seeing your reaction when Mummy parks the car, and you can see me standing in the doorway waiting for a cuddle and a chat. I love how much you giggle when I blow raspberries on your body.

This year has been like watching the perfect TV show. It has a fascinating and compelling central character who changes and learns new things every day. The show is entertaining; it's often hysterical and terrifying, and certainly hard watching at times. But it's immensely satisfying. And the producers of the show know they're on to a winning streak because they keep churning out new episodes every day. In fact, there is so much new content involving this fascinating lead character that you might as well call it a channel – a channel that's accessible for me to enjoy every minute of every day.

And the great thing about this channel is that, barring any unforeseen tragedy, I will never see the end credits. For me the show will never end.

How awesome is that?

The urge I feel to protect you is as fierce as anything I've ever encountered emotionally – or anything I thought emotionally possible. Before I became a father, I heard other parents describe the feelings they harboured for the safety of their children.

I understand them now.

You sometimes hear about these horrific stories, how a parent gave their life to save their child from the most tragic of circumstances, like a house fire or something equally horrible. But now I know that those parents couldn't have played out their sacrifice any other way. The protective urge I feel for you is an expression of the raw biological files of my DNA scripts. Nothing could possibly override them. I, too, would walk through fire for you if it meant I could save you from danger – though, between you and me, I hope neither of us is ever in that position.

Something I knew from the moment I met your mother all those years ago on a merry-go-round was that she would make a wonderful mummy. And she does. She has been phenomenal this year. I can say without a doubt that her efforts as a mother have allowed me to enjoy mine more as a father. She makes all the difficult and complicated pieces of parenthood that bit easier. She is a natural, which is something I knew beforehand, but I'm blown away by how she is able to do what she does every day. And as a result of her maternal instincts and natural talent for loving and caring for you – for us both – we have all enjoyed this year much more than I was expecting. In the face of a dark moment in modern history, this has been a gift for our little family.

A few weeks ago, Mummy was cuddling you, and she said to me: 'If I could bottle up this feeling and sell it, we'd be millionaires.' I think that sums up our first year as parents.

# Some Things Never Change
## Wednesday, 18 November 2020

### 365 days old

Mummy and I have blown up eighty-five balloons to create a balloon arch. Mummy insists that I blew up only seven of the balloons, but who's counting? ... I guess Mummy is. Truth be told, I hate balloons. They're such an unnecessary kick in Mother Nature's testicles, but I let Mummy have this one. She's spent most of the day crying because you're about to turn one.

Your birthday was going to be animal themed – 'aroarable', if you want to drill down to the specifics. But because of this stupid fucking virus, you can't have any birthday guests, so Mummy has decided to reconfigure the theme to rainbows instead, in tribute to the NHS – though I'm sure they'd prefer a pay rise to knowing that we've blown up a rainbow-coloured balloon arch.

Next, we stick up a banner that has a picture of you from every month of your first year. My favourite is you standing in nothing but your rocket-pattern reusable nappy and baby-blue glasses. You have this vacant-gormless expression on your face that cracks me up every time I look at it.

You have a cake. It's white, but apparently, when you slice into it, we will once again find the colours of the rainbow.

Sticking with the rainbow theme, we've drooped paper streamers down from the upstairs landing to create a curtain of sorts. The exercise takes us ten minutes, but I know it will take you considerably less time than that to pull it down.

Finally, we take all your presents down from the loft and Mummy arranges them on the table. I bring your climbing gym down and put it on the floor ready for you to explore in the morning.

Today is a sad day for me, Arlo. I thought I'd be happy but this year has gone too quickly. The first year of our parenthood journey is all but finished.

I take another look at your climbing gym, and a thought occurs to me. 'Can I ask you a question? And please don't take offence, or be embarrassed,' I say to Mummy.

'Yeah?'

'Did you change the theme of his birthday to rainbows because you honestly wanted to pay tribute to the NHS, or was it because the rungs on his climbing frame are also of a rainbow design, and you wanted everything to match up?'

'Er … well … yes, I suppose I did …'

Some things in life change, Arlo, like when a baby grows and develops every day from birth onwards.

Other things … not so much.

## Happy Birthday (Again)
Thursday, 19 November 2020

366 days old (remember. it's a leap year)

The sound of a happy and content one-year-old baby boy talking to his monkey wakes me up: still my all-time favourite alarm clock – at least, when it goes off *after* 7 a.m., which it has done today.

I swing my legs out of bed and the first thing I notice is a small pile of children's books on my bedside table. There's *The Very Hungry Caterpillar*, *That's Not My Badger...* and *Where's Mrs Ladybird?* I walk around our bed and past Mummy's dresser, which has a stack of clean, neatly folded baby clothes on it.

I head downstairs to get you some milk.

In the living room, strewn across the wall, are photos taken from when you were nine days old. In one corner is a yellow bike that, when switched on, has the voice of a well-spoken elderly gentleman singing songs and nursery rhymes. In another corner is your wicker basket that has all your other toys in it. Everywhere else there are decorations for your birthday.

In the kitchen, there's an empty space in the corner. Only last week it housed your bottle-prep machine and steriliser. But they're not there any more. They've been returned to the friends who lent them to us. Hopefully, we can ask to borrow them again one day.

I warm up your milk and add your vitamin D, your DHA and your probiotics into the bottle. Then I go back upstairs to find you cuddling Mummy.

You weigh 10.35 kg, and your hair is a sandy-blond colour – and is in desperate need of a trim. Your eyes have lost some of that deep sapphire-blue look that they had when you were born. There's now a faint shade of green in them. You have my eyes and your mother's smile.

As soon as you see me, you spit your dummy out and a sparkling smile spreads across your face, one that would illuminate the deepest and darkest regions of the universe. *My universe.*

'Dadda?'

I'm here, buddy. *Always.*

Happy Birthday.

# Acknowledgements

I'm indebted to a number of people who helped make this book what it is.

I had two phenomenal editors standing in my corner. Their contributions to the project have ensured I appear, at least to the reader, to be a much better writer than I truly am. Ian McIlroy: you fix everything. Ross Dickinson: please don't ever change jobs! And if you do, you have to promise to still work with me. Forever!

I'd like to thank those people who read an early draft of *Dear Arlo* and provided invaluable feedback. Those people include Steph Kater, Martin Birse, Laura Mutlow, Kat Viglaska, Gail Roberts, Faye Ranger, Laura Day, Mark Jackson, Marc Mason, Jess Clare and Gareth Bartley.

To Jamie Allerton, my go-to guy for all things joke related: thanks for once again reviewing the book's humour and providing ideas and suggestions, and even writing a few jokes for me to use and take credit for.

To the folks at MiblArt who designed the book cover and the layout: thank you for your unending patience, your support, and your unwavering commitment to collaborating with authors.

A big thank you to Chandana Wanasekara, who created all the illustration artwork in the book. You are one superbly gifted graphic designer.

And to Andrew Roberts: thank you for once again narrating the audio book.

To the NHS operations manager of the 111 services: I'm sorry for flooding your call centre this year, but not sorry enough to say it won't happen again.

To 'Dawn', the health visitor who wouldn't listen to me when I told you about Arlo's eye: I've since learnt you've moved on career-wise. Good!

To every midwife, nurse, doctor and healthcare worker who isn't 'Dawn', and to all other key workers and individuals who have put themselves at risk so that we may overcome the biggest global threat we've seen in modern times: thank you.

I used to believe that *Star Wars* and Marvel movies were the best thing in the world. That was until I sampled this wonderful thing called childcare. Thank you to Arlo's grannies, and to Lisa, his auntie, for being there for him whenever he needs you. He loves you guys. I'm also fond of you all.

To my partner, Charlene: you make parenting just that little bit easier for me. You are a wonderful mother, and Arlo and I are extraordinarily lucky to have you. By the way, I went a lot easier on you in this book than I did in *Dear Dory*. You're very welcome.

To my son, Arlo, my personal CPR machine that I never knew I needed: without you, I may never have even realised my dream of becoming a writer. So first, thank you for that. Second, can you please stop turning the washing machine off while it's midway through its cycle? I don't think Mummy has many more blood vessels left to burst. I love you, buddy.

To parents anywhere and everywhere: just keep going. It's a tough gig, but it's also an inspiring, rewarding, entertaining and damn-well critical gig – so keep at it every day, and aspire, to raise your children in the best way that you can. They are our future, so let's equip them with everything they need. And let's try and have fun doing it along the way.

# A Note From The Author

I'm a new writer, but I'd love to become an old one!

If you enjoyed *Dear Arlo*, please consider heading over to Goodreads or wherever you buy your books and leaving a review. Tip: you can copy and paste the same review on more than one platform.

I cannot overstate how valuable and important reviews are to an author, so believe me when I say that your support is greatly appreciated.

And if you're planning to tell your mates about *Dear Arlo*, they can find it on sale at all the big retailers (Amazon, Apple Books, Google Play, Barnes and Noble, Kobo and many more outlets). It's available in paperback, hardback, e-book and audio.

# About Tom Kreffer

Tom Kreffer is the author of *Dear Dory: Journal of a Soon-to-be First-time Dad* and *Dear Arlo: Adventures in Dadding*, and he is the creator of the *Adventures in Dadding Newsletter*. He loves *Star Wars* and Marvel movies, and he has a degree in film and television that he firmly believes to be worth less than a second-hand toothbrush.

He lives in Northampton, England with his family, whom he intends to exploit for many more story opportunities in the years to come.

## Say Hello!

My website www.tomkreffer.com
email at tom@tomkreffer.com

www.goodreads.com/tomkreffer
www.twitter.com/tkreffer
www.instagram.com/tom_kreffer
www.facebook.com/officialtomkreffer

# Want Free Stuff?

**Free ebooks**

I didn't write *Dear Arlo* as a guidebook, but I have since created a series of e-books that focus specifically on dads during pregnancy and labour, and on dads and their newborn babies. These might be useful to you if you're a soon-to-be new parent or if you're expecting another child. If you head over to my website (www. tomkreffer.com), you can grab your free copy.

**Adventures in Dadding Newsletter**

I invite you to come and have a laugh at my expense: every month I send out a bite-size, scaled-down version of my dadding adventures, summarising the most recent tortures that parenting has thrown my way. Visit www.tomkreffer.com to join the fun.

Out 2022

TODDLER INC.

A
B C

TOM
KREFFER

cover art not final